THE
GOSPEL AND
THE
AMBIGUITY
OF THE CHURCH

Institute for Ecumenical Research
Strasbourg, France

The Gospel Encounters History Series
Edited by Vilmos Vajta

In cooperation with Gunars Ansons, Günther Gassmann, Marc Lienhard,
Harding Meyer, Warren A. Quanbeck, and Gérard Siegwalt

Already Published
THE GOSPEL AND UNITY
THE GOSPEL AND HUMAN DESTINY

The GOSPEL and the AMBIGUITY of the CHURCH

Edited by Vilmos Vajta

Philadelphia
FORTRESS PRESS

Table of Contents

Preface

This third volume in the series produced by the Institute for Ecumenical Research in Strasbourg examines the ecclesiological problem which has again become a burning issue. It is not only the ecumenical movement and with it the scandal of the division of the church which has caused the reemergence of the problem. Nor is it solely the result of the Second Vatican Council, which was obliged to reexamine the fundamentals of the church. Today the whole mission of the church in a changed world and the question of the salvation of mankind appear in a new light.

A well-known formula of Catholic modernism reads as follows: "Jesus proclaimed the Kingdom of God; the result was the church." As one-sided as this formula might sound, it nevertheless reveals the problems which Christianity is never permitted to ignore but which have to be reexamined by each generation. For the question is that of the relationship between the origins and the present form of the church. How has the church passed on the message of Jesus Christ, and how has it established its own existence in the world? Has it identified the salvation of mankind inseparably with itself and with its historically developed structure, or has it recognized the activity of the Triune God as the horizon of its self-perception? These questions, closely connected with the problem of the church's historical existence, are the ones which have to be reexamined today. The present volume does this by investigating the "ambiguity" of the church in its confrontation with the gospel. At the same time a critical inquiry into the present–day structure of the church must take into consideration its historical continuity. For this reason it is not only a theoretical explanation which is attempted here, but also a crystallization of the problem as it exists even in the remotest contexts of the church's life-style.

The volume rests upon the united conviction of the authors that the church can realize its function in today's world only when it is made aware of its historical character and thus also of its ambiguity. Under these conditions it must strive towards a suitable form for its existence and function. In undertaking this critical analysis the church will have to take into account its origin and the structure it has developed during the course of history. Struggling for the continuity of its mission, the church is obliged both to pursue its path and to find a suitable form for each successive generation. The present volume serves this end, although these problems can be investigated here only in a few essential aspects.

It is our particular regret that we failed to receive the contribution originally planned for this volume on "The Church as a Minority." This theme, so significant for the church today, was to have been treated by a theologian from Eastern Europe; as a result of other academic commitments, however, he was unable to participate in this symposium.

We are grateful to Fortress Press for accepting the publication of this volume as a service to the current ecumenical discussion among the churches.

November 1973
Strasbourg, France

THE EDITORIAL COMMITTEE

I.

THE MISSION
OF THE CHURCH

Chapter 1

The Gospel of the Kingdom of God and the Church

I
A New Affirmation of a Theology of the Kingdom of God

In spite of the fact that kings and kingdoms are out of fashion in the modern world, the current theological scene has witnessed a reaffirmation of the biblical symbol of the kingdom of God. This is all the more surprising in view of the almost universally accepted requirement that for a religious symbol to be relevant it must be translated into language that is culturally significant. Since we are lacking the cultural medium to facilitate a translation with the power of equivalent effect, we are faced with a hermeneutical hiatus between the symbol itself and our life situation. The fact, however, that the symbol remains useful suggests that some of its original scope and meaning are able to break through the cultural barrier and speak to the deepest concerns that men display today.

There are a number of reasons that the symbol of the kingdom of God has surfaced with a new impact. Two are most noteworthy. First, the ongoing crisis of Christian identity has drawn theology into an ever more radical inquiry into the origins of its history. This is the abiding meaning of the "quest of the historical Jesus"— whether old or new. The result of this research is well established: Jesus of Nazareth proclaimed the gospel of the kingdom of God, calling for repentance and faith. In rebuilding the foundations of Christian faith, against the backdrop of the universal collapse of Constantinian orthodoxy, it has been necessary to get back to the original meaning of these major terms—gospel, kingdom of God, repentance, and faith—and to interpret them in light of their original contexts. A controlling criterion has been the desire to remain faithful to the message of Jesus and to understand its inner connection with the christological kerygma preached by the apostles. Harnack formulated the problem: "Jesus preached the Kingdom of God as good news, but the apostles preached the Lord Jesus Christ."[1] It is in striving for a solution to this problem that the notion of the kingdom of God has assumed a new importance in our theology. That is, we do not see how we can claim the kerygma of Jesus as Lord without going back to the gospel of the kingdom he preached.

The second reason has to do with the timeliness of the message of the kingdom of God in relation to the aggravations and aspirations released in the process of moving toward a "planetary totalization of human consciousness."[2] Something has been stirring—since how long?—within the life of mankind to accelerate the drive toward a highly complex social organism, composed of superconscious units of personalized existence. If something like this is happening at the present time, there is need for a religious symbol both broad and deep enough to focus and illuminate the process and to make it a sacrament of a transcendent future in the fullness of God. The kingdom of God may be just such a symbol. It is the most powerful symbol of hope in the religious and social history of mankind. It combines social, political, and personal dimensions of fulfillment; it unites spatial and temporal elements in an eschatological synthesis; it promises healing to bodily and spiritual illness, liberation from authoritarian bondage, justice for the oppressed, righteousness for sinners, homecoming for exiles, etc. The kingdom of God is a transcendent aggression against the demonic power structures which rule in history and personal life.

We have stated that the kingdom of God is at the core of Jesus' preaching and thus gives foundation and content to the quest for Christian identity; we have also stated that it answers to the quest for total personal and communal fulfillment, offering a future in which love, power, and righteousness work in perfect harmony for the good of all. But there are other advantages. To us in America it takes up and carries forward the theme of the kingdom of God that was abruptly discontinued with the great influx of neoorthodox theology. Thus, it reestablishes continuity with an idea that is deeply ingrained in American experience. H. Richard Niebuhr, in his masterful way, has written the history of the idea of the kingdom of God in the workings of American history.[3] It is astonishing to discover that

THE KINGDOM OF GOD AND THE CHURCH   5

the great outbursts of religious enthusiasm and theological creativity
in America are stimulated by belief in the coming kingdom of God.
This religious faith also shines through cultural history, so that it is
not farfetched to say that American history from the beginning
has been a pioneering movement pushing back the frontiers to ex-
plore the realm of the future, to receive what the Lord has in store
for his people.[4] The fact that this quasi-messianic dimension of
American consciousness has recently been corrupted by the demonic
powers of national haughtiness, industrial greed, military blood-
thirstiness, and ideological arrogance, should not dissuade us from
appreciating its positive contributions to Christianity in America.

In European theology a similar thing is accomplished. One Lutheran theologian has been quoted as stating that "generally speaking
contemporary Protestant theology in all its fields has lost the basic
idea of Jesus' preaching."[5] He meant that the various crisis- and
word-oriented theologies after World War I displaced the theme of
the kingdom of God that had had an illustrious history from Kant
through Ritschl. Pannenberg states point blank that "the dogmatics
of recent decades is marked by a steady erosion of the notion of the
kingdom of God."[6] Thus when systematic theology today recovers
the centrality of the idea of the kingdom of God, it is reestablishing
continuity with nineteenth century theology that not so long ago was
written off as a neo-Protestant heresy. But in doing so it offers an
eschatological understanding of the kingdom as a corrective to the
dominantly ethical model that prevailed in the Kant-Ritschl line
of thought.

The most important thing about the new affirmation of the kingdom of God in theology is what it might mean for the renewal of
the church. The organized church has become the religious honey
on the comb of our "one-dimensional society." The church tends to
serve as the religious function of society, and is expected to act as
one of the smooth-running parts of that society, along with business,
labor, government, education, and entertainment. To the extent to
which this is so, the church has lost its power to mediate transcendence. Mediating the sense of transcendence is experienced in terms
of prophetic aggression against the establishment of the status quo,
overshooting the present by following the signals of hope, and height-
ening the existential sense of alienation under the conditions of
history. The symbol of the kingdom of God offers the church a
horizon of transcendence, opening up a distance between the future

of life it proclaims and the conditions of the present that resist its advent.

II
The Contemporary Quest for an Adequate Eschatology

The struggle to regain a position of centrality to the Kingdom of God in theology may be characterized as a quest for an adequate eschatology. A special problem of this quest has been how to handle the theme of the future. With the rediscovery of the apocalyptic framework within which Jesus proclaimed the kingdom of God, notably through the studies of Johannes Weiss and Albert Schweitzer, the dimension of the future in the structure of Jesus' message has come more forcefully into its own. The kingdom of God is immediately at the door; it is an event very near, but not yet altogether here. The power of this future has a present impact, to be sure, but it does not cease to hold open a temporal distance between what is already the case and what the future will bring. An eschatology that is not centered in the future is not genuine eschatology, but may only be axiology (a theory of values) or mysticism. Numerous attempts have been made to absorb the future into the present in some form of realized eschatology. The category of hope in the oncoming future of God has often been transposed to the experience of faith in his transcendental presence. Platonism once provided Christianity with the conceptual means to defuturize its own eschatology. In modern times this role has been played, first by idealism, then by its stepchild, existentialism. Eschatology then becomes the doctrine of the eternal shining through the presence of all being or through the existential moment. Then Christian faith may look upward, inward, or backward; but the foreward movement of hope, fired by the promise of God that drives the world, is arrested on its way.

Karl Barth elevated the place of eschatology in Christianity when he stated, "Christianity that is not entirely and altogether eschatology has entirely and altogether nothing to do with Christ."[7] In the various theologies that were born under the spell of dialectical thought, the future never wholly drops out of sight. We shall try to trace out the fate of the future in the vise of the eternity/time dialectic and in the subjectivism of existentialist theology. Here and there the theme of the future appears as an oasis in systems of thought that have otherwise defuturized eschatology.

Beginning with Karl Barth we can hazard some generalizations. There is no doubt that all parts of Barth's theology are threaded together by eschatology; it is only a question of *what kind*. As a theologian of crisis Karl Barth juxtaposed the world of the eternal God above to the world of man here below. Eschatology which has to do with the future destiny of this world is lifted into a transcendental realm above it. The eschatological event is the *nunc aeternitatis* which can only touch history at a tangent, but itself cannot have a history. Eschatology lies outside of history, in a prehistory or a suprahistory. The history of Jesus Christ shrivels up to a bare mathematical point so far as it is the eschatological event. The resurrection of Christ, for example, is called an eschatological event, and that means it cannot be an historical event. The *parousia* has nothing really to do with new events which hope expects from the future of God. It is swallowed up in the eschatological present of the eternal now. Eschatology is thus not a doctrine of the future, neither the future of man and his world, nor the future of God and his approaching kingdom. It is wholly absorbed into the transcendence and eternity of God, coming down vertically from above. The horizontal categories of history and the kingdom of God in the Bible are spiritualized into the beyond of eternity.

For a time Barth seems to have become more aware of the inadequacy of an eschatology that relocates the future of hope from ahead to above. In a number of essays he tried to break out of a starkly abstract dialectic of eternity and time,[8] giving expression to hope for a real fulfillment in the future. He says, "Not that the kingdom has come, but that it has drawn near is the meaning, after as well as before the appearance of Christ, of the word that the 'time is fulfilled' in Mark 1:15."[9] Here Barth glimpsed the function of eschatology to keep hope alive and the future open. It is this tension between the promise of the kingdom and its future fulfillment which drives the church as mission of hope into the arena of world history.

In the end Barth never wrote the volume on eschatology for his *Church Dogmatics.* It seemed that as he approached it, there was nothing new for him to say that had not already been contained in the incarnational revelation. The future can only have noetic significance, bringing a fuller *knowledge* of the revelation in Christ. Eschatology does not deal with new events, only with the final unveiling of the accomplished revelation of God in Christ. Does this really give us an adequate eschatology? And does it properly spell out the relation between the horizon of the coming kingdom and the reality of the church? T. Stadtland poses the revelant question: "For many it was painful that Barth declared that he no longer wished to write his eschatology (*Church Dogmatics*, Vol. V). But could he really do that from the starting point that was his?"[10]

Eschatology also holds a key position in Bultmann's theological thought. However, it does not succeed in breaking out of its confinement in existential futuricity. The idea of the priority of the future is expressed, but only in Heidegger's sense as "the primary phenomenon of primordial and authentic temporality."[11] Yet, in his book on *Jesus*, Bultmann has not suppressed the futurist aspect of the kingdom of God. He clearly depicts Jesus' message as an eschatological gospel of the coming of God's Kingdom. This kingdom is "a power *which, although it is entirely future, wholly determines the present.*"[12] The pressure of the future bears down on the present moment, making it for me the "final hour."[13] In reaction to the nineteenth century evolutionary view of the kingdom, Bultmann states that the future kingdom is not the consummation of the creation, as if it were already there in germ from the very beginning. The end is not a mere seed that lies latent in the beginning.

The horizon of the future shaped most of Bultmann's basic concepts. This is a legacy that present-day theology would be prodigal to surrender. Thus, man *qua* man exists in radical openness to the future; bondage to *sin* is enslavement to the law of one's past; authentic existence is the openness of trust toward the future; *faith* is freedom from the past; it is essentially *hope* directed toward the future. *Salvation* is an ever-coming occurrence out of the future, to be grasped through faith alone. The *grace* of God is the power to assure the future as life, in contradiction to the future as death.

Bultmann's quest for an adequate eschatology was hampered by too great a dependence on existentialist philosophy. This means that the eschatological future of God's Kingdom tends to be reduced to the element of bare futurity in the structure of time in human existence. Eschatology becomes scarcely more than the significance of the factor of futurity for the individual. However, the future of eschatological hope must have a new basis in reality that transcends the futurity of existence. Why? Because *death* is the eschaton of existence as such. This new basis is announced by Christian faith in the resurrection of Jesus of Nazareth. It is necessary to trespass the limits of existentialist analysis to speak of a future of existence that spells life rather than death. And there is another crucial point. The future of the kingdom is not merely the hope of existence; it embraces the future of the world, history, and human community. The eschatological future in the biblical kerygma is not reducible to existential futurity.

The ultimate ground for speaking of the future of existence and the future of the world must be located in a theontological doctrine of the future. God is the power of the absolute future. Bultmann's language concerning the future became impoverished by its existentialist reduction since it was not mounted on an adequate doctrine of the being of God within the horizon of biblical eschatology. So finally there is no way to prevent the future from being reduced to the ever-receding horizon of man's openness, without shape or content, power or reality of its own. The power of the future is rendered sterile by being absorbed into the existential now, into the subjectivity of the self.

Paul Tillich made the greatest contribution to the interpretation of the doctrine of the kingdom of God among the theological leaders of the last generation. He defined the problem of eschatology as the question of the meaning and goal of history, and therefore as the quest for the kingdom of God. The symbol of the kingdom of God has two sides—an inner-historical and a transhistorical side. The prophetic revolutionary aspect of Tillich's social thought drew its power from the dynamics of the kingdom of God in history. He saw history as a movement in which the new is created, in which unique and unrepeatable events occur, and which runs toward a future goal. In plain terms Tillich stated: "Christianity is essentially historical"[14] and "Biblical religion is eschatological."[15] This means that the Christian faith looks ahead for the future transformation of all reality, interprets the past and acts in the present in light of the future goal toward which history runs. The New Being is expected predominantly in a horizontal direction rather than a vertical one; there is an expectant hoping for the realization of the kingdom of God, the divine rule of peace, love, and righteousness in a new heaven and a new earth.

Tillich's eschatological interpretation of history, however, did not win the undivided loyalty of his mind. It can be shown that it stands in tension with, perhaps even in contradiction to, the categories of his essentialist ontology. He introduced a suprahistorical ontology in order to overcome the antinomies of strictly historical thinking. The end result was that the problem of the future was solved by dissolving it into the permanent presence of eternal life. His notion of "essentialization"[16] works to translate the eschatological future into the mystical presence of being itself. Theological eschatology becomes a little wheel within the big wheel of a philosophical ontology. Essentialization bears a suspicious resemblance to the classic doctrine of the cycle of time in Neoplatonist philosophy in which "the end is always like the beginning." The horizontal expectation of the kingdom of God takes a vertical leap into eternal life; the vision of the eschatological end curves back upon the ontologized myth of origins.

The final translation of the symbol of the kingdom of God into eternal life is the door which lets in the transcendental mysticism that deprives the future mode of being of its power and meaning. Tillich was right in striving to formulate a doctrine of transcendence. The question is whether Christianity has to borrow the categories of Neoplatonic mysticism to develop a doctrine of transcendence, or can it be more adequately achieved within an historico-eschatological framework? It is doubtful that the conceptual difficulties we face in handling the idea of the future of the coming kingdom can be eased by shifting to the spatial symbolization of mysticism. In fact, by so doing, real transcendence is not achieved at all, since it passes over into the immanence of the eternal now, understood as an ecstatic moment extending into its own depths.

The quest for a more adequate eschatology has been continued beyond Barth, Bultmann, and Tillich by the present generation of systematic theologians. Both Wolfhart Pannenberg and Jürgen Moltmann, whatever the differences between them, have criticized an eschatology in which the horizon of the future is swallowed up by the eternal blitzing in from above. Dialectical theology did not think of eschatological hope as having anything to do with the concrete future. Future tenses were as often as possible converted into talk about the presence of the kingdom of God here and now.

According to Pannenberg, theology must accept Jesus' message of the kingdom of God as the basic starting point for any christology or doctrine of salvation. He says, "This resounding motif of Jesus' message—the imminent Kingdom of God—must be recovered as a key to the whole of Christian theology."[17] The kingdom of God is the eschatological future which God himself brings about. This is to be thought of as the power of the future determining the destiny of everything that exists. It is possible to call God eternal, not in the timeless sense of Plato and Parmenides, but in the sense that he is the future both of our present and of every age that is past.

Moltmann also speaks of the future as a "new paradigm of transcendence."[18] This future is not to be thought of as the progress of the world developing out of the present. There is no transcendence in that. Rather, the future can be a paradigm of transcendence only by bringing into the present something qualitatively new. If we blow up the present into the future, without radical change in the foundations of personal and social reality, the power of evil is magnified along with the good. And our last state is not better than our first. The transcendent future is a power to attack the conditions of evil in the foundations of reality, and to lead it forward through a process of revolutionary transformation. From within history and suffering the pain of its conflicts, it is possible to project a transcendent future of history, which is qualitatively other than just future history. A better future in history can be hoped for on the basis of the power emanating from the transcendent future of history, which opens up new prospects and new possibilities.

It is the case that the theological trends we have been tracing in Protestant theology have stimulated Roman Catholic theologians to rethink their own eschatology. Each of the great Protestant theologians—Barth, Bultman, and Tillich—attracted a significant number of Roman Catholic thinkers and left an indelible mark on their new constructions. Similarly, the trend to give a larger place to the concept of the Kingdom of God, and especially to restore the dimension of futurity so essential to it, has its following in the sphere of Roman Catholic theology. Here we have the profoundest basis for new insights and new reflections on the theme of "Christ and his Church." The eschatological perspective has the force of relativizing the traditional doctrinal differences between Protestant and Roman Catholic theology.

III
The Eschatological Horizon of the Church in History

We have given so much attention to the idea of the eschatological future of God's approaching kingdom because it forms the horizon for understanding the nature and mission of the church. Both Roman Catholic and Protestant theology have had to reconsider the question of the proper starting point for developing a doctrine of the church. In the nineteenth century there prevailed a tendency to identify the church with the kingdom of God. Roman theology conceived of the kingdom as a hierarchically structured church in history, in analogy with the monarchies of Western Europe. This juridical concept of the church was challenged by a resurgence of Pauline studies, yielding the emphasis on the mystical notion of the church as the "body of Christ." This organic symbolism of the body proved, however, to offer too limited a grasp on the church's reality. It tended to be too static and ecclesiocentric, insufficiently oriented to the world and the future of the kingdom. With the beginning of Vatican II, Roman theology had moved on to appropriate a new symbol for the church, namely, as the "people of God." This is the primary image that won its way into the *Dogmatic Constitution on the Church*.

The image of the church as the "people of God" is rooted in Yahweh's election of Israel in the old covenant. The idea of "the chosen people" is also an image that can curve in upon itself if it is not placed within the universal horizon of the kingdom of God. Therefore, it was a stroke of good fortune when Vatican II integrated the eschatological horizon into its reformulation of the doctrine of the church. We read, "The mystery of the holy Church is manifest in her very foundation, for the Lord Jesus inaugurated her by preaching the good news, that is, the *coming of God's Kingdom*."[19] In an explanatory footnote of the American edition we have the further reassurance that "The kingdom of God, which Jesus inaugurated in His public life by His own preaching and by His very person, is not fully identical with the Church. But since Pentecost the Church has had the task of announcing and extending the kingdom here on earth, and in this way initiating in itself the final kingdom, which will be realized in glory at the end of time."[20] Here we have a common root for an understanding of the church today that both the church of the Reformation and the church of Rome can share: Jesus inaugurated the church by preaching the good news of God's coming kingdom. The mystery of the eschatological future is represented already in the very foundation of the church.

In response to the ecumenical situation today and through reflection on the results of biblical scholarship, we as Lutherans are challenged to ask whether our own definition of the church in Article VII of the Augsburg Confession is not too limited.[21] First of all, there is lacking in the definition any reference to the eschatological goal of the church, and second, there is no mention of her essential missionary function in world history. If we are asking about the nature of the church, we cannot omit the fact that it is constituted essentially by its relationships, forward to the kingdom of God and outward to the world. If the church is a gathering of saints to hear the gospel and receive the sacraments, it is also a people on the move in history, pioneering the future of the world toward the fullness of the kingdom. As such it is both a *sacrament* and an *instrument*, as Vatican II stated: a sacrament of the coming kingdom and an instrument for the salvation of mankind. The church is already a sign of the eschatological future it proclaims for the whole world. A doctrine of the church must be developed in terms of the tension between the kingdom of God and the world.

The widespread notion that the church is a voluntary association of persons who are united by a common experience may touch the reality of the church at the sociological level, but theologically it is disastrous. For then it is difficult to overcome the idea that the church is like a social club whose main purpose is to cultivate experiences that hold the group together. If the primary aim of the church is to generate and stimulate Christian experience, then the outward missionary thrust to the world will be felt as a risk to Christian identity and a source for the possible attenuation of its particular types of experiences. "Don't-get-mixed-up-in-the-world" is an attitude of mind that can exist even when Christ is placed at the center of the Christian fellowship. Christ is Lord of the church *and the world*, inasmuch as his universal Lordship possesses eschatological finality with respect to the totality of the created world. There is no way that the church can claim to possess a private relation to Jesus Christ that does not involve it in an outward thrust of mission to the world. To believe in Jesus as Savior and Lord is not merely a matter of having an I-Thou relationship; it is more a matter of acknowledging him as the One through whom God's rule is being represented for the salvation of the world. To know Christ is to know the divine intentionality for the world; to have faith in Jesus as Messiah implies an awareness of the dawning of the messianic age in the midst of worldly events; to believe in Jesus as God's representative is to have hope for the world, to believe that the world's future can participate in the victory of Christ's resurrection over death.

There has been a lot of talk in modern biblical theology about a "realized eschatology." In recent years we have seen a swing away from that, with stress on the fact that the future of the kingdom retains its futural dimension in the very process of making a present

impact. It never becomes perfected, realized, an accomplished fact.
It is important, however, to guard against a total surrender of the
aspect of realization. The claim of Christian faith is that the eschatological future of God has already arrived in Jesus of Nazareth, in his
person, his ministry of word and deed, and in his passion, death, and
resurrection. What we are trying to say is that its arrival in Jesus of
Nazareth so futurizes his person through the resurrection that his
life becomes our Christian future and the future of the world. On
the basis of the presence of the future in Jesus Christ, the church
becomes open to the future when Christ becomes really present in
and through the church. To be open to the future is to share in the
freedom which the gospel of Christ brings. So in the church too the
kingdom of God becomes actualized in faith, hope, and love. This is
actualization through participation in the new reality of Christ.
This participation is made possible by the proclamation of the good
news of the kingdom of God that has arrived in Christ and by the
administration of the sacramental forms in and through which Christ
is experienced as present in the community of believers.

We are saying that our doctrine of Word and Sacraments needs
to be quickened and contoured by the eschatological perspective.
Dogmatics cannot simply provide commentary on sixteenth century
confessional texts. A total recasting is demanded in light of the
recovery of the eschatological horizon of authentic Christian faith.
This will disclose that to the extent that the eschatological future of
the kingdom is operative within the church, it becomes a revolutionizing anticipation of the new world that is being created through the
dying of the old. Word and Sacraments are means by which the
promised future is already being made present in faith and hope and
love. So Christians can live from the power of the "already"—ahead
of the times, so to speak—because they live as though the end is now
in force. The church is *simul iustus et peccator* until the rule of
glory (*regnum gloriae*), because the eschatological righteousness it
appropriates in faith reveals the sinful imperfections of its concrete
life as a church.

The eschatological power of the gospel relativizes all the structures of the church and of its tradition. Nothing in and of the
church can be exempt from the criticism that emanates from the
eschatological word of God in the Christ-happening. The church in
history meets every new situation with reference to that future which
has already been previewed in the coming of the crucified and risen

Lord. The anticipation of this future reacts upon the church's traditional structures and keeps up the pressure from within. The overriding question must always be whether the structures of the church can still serve as sacraments and instruments of the coming kingdom of God. The mere fact that a given structure has a long history, that it can be traced back to the church fathers or so-called biblical times is no sufficient warrant to retain it. Needless to say, the very authority of Scripture itself is not based on its antiquity. The authority of any structure in the church must be derived; it cannot be *ex sese*, a self-constituting authority. Even the best statements and institutions from the past are subject to the eschatological life and relative to the historical situation in which these forms must function.

A burning eschatological consciousness can shed new light on the structural problem of the church today. This problem looms up as still the major hurdle on the way to the reunion of the churches. What can we say about this without giving in to a romanticism which blinks away the tough realities of our divisions? On the other side, however, we should not yield to a realism which is willing to say only what is politically feasible or convenient. The appeal to realism is often a way of escaping responsibility for the crtcial truth.

I think we can say as Lutherans that we recognize the need of the church for *servants* and *signs* of the union we have with Christ and the unity we hope to share with all mankind. The episcopal and Petrine offices can be affirmed by Lutherans under certain conditions.[22] There can even be a high appreciation of them for the services they have traditionally rendered in calling attention to the importance of apostolic succession, in caring for the unity of the church, and in symbolizing the catholicity of the vision. These offices remind the church of its historicality; it must not let its eschatological vision make it a fugitive from history. The church is called by the gospel to the front line of world history, bringing light to the nations, and always seeking better social embodiment of the coming kingdom. The church needs the kinds of offices that are a force for unity among believers, that send them forward into world mission, that tie their memories to the holy events on which the church is founded, and that signal a wonderful future in which all the separated on this wretched planet will enjoy a rendezvous in the kingdom of God. If the episcopacy and the Pertine office have been betrayed into captivity, so that they no longer function in these many respects, then the thing to do is to liberate them. I think that is all

that Luther wanted. He did not want to forget about those in captivity, but to free them for effective service under the gospel. The
matter in this regard is not different in principle from all the other
structures of the church—the process of reform and renewal is continually needed to reorient them away from the hierarchical model
and its authoritarian features toward the image of the servant and an
evangelical concept of leadership. "Whoever would be great among
you must be your servant, and whoever would be first among you
must be slave of all" (Mark 10:43b-44) .

The unity of the church can be forged anew only by putting the
concern for the truth of the gospel ahead of the institutional structure of the church. A reunited church of the future which would
subordinate the concern for a true preaching of the gospel to a form
or organizational unity could easily become the temple of Baal or
the throne of the antichrist. The unity of the church cannot be
guaranteed by the ecclesiastical office, but only through a sharing
in the movement of faith that was inaugurated by the history of
Jesus Christ. The norm of truth that counts in the church is the
Scriptural witness to God's revelation in the person of Jesus Christ.

If the kingdom of God is the starting point for the church's self-
definition, the church will not withdraw behind a wall of privatized
religion, sealing itself off from the social and political realm of life.
The question about the political relevance of the kingdom and the
mission of the church in the social realm is very much disputed
today in all the churches. There has been a tendency for the church
to involve itself in the public sphere at the upper levels, lobbying
for special privileges and immunities. This alliance of the church
with the upper crust of society, or at least with the relatively advan-
taged middle class, is having bad reprecussions on the church's mission to minorities and subcultures today. So the church tends to be
part of the established order, joining the fight for the *status quo*
against the revolutionary struggle for a new order. Where should the
church stand in the polarization that occurs between establishment
and revolution? Again the perspective of the kingdom offers a
guideline.

The Holy Spirit is the personal presence in the church of God's
eschatological future in Christ. He is the Paraclete, the promised
Comforter. Can we deny that Christians have appropriated the
Paraclete to keep themselves comfortable in the establishment—as
long as it favors them? The Spirit has often been applied as a non-

revolutionary principle in the church, keeping it quiet and submissive. In the U.S.A. there is a saying that the Episcopal Church
is the Republican party at prayer; but it is just as true about the
posture of Lutheranism. The church must be on watch lest the
appeal to the Spirit becomes a word to keep Christians warm inside
their ecclesiastical huddles.

The Spirit, rightly understood, is not a principle of comfort for
those who "have it made." He is a revolutionizing presence, the fire
of the spiritual movement that is spreading around the world in the
name of Christ, and the chief source of inspiration in the advocacy
of a world-transforming truth. Literally, *parakaleo* means "called to
the side of." This suggests that we can think of the Spirit as the
principle of one-sidedness—not the presider over the lukewarm middle. The Spirit calls men to one side, to take sides; that can very
well spell offense to the trustees of the establishment. In the history
of the church the Spirit has not only been the comfort of the conservatives, but also the fire of the radicals. In retaliation the ruling
structures always erect a cross for those who threaten their positions
of power and privilege. The Spirit is the defender of those who take
up the cause of the Man who died on the cross outside the gate.
Thus he became an outsider so that all those outside may be given a
place inside the kingdom of God.

IV
Permanent Tension in the Doctrine of the Church

There are three ways that the church can distort its true nature,
and that is by a reduction to a single pole of reference, to the kingdom, the church, or the world. If the church commits the fallacy of
reduction to the kingdom, it places all the fullness of the future
against the emptiness of the present. It does not really get involved
in the present, since it is a mere waiting room. All we have in the
present is hope; the future has all the blessings. This life is written
off as a bad mistake; the only thing it is good for is to make a decision to leave it in favor of another that comes in the "hereafter." The
picture is only a little less bleak when this life is thought of as only
practicing up, or getting ready, for something much more glorious
in the future. This means that the past and the present are sacrificed
for the future. There are eschatological sects that have betrayed this
attitude. The reduction of spirituality to the kingdom can result in

a sneer against creation, against the present time, against the body, against secular pursuits, against feelings of joy and happiness that a person can find in his daily vocation, his friendships, his family, his aesthetic creativity, etc. This is the wrong way to relate the eschatological future to the past and the present. In the history of Jesus Christ we are confronted with the paradigm of the sacrifice of the future for the sake of the present. The gifts of the Spirit are released into our life now; we can experience freedom now, peace now, joy now, love now. We don't have to wait around for these qualities of eschatological life. On account of Christ and the outpouring of his Spirit we can let the future be in the present.

The second fallacy is reduction of the church to itself. We have already used the word "ecclesiocentricity." The church exists out of itself and for itself. It controls the means of its own creation and perpetuation. The kingdom is so fully realized within it, that it has only to take stock of its past and live from its own precedents. It does not need to be open to the present or lean toward the future. It lives self-protectively, suspiciously, and defensively vis-à-vis the world. Perhaps it goes into the world to find new recruits, but basically it senses no solidarity with those outside its own walls. Everything that it is and has comes down from eternity, and derives its justification supernaturally. It has the divinely appointed administerium, the apostolically founded magisterium, the dominically instituted sacramentalities, the patristically established liturgies, and with all this triumphal self-assurance it squares off against the world. In terms of this model the church's task is to hold the line or to restore the past. Its diagnosis of each ill is that modernists have changed the church to conform to the present culture. Faith is equated with fidelity to the tradition, not openness and trust toward the future. Her solution to the world's problems is for the world to listen to the church; her solution to her own problems is to listen to her echoes in the past. The meaning of Vatican II can be seen as the attempt to correct this type of fallacy.

The third fallacy has been amply represented by the modern exponents of secular Christianity. The church is then called to catch up to God's activity in the world. The world determines what is *avant garde*, and the church, not wishing to be left behind, goes about trying to be relevant and "with it." The church joins in a litany of self-condemnation, coupled with exhuberant praise of the virtues of humanists and all men of goodwill. In this reduction, the tradition of the church is sneered at as so much baggage, the Bible is honored as one of the classics in our Judeo-Christian culture, the structures of the church are *only* instruments for the improvement of society, and a Christian is a secular man celebrating the "world come of age." Jesus of Nazareth is made to suffer what one scholar called "the peril of modernizing." The trend of *aggiornamento* in the modern church will surely bring about its demise if what is up-to-date is not itself criticized and relativized by the horizon of the eschatological future. The "latest thing" is as likely to be a tool of the demonic as of the divine power. God has no monopoly on the action in the contemporary world. The antidivine powers have seldom had it so good, because they hide behind the widespread illusion that ours is a Christian culture. The secularist's fascination for the contemporary must not be equated with the Christian's anticipation of the qualitatively new that cuts into the present as a two-edged sword, bringing aggressive criticism and truth transcendent.

It has been said that we must retain the right order in speaking about the church. "That order is God—World—Church, not God—Church—World."[23] I think that the mere switching of the positions of church and world in the series is unfortunate. What is the *order* in question? In traditional Lutheran terminology we could say that the world, of course, comes first in the order of creation, but that in the order of redemption the church comes first. But such competition for priority doesn't accomplish anything. It is better to think and speak of the church as a special instrument which God has created to lead the world forward to the kingdom of God. There is no competition between the church and the world. The church is the sacrament of the world's future; within its life appear the signals of the future which the world, as well as the church, has in store for itself. The church lives not a monological existence in relation to the world, but a dialogical existence to test everything that happens in relation to the future of truth that has been previewed in Jesus Christ. The church can learn from the world because God's Kingdom is present to the world in a penultimate way, just as the church is present to the world as a prismatic reflection of its ultimate destiny.

In the revolution of faith and the institutionalization of the church, a twofold dilemma has accompanied the historical church from the beginning: how can faith be transmitted through the established structures of the church when it is only the Spirit that can create genuine faith, and he blows "where and when he wills." And once faith is created, how can it go on living in the traditional institutions of the church without blowing them apart? The institutional church always tries to domesticate the living faith of its members, to create channels that can be planned, supervised, and recycled into the systems of the established church. When faith gets overly heated by the fire of the Spirit, the governing bureaucracy of the church tries to cool it down to room temperature. The two leading traits of the institutional church since Constantine are state licensing—in one form or another—and infant baptism. Thus the church has come to rely on the state and the state on the church in mutual cooperation. The state has even played the role of persecuting the dissenters within the church, before, during, and after the time of the Reformation. Infant baptism acquired the effect of discounting the need for the personal decision of faith. In reaction to this, there has arisen in the underground church the demand for strictly believers' baptism. The church is then composed of the nucleus of committed Christians, who know whether and what they believe, and the difference that ought to make in their style of life. In the nature of the case the church becomes a movement that goes counter to the worldly society. More than that, it also goes counter to the established form of Christianity that lives a hyphenated existence with the existing culture. The institutional church is seen as a monstrous accommodation of social religion. To be a Christian and a good citizen come down to the same thing; birth and baptismal certificates are virtually interchangeable in culture-Christianity.

From the viewpoint of the believers' church, the official church is always in danger of becoming the church of the antichrist when it exists in fusion with the dominant powers of state and the approved patterns of culture.[24] The church is to be holy; that means to separate itself from the visible world-that-is in order to be a sign of the invisible world-that-is-to-come. The believers' church is a free community constituted by personal conversion and spiritual discipline. In contrast, the institutional church appears as a Judas-church. It is an organized system of religious works without true faith.

That is only half the story. The tragedy of the believers' church is that in trying to transmit the faith of the first generation to the second and third generations, it is forced to improvise forms that bridge the generation gaps. With each passing generation the forms are maintained in the service of a diminishing content. The process of accommodation to make room in the fellowship for the lukewarm and half-committed creeps into the believers' church, betraying the very signs of formalism it found so despicable in the established churches. Ironically, this becomes most evident in the handling of baptism. The first generation offers baptism to those who make a personal decision for Christ; by the third generation it is decided by adults that age thirteen, say, is the right time to be baptized; what then counts as personal conversion is subject to considerable qualification.

Once the believers' church becomes established, it ends in becoming a shadow of the historic church from which it took its departure. But cutting itself off, it loses access to the great storehouse of tradition that the historic church has faithfully garnered with the treasures of faith. In time the "sect" will wend its way back to the main stream of the church's tradition, or it will live alongside in a parasitic way. The historic church attends to the ongoing process of transmitting the traditions of faith, preaching the words, writing the commentaries, remembering the events, commemorating the saints, celebrating the liturgies, etc. This process cannot guarantee the transmission of faith, but it still provides the occasions and stimuli that can turn a person on.

The radical churches have been in hot pursuit of the Kingdom. The heat and light they generate along the way have been of inestimable value to the historic churches. We could even say that established Christianity lives parasitically off the revolutions of radical faith that explode around her fringes. The sectarian movements in church history have often brought needed judgment and even hope to decaying forms of official Christianity. There is a continuing need for the revolutions of radical faith, precisely for the sake of the survival and integrity of the institutional forms of Christianity.

The love of God that has been revealed in the redemptive work of Jesus Christ and that has been appropriated by the faith of the Christian church—does it have any relevance for the wider human community outside? Does the gospel of the coming kingdom of God make an impact for good in the wider social and political community? Modern anthropology has driven home the point that man is not man as an isolated individual; rather, he is what he is as man in a universal network of social and political conditions of life that he shares with his fellowmen. A purely existentialist anthropology is

an abstraction; a Christian doctrine of man must incorporate the
sociopolitical dimensions of anthropology. Therefore, if the gospel
is for the whole man, it must encompass the meaning of the social
and political conditions of human existence. Is it any longer possible
to hold back the revolution of love triggered by the gospel from
entering the social sphere of human life? In the language of classical
Lutheranism, is it possible to segregate the *regnum gratiae* from the
regnum potentiae in a clean-cut dualism of two kingdoms? Are not
both of these spheres of God's rule linked to the *regnum gloriae*,
which is not so much an addendum to world history as the oncoming
power of his rule that he presently exercises both in the church and
the world?

The Lutheran doctrine of the two kingdoms, at least in the form
we received it from the nineteenth century, has led to a static conception of the church and the world standing alongside each other,
each one jealously guarding its own turf and refusing to be en-
croached upon by the other. At its best this doctrine has worked to
police the borders between the church and the world, and even to
encourage harmony, cooperation, mutual goodwill, and functional
interaction. However, the essential eschatological basis of the social
and political dimensions of the church's relation to the world has
not been adequately articulated in the doctrine of the two kingdoms.
It would at least have been better to have a doctrine of the three
kingdoms—the *regnum potentiae*, the *regnum gratiae*, and the *regnum gloriae*. But even that would not help if they are kept un-
dialectically outside each other.

Theological attention must be given to the fact that Lutherans
in America, perhaps more than Lutherans in Europe, have become
involved, not merely as citizens but as members of the church, with
the issues that concern the entire human community. This is a new
experience for the Lutheran churches. For most of their history they
have dealt with merely internal questions, questions of doctrinal and
parochial concern. Recently a restless social consciousness has been
aroused in the church, and Christians are developing a sense of
responsibility for the world, its political, social, economic, and
ecological well-being. Lay Christians and many pastors are demanding of their church bodies articulate pronouncements on social
issues and even concrete programs of service in the secular realm. In
the Lutheran church there has arisen an urgent quest for a theological legitimation of the investment of time, energy, and money in the

public domain. Some feel that the church should stay out of politics, and stick to its own expertise—the preaching of religion and the work of women's auxiliaries. Others feel that the beautiful rhetoric on Sunday is obscene if there is no practical pay-off on Monday. Religious words must produce dividends in deeds. The theological ethic that the church has operated with has spoken of "faith active in love." A living faith is expressed in loving service to the neighbor in the secular realm. This is the realm in which the phenomena of law and justice, reason and power, threats and punishments, hold sway. In regard to this realm Lutherans have derived their theological position mostly from the doctrine of creation. In contradistinction to this realm of creation there is the realm of redemption, based on God's saving work in Christ, realized on earth through the church's preaching of the gospel and the ministry of sacraments. In this realm the phenomena of faith and love, of joy and peace, of hope and freedom, prevail. The juxtaposing of creation and redemption can result in a dualistic antithesis, in which the two realms are insufficiently linked to the eschatological goal of both the church and the world in the future of God's coming kingdom. The Lutheran stress on the *two* kingdoms has the merit of guarding against the dangers of either a "Christianization of society" by ecclesiastical heteronomy, or a "secularization of the church" by legalizing the gospel. The church has no monopoly of insight and right action when it comes to the way in which love is to be expressed through justice, justice through law, and law through power.

The rule of God's power in the secular realm goes forward also outside of the church's sphere of influence, and oftentimes against its organized opposition. When this happens, this becomes a scandal of the church, and God's judgment will surely strike against it for obstructing his will. When the church happens to be behind the world in the struggle for more humanizing forms of social and political life, it has forgotten the total obedience expected of it in relation to the kingdom of God. It has forgotten that the gospel of the kingdom embraces the *total man*. The revolution of love released into the world by the preaching of the gospel cannot be confined to the inner life of the private individual, but extends its impact into the social sphere. Faith active in love needs to be supplemented by a love active in hope.

The fear of the social gospel that has gripped many Lutheran churches is right insofar as it warns against the tendency to reduce the gospel to a means to improve society. The ultimate future of which the gospel speaks is then emptied into the penultimate aims of a particular society. The gospel announces an ultimate horizon of fulfillment that overshoots all the objectifiable goals of the social and political order. The gospel affirms the infinite value of the individual person in such a clear way that it withstands every effort to exhaust the definition of an individual's worth in terms of his role in society or his contribution to the state. The gospel is the enemy of every totalitarian usurpation of the individual by society or its government. It holds out a promise of fulfillment that answers to the deeply personal longing to be somebody, to be an individual person, to be free, just to be. The church has the function to keep the revolution of hope alive, for the sake of reinforcing the highest possible self-definition of man at any time. The symbols of man's final destiny in the kingdom of God, interlocked with the whole creation that is now experiencing the agony of its imperfection, even now inspire the imagination to hope for an ultrahuman fulfillment in the boundless being of God.

The revolution of final hope does not postpone the outpouring of its regenerative force until the end of time. The final revolution already now enters into fusion with particular revolutions of hope for the oppressed and alienated people of history. The master model of how hope for a final future can bring an infusion of hope into the present situation of desperate people is pictured for us in the story of Jesus Christ.

The eschatological hope functions also to relativize all social and political achievements; at their very best they are only partial and provisional signs of the future of the kingdom. The church keeps open the awareness of the distance between the better society we seek in the future and the ultimate kingdom that arrives from the future of God. This gives it a prophetic realism; the church goads men on to better forms of life without suffering the illusion of secular utopias that such forms can be achieved apart from the apocalyptic intervention of God in judgment and grace.

And what will the final future of life in the kingdom of God be like? Man is possibility limited by finitude. But there is also a drive toward infinite freedom within man that seeks an unburdening from every limitation. He has an unquenchable thirst for the infinite. "Man's heart is restless until it finds its rest in God" who is pure and unlimited freedom. Man is not satisfied to stand still within the confines of finitude; he must go forward to new being and live from the unfettered source of freedom—God. Is the final goal of the kingdom to be thought of as a static finale to the dynamic struggle for freedom? Is man now in motion only to stand still in the end? Is there a final resting place—a mansion—to which everyone will retire from the struggle of life? Then the kingdom of God would resemble a Nirvana—an eschaton of nothingness. It would be better to think of the kingdom of God as the power of the future which ceaselessly opens up new possibilities. The essence of God is the pure freedom which man is seeking when he is in search for the truth and reality of his own identity. God is pure freedom—free to be—because the reality he enjoys is underived freedom as such. The freedom man seeks is derived from beyond himself—from the source of freedom in the future of God. The salvation man seeks—paradise, heaven, eternal life—is not the peace and quiet of an old people's home. It is an ecstasy of life—*ek-stasis*—a vital movement beyond every stasis. The symbol of the resurrection is just such an ecstasy of life beyond the stasis of death. The final Christian hope is to share in the victory of the resurrection and the life of the risen Lord.

NOTES

1. Quoted from Willi Marxsen, *Mark the Evangelist*, Abingdon Press, 1969, p. 145.
2. Teilhard de Chardin, *The Future of Man*, Collins, 1964, p. 115.
3. H. Richard Niebuhr, *The Kingdom of God in America*, Harper & Row, 1937.
4. See my chapter, "American Historical Experience and Christian Reflection," *Projections: Shaping an American Theology for the Future*, Doubleday, 1970.
5. Attributed to Gerhard Gloege, quoted by Wolfhart Pannenberg, in *Theology and the Kingdom of God*, Westminster Press, 1969, p. 51.
6. *Ibid.*
7. Karl Barth, *The Epistle to the Romans*, Oxford University Press, 1933, p. 314.
8. For example, "Verheissung, Zeit—Erfüllung, Biblische Betrachtung," *Zwischen den Zeiten*, 1931, p. 459.
9. *Ibid.*, p. 459.
10. Tjarko Stadtland, *Eschatologie und Geschichte in der Theologie des jungen Karl Barth*, Neukirchener Verlag des Erziehungsvereins, 1966, p. 189.
11. Martin Heidegger, *Being and Time*, SCM Press, 1962, p. 378.
12. Rudolf Bultmann, *Jesus and the Word*, Charles Scribner's Sons, 1934, p. 51.
13. *Ibid.*, p. 131.
14. Paul Tillich, "Historical and Nonhistorical Interpretations of History," *The Protestant Era*, University of Chicago Press, 1948, p. 20.
15. Paul Tillich, *Biblical Religion and the Search for Ultimate Reality*, University of Chicago Press, 1955, p. 41.

Chapter 2

The Church in History

To discuss "the church and history" in the space of a few pages is an impossible task, as anyone who knows the subject will recognize. The following can, therefore, only be seen as an outline presentation of a number of problems raised by this title.

Our aim is to demonstrate the unbreakable link between the church and history. A discussion of the relationship between the two entities demands an investigation on a number of levels. It is important to keep the different levels apart while at the same time recognizing the relationship between them.

After an introduction we shall try to make clear the fundamental relationship between the faith of the church and history. What does it mean from a theological point of view that the church is historical? The question of the historicity of the church has to be seen clearly: the church knows that it is grounded in history; its faith is basically an interpretation of history. Christ entered human history. In his incarnation he, in a sense, became history. Thus we have first to try briefly to explain the expression "the historicity of the church."

Second, however, the word "historicity" is not unambiguous. This becomes evident when we turn our attention to the subject of "The Church *in* History." The existence of the church in history contains an inner ambiguity because the history of man itself is marked to its core by an ambiguity. We know no "pure historicity" but only a historicity *in statu peccati,* in the state of sin. On the basis of *this* factor how should one understand the relationship between the church and history?

In order to come to the heart of the matter as quickly as possible, two diametrically opposite ways of viewing the relationship between the church and history are mentioned below, if only briefly.

I
Two Views—and the Suggestion of a Problem

Over long periods of this history of the church the relationship between the church and history could be described more or less in the following way:

Fundamentally, there is only an accidental relationship between history and the church. Of course, the church claims a basis in historical facts, as recorded and witnessed to in the Bible and the confessional writings of the churches, but in the final analysis the church is something which is *above* the history of mankind and is only affected by history on the fringe of its existence. In fact history is "merely an accidental change in an eternal core of being"[1], a change which never essentially affects the church. For, as the church of God, the church is beyond history. It has its own sacred history, basically self-contained, from the resurrection of Christ to the *parousia,* that is, to use the usual terminology, a *church* history in contrast to *secular* history. The relationship between the two is in reality only external. Of course, the church exists *in* history, but it is there as a fundamentally unchangeable entity established by God with its own existence in the midst of the history of mankind. Because the church is divine it is beyond history. The consequences of this view is the almost inescapable conscious or unconscious and perhaps very "humble" superiority complex of the church. It is safe and protected because it is the People of God.

I can still remember quite clearly how I was once filled in my early youth with the comforting, exalted insight: the Christian culture can never be destroyed. All other cultures have had their time, but the culture which is based on Christianity can never finally be overcome. God himself is the guarantor of this. This pious feeling of grateful certainty is accompanied by a sense of superiority to the world. Of course, the church has its bad times; it also has its sinful times. It has always been very difficult indeed to talk about the sin of the church. For some churches it was impossible and for others a little easier. The sense of security in the midst of the flow of history with its movements to and fro, its uncertainty and its dangers, was deeply rooted in the churches. But is this sense of security not justified? Is it not part of the essence of faith that the gates of hell will never prevail against the church of Christ? Certainly! The only question is how that should be understood. There has been and there still is a sense of the final victory of the church in the flow of history which has nothing to do with faith. In this connection I think it is useful carefully to read Jer. 7:1-15. We shall come back to this question later. According to this view history is, naturally, not superfluous. That would be pure heresy. It plays a necessary part—in two ways. At the time of its founding the church was built up on the wonderful, historical deeds of God. And later history could show traces of the divine which would indicate God's blessing and support. In many cases the writing of church history was only apparently a *historical* discipline. Often it was a semidogmatic, careful rearrangement of the facts, more apologetics than history. "Many historical monographs were nothing more than a further ballot paper for a predetermined hypothesis. With a cloud of witnesses the attempt was made to suppress the other point of view." That "historical thinking is by nature critical thinking" was ignored in many cases.[2]

A form of Christian thinking based on political, sociological, economic factors, related to a certain period, was often seen as genuine Biblical Christianity, as *the* Christian tradition. A theoretical distinction was made between *tradition* and traditions but in practice what one had inherited was considered to be the genuine tradition. It has always been extremely difficult to distinguish between the divine and the human, between the unchanging and the changing.

The church was not only the infallible instrument of salvation in a sinful world; at the same time it provided the necessary guidelines for the life of the world. It was almost always, consciously or unconsciously, sumultaneously playing a political and social role. The church was aware of its responsibility for the world. It is one of the fundamentals of the religious and moral cosmos of the influential Western world. In a way it constitutes the metaphysical basis for faith and morals in life as a whole. One could obey or not: the basis remained unchanged. If one wished to escape one had to *decide* to do so[3]. It was not automatic. The forces which opposed this link between the church and history, in which the church as a suprahistorical entity was the determining factor, had to fight against a strong spiritual power rooted in metaphysics. Despite this strong reference to history, strangely enough it is as clearly established: as an institution established by God the church as church had essentially nothing

to do with human history. Its God-given task was to exercise an influence on the world but in itself it could basically not be influenced.
This was what constituted its humble pride.

As I have said, the Christian revelation was historical because it
was based on historical facts; in reality, however, the revelation was
only a manifestation *in* history of divine truths of a dogmatic and
ethical nature, which God brought to light by means of the "history
of revelation" for man's salvation. What was really meant by historical was not taken quite seriously. What was most important was not
history but the dogmas. History itself became secondary, being
viewed and used merely as a "channel" for the eternal, divine, saving
truths. A typical example from the Roman Catholic realm is the
definition of revelation given by the Thomist Garrigou-Lagrange:
"The revelation is the free and essentially supernatural act in which
God—in order to lead the human race to the supernatural goal—
speaks to us through the prophets and finally through Jesus Christ
and, thus, in a certain obscurity *(sub quadam obscuritate)*, reveals
the supernatural truths and also the natural truths of religion, so
that they can be presented infallibly by the Church one after another
without any change in meaning *(sine ulla significationis mutatione)*
until the end of time."[4] Here revelation is seen essentially as the
transmission of truths. There was a docetic sheen about this conception of revelation. The living figure of Jesus in the synoptic Gospels,
his relentless struggle with the tradition of the established Jewish
church, his "new wine" in the midst of the stabilised *status quo* of
religion, the way of the suffering servant of God to the cross, the
resurrection of the obedient one—all this which was historically new
and unexpected was often forgotten in history and preference was
given to a dogmatic system.

The Bible and the New Testament in particular were seen finally
as the source of a system—although often mitigated by a religious
experience—of indisputable dogmas and ethical prescriptions. It is
interesting to observe how, despite its passion for the historical,
mutatis mutandis, existentialist theology becomes after all unhistorical, for here, too, there is a danger that history will be restricted to a
"channel" for a "historically" existential proclamation. Here, too,
history itself becomes secondary. To sum it up: according to the
view outlined here the relationship between the church and history
is external. They do exist side by side and are not able to separate

themselves from one another, but the contact between them is basically that between two unrelated entities.

The second conception of the relationship between the church and history with which we shall deal here follows a diametrically opposite line. In the previous view the church existed in the final anaylsis, independently of history and was superior to history. In the following the opposite will be the case. Here history becomes the factor which governs and is superior to everything else. Everything is swallowed up in the flow of history, nothing is permanent, nothing is absolute, everything becomes totally relative. The name for history is development; and development means unceasing change. There is no unchangeable being, no metaphysically permanent, unchanging nature. In this connection tremendous importance is attributed to the development of science in all its branches; the recent trends in philosophy, psychoanalysis with its understanding of man on the basis of the subconscious, linguistic structuralism which has made man into a sort of instrument of language so that basically it is not man who speaks but, on the contrary, language with its various structures which speaks through man. It is language which invented the idea of a man who would speak a language. Here is the danger of denying that man is a spiritual being.

In short, the extraordinary discoveries in all fields seem seriously to undermine the Western Christian view of man as the center of the cosmos, as God's creation. The all-pervasive characteristic of this new spirituality is its radical this-worldliness, its secularism. There were, of course, people in the past, either individuals or groups, who protested against a metaphysics marked by Greek spirituality and against a culture interwoven with the Chistian faith. But what used to exist only on the edge, as it were, now embraces large portions of the modern world. A lot has been written about this in recent years. What once took place in secret is now shouted from every rooftop.

Few people have recognized this situation so clearly and described it so vividly and urgently as Dietrich Bonhoeffer in his letters from prison. But he was neither the first nor the only one to recognize it. Naturally, the church is also drawn into this historical development. How does the church appear to the eyes of this new world? One can put it in approximately the following way: the church came into existence at a certain point in the history of mankind. As a result of a number of historical, religious and sociological factors it became widespread; in the West in the course of the centuries it has developed into a religious, spiritual, and cultural major power; without it Western European culture would have been impossible. It embodies a complicated synthesis of the Israelite-Christian religion of revelation, the oriental religion of salvation and of Greek philosophy, which formed the basis of the so-called Christian Western world for centuries. As such it was of historical significance, but only for as long as the presuppositions existed. It is in fact so closely related to the image of history of the so-called Christian Western world that it can only continue to exist against this background. At the moment when these presuppositions come to be doubted its time has also come. It can fight for its life, it can try by means of a number of *aggiornamentos* to adapt itself to the new period, but this will be to no avail because it is so fundamentally identified with certain presuppositions of a particular period that it must of necessity die in a radical process of transformation.

For Feuerbach and Marx there is no doubt that religion is outdated. It belongs to the category of illusion. The church is the place of refuge for alienated man; it offers comfort and peace when what is needed is fight and action. It is not only meaningless, it is clearly harmful because it works directly against the course of history. It is of no relevance to the process of man's liberation, to the movement for a classless society. It is an *opponent*. That which was positive in early Christianity, especially its utopian hope for the future, has now become so bourgeois and related to an overemphasis on the life to come as to be fatally fossilized.

Its eschatology has been adopted today by Marxism: the kingdom of liberated man who has discovered himself will come. This has made history meaningful again. The historical process has two aspects: on the one hand it must of necessity reach its goal (the "metaphysical" aspect), on the other it demands the total commitment of the man who decides for it (the moral aspect).

In historicism we meet a philosophical approach which has exercised a tremendous influence over the past two centuries. Few people have seen the final consequences of consistent historicism as clearly and unflinchingly as Ernst Troeltsch, especially in the book published after his death, *Der Historismus und seine Uberwindung* (Historicism and the Overcoming of it). "In that not only all revelations and absolutes but all normative commitments to ideals are transformed into historically conditioned and thus relative matters, every culture disintegrates into an aggregate of more or less coincidental and transitory values, all of which have lost their binding authority for the uninhibited observer, and everything dissolves into a great river of historical becoming and perishing."[5] The whole of our knowledge, our spiritual world with the state, law, morality, art, and religion, can only be understood as a part of a historical development. Troeltsch sensed and presented most energetically and uncompromisingly the consequences of historicism for the church and its theology, and especially for its dogmatics. "The person who thinks dogmatically is the one who fails to recognize that all truth is historically conditioned." "Dogmatics is a science which exists today only in the most intimate theological circles and even there it is hardly really present."[6] How can one avoid this total relativism which permeates everything? This was a question which Troeltsch clearly recognized, and he devoted all his intelligence to overcome these consequences of historicism.

One final factor must be mentioned which is of great importance in our context. The critical view of the church has found its way into the churches themselves. The church has become a problem for the churches.

In 1970 in Germany appeared a book entitled "Warum bleibe ich in der Kirche? Zeitgenössische Antworten" (Why Do I Stay in the Church? Contemporary Answers). It had been written by people who were consciously Christians, seventeen Catholics and fourteen Protestants.[7] Only very few of the writers could maintain a total identification with their church and these few often for paradoxical reasons. Most of them found themselves compelled, for the sake of honesty, to be satisfied with an often critical partial identification. For several, personal faith in Christ did not depend on the church as it is; rather their attitude to the church was critical as a consequence of this faith.

The criticism expressed by these persons was not negative. Behind it all there was a hope, although they were unable to give concrete expression to this hope. Behind such articles is there not a feeling that, in order to become churches again, the churches will have to undergo a painful transformation, that they will have to be purified in a melting pot?

A large part of the protest of the youth is directed consciously or unconsciously against the scientific treatment of the world, an artificial, increasingly lifeless world, built by man the manipulator with

his fantastic technical capabilities. They are protesting against a
world in which that which is immediate, unobservable and thus living is being transformed into a world which is controllable on the
basis of an operational "cybernetic ideology."[8] In their despair at
being powerless against the inhumanity of this world they run amok.
Their critical rejection also applies to the church which they see as
inseparably bound up with this alienated world. In their view the
church, too, has fallen victim to hollow systematization. The young
people, to whom also a large number of older people is to be
counted, see in the established, dogma-ridden, liturgically rigid
church an expression of the manipulated, controllable world of
man's making.

The criticism of the church is an attack especially on its language. Church language has, of course, its own structure. One can say
nothing against this. Faith expresses itself in a different language
from science, philosophy, or politics. But when this language becomes sealed and inaccessible, a process of alienation inevitably takes
place. It is not "understood." It finds no point of contact, no frame
of reference.

The language which the church uses for preaching and liturgy, for
church hymns and everyday religious life has changed slowly and yet
it is so closely tied to the piety and concept of faith of earlier generations that it has a frustrating effect: it does not apply to man, it answers no questions and causes only very few people to face the ultimate questions of life.

Despite earnest and profound endeavors to take the problem of
language, preaching, and theology seriously, both scientifically in the
case of hermeneutics and in pastoral teaching, the church has on the
whole not succeeded in making its language into a living, meaningful language as the servant of the good news of God in our time.
How can the two words "Jesus Christ" or the word "salvation" be so
interpreted that, in a context which is very different from the situation of the Early Church and of the Reformation, the reality and
meaning of the Christian faith can break through? The hermeneutical task demands a spiritual intellectual effort which cannot achieve
its aim either without strict scientific method or without the illumi-
nation of the Holy Spirit.[9] But what does "aim" mean here? We
keep coming back to the beginning again.

In what was said above we have outlined two different views of the
relationship between the church and history. The former was based

on the presupposition that the church is finally an entity which is above history. As the People of God it is safe and, thus, finally impervious to the laws of history. As the instrument of salvation it can fundamentally only have a relationship of vis-à-vis to the history of sinful mankind. It does exist *in* history but is in reality *above* history.

In stark contrast with this, the latter view presupposes that the church is a historical entity among others. It is totally part of the history of mankind and is swallowed up by the flow of history.

Each of these views is subject in its own way to an internal error of reasoning: the former errs by "too much" and the latter by "too little." In both cases the unique nature of the church is overlooked.

In passing, we have also referred to the crisis of the church today, where there is a radical protest against the first view but also opposition to the second, because people are turning to the church with *questions* and *demands* in the hope that they may still receive an answer.

Our further examination will now be conducted on two levels. First we must, however briefly, make clear that there is an essential link between the Christian faith, the church, and history: faith is based on and nourished by history, namely, the history of God with man, as this was interpreted by the people of Israel and later by the church and handed down both orally and in writing. Here we face the fundamental question of the relationship between faith and history.

Second, the following question must be tackled: What is the relationship between this church as it confesses and interprets its faith and the history in which the church lives and must live and from whose laws it cannot escape as an earthly historical entity? In what way does the church of Christ exist in the history of man?

While discussing this last question we shall be confronted time and again with the internal and outward crisis of the church. The church's progression through history is marked by true and false decisions, by faithfulness and unfaithfulness from inside and by opposition and temptation from outside.

II
Reflections on the Problem, "Faith and History"

According to the church's own self-understanding, its basis is neither a final metaphysical truth nor profound myths or symbols which support and illumine human existence. This does not mean that mythical and symbolic language has no part to play. On the contrary. But its fundamental basis is history, understood both as historical words and historical deeds, which were "experienced" as facts of salvation, interpreted in faith with the help of the human *logos*, formulated or recounted in language and handed down by the tradition. The Christian and the historical are entities which cannot be separated. In order to explain this further we shall look briefly at the difference between a philosophical view of life such as we find in Plato and the Israelite understanding of life.

In the Platonic world-view, the real or being was not to be found in concrete, earthly things which were merely a shadowy reflection of eternal ideas. Therefore, it was the philosophers who had the ability to recognize ultimate truth. The less one was involved with earthly things, the nearer he was to the truth and to God. Salvation was simply a liberation from the earthly, the shadowy, from time with its movement and change, from the emptiness of temporal life. Only after death was man redeemed from time with its constant succession of finite "facts" which disturbed the philosopher. Only then could true life begin. This is how Plato presents the situation in *Phaidon*. By virtue of his nonmaterial intellectual capacity, man was able to rise above unredeemed time and, thus, become aware of reality. Salvation meant the sight of the eternal ideas and finally becoming united with them.

Naturally, the Platonic Greek was also familiar with history and the writing of history. But history could not offer that which was essential and final. Naturally, the thinking Greek also lived within a tradition.[10] No one was born ready-made. In this sense he was also a historical being. Tradition means that one receives something and passes on something. For Plato tradition was a main concept, and he valued the oral tradition much more than the written transmission. But that which was received here was basically the "property" of the person receiving. He did have to listen, to learn, to develop; he could not "be" automatically, he "became." And yet from the very beginning it was "his own," because he had everything true and good deep within himself in his memory. He had the ability and, therefore, also the possibility of verifying it all alone or, at best, in dialogue with others.

The Israelite understanding is quite different. The Israelite's life is not based on eternal, essential reasonable truths but on "history."

What does that mean? The Israelite also lives within a tradition. Something was handed down to him; but what was handed down to him was not his own property but what had happened to his forefathers, what spoke to them directly, what brought the truth home to them.[11] All of this was transmitted to him by a living tradition. History was like words: in the things that happened a word of promise, of judgment and of salvation became audible, a word which called for an answer. That answer could not be a *philosophoumenon*, a philosophical concept; rather it took the form of a story of praise. The Israelite faith did not imply a coherent total view in which, at least by implication, all questions had been answered. Often the Israelite remained in great trouble and profound doubt. Hence the many complaining, despairing people in the Old Testament,[12] including those who complained against God. There were times when everything became obscure, when the questions remained unanswered, times when the people was led to the edge of destruction, but also times when God's salvation was received and praised with great joy and rejoicing. Here it is not a matter of "essential reasonable truths" but indeed of "chance historical truths"; and here the "ugly chasms" which Lessing could not cross were really bridged. It was on the basis of such historical events that the God of Israel was recognized as God. Here history and knowledge were closely intertwined.

In worship this *Heilsgeschichte* was experienced and believed over and over again as a source and goal. Here the meaning of existence was experienced and acknowledged. The classical example of this is the much discussed so-called "historical creed" in Dtn. 26:5-9.[13] This brings together an account of the mighty saving acts of God, praise and thanksgiving, instruction and exhortation, and his sharing in the history of the people. The hearing of this word of history leads to the creed. Could the Greek tradition bring one to a confession of faith? Or did it end in a form of final knowledge which could cause joy and could mediate peace even in the midst of the apparently absurd, but which could not experience any history in the midst of history as the basis for praise? The unique characteristic of this creed is that it does not only refer back to the past but that it is above all related to the present and open for the future. The confession of faith portrays what applies *today* and for the future.[14]

The same is true of Ex. 15:1-19, the hymn of victory by the Red Sea. This account, too, is based on a particular historical event, the miraculous redemption of Israel from Egypt. But it is of typological significance for the whole history of Israel. Many individual aspects of the hymn refer to later events in the history of the people. The story is open to the future saving acts of Yahweh. Later facts of their salvation could be included, in particular Israel's return from exile as a new exodus. Thus, a memory became the living present.[15] In early Christianity and in the liturgy of Easter night in the Early Church, Ex. 15:1-19 was related typologically to the resurrection of Jesus.

For the Israelite, God was not the ultimate, immovable ground of being, nor an *a priori* for all human culture and intellectual activity, nor a mystical origin of all being, but a personal power, a "Thou" who is lord, who intervenes actively in history. History has meaning because God is God, not because the people are able to philosophize and discover some "immanent" meaning. Israel lived from and in history but had no philosophy of history. This faith which relates to history is also the basis of the relationship to the future. Gradually, the Israelite faith also became a hope which was expressed in many eschatological forms.

This faith based on history also had an effect on the young church. We do not need to go into that further here. In a very fundamental sense everything depended on a history, namely, the history of Jesus Christ. Here a "contingent historical truth" constituted the only basis for a faith on which life and death depended. *Now* the fulfillment of the promises of the old covenant was taking place. *Today* is the day of salvation. Through this one person the kingdom of God has become a reality here and now. *His* day is the day of days. In the life, deeds, and words of Jesus, in his death, resurrection, and exaltation God was acting for the salvation of the world.

For a Greek, then and now, this was nothing less than a shock. "Christianity rebelled against the Hellenistic world by introducing a time of events, of crises and decisions." "The Christian revelation scandalized the Greeks with its holy stories: creation, fall, covenant, prophetic anger, and still more radically with words like incarnation, cross, empty tomb, resurrection, outpouring of the Holy Spirit, etc." This is how Paul Ricoeur puts it.[16] And he adds: this conception of a living history also has an effect on a concrete understanding of man. He, too, is understood in "historical" categories: he can rise up in revolt, he can be converted, he can lose or win his life. Even a nation has a "personal" existence and can gain or lose its life. In this

Christian view history acquires a positive significance where man is called forth from the anonymity of nature. He makes history by also integrating nature in his history. The Early Church was soon faced with a very big problem because as it spread it inevitably came up against the Greek world. We can already find traces of this confrontation in the New Testament. Very early the Christian faith developed its own historical creed, for this is how one must describe the Apostles' Creed from its earliest beginnings up to its finished form. This creed, like all the original kerygmatic-liturgical credal fragments, is thoroughly "anti-metaphysical," unphilosophical, simply *historical*. It includes creation, salvation in Jesus Christ, the whole history of Israel in its liturgical expression, the historical activity of the Spirit, the earthly existence of the church and an eschatology relating to the future.

Christianity, as Joseph Ratzinger states in his interpretation of the Creed, opted for the *logos* against the *mythos*, "*for* the God of the philosophers *against* the gods of the various religions."[17] Something can be said for this bold statement. It is appropriate, first, in that from the very beginning Christianity was everywhere vigorously opposed to the mythological. We have already mentioned this. Faith was *not* mythological, based on myths; rather it was based on historical facts from a particular, dateable period of time. The Christians lived on a history which was illuminated by the Holy Spirit and which they understood and interpreted as God's history of salvation. Faith became a reality in the full light of day, not in some esoteric, mysterious, religious darkness. The term "symbol"[18] did not mean a language of ciphers understandable only to the initiated, but was an express reference to a very definite historical fact which was explained and interpreted existentially in preaching and catechetical teaching.

The other thing which Ratzinger maintains—that Christianity opted *for* the "God *of the philosophers*" against the gods of the religions—is rather more difficult and requires careful reflection. On the one hand it is true that faith is an understanding faith, or perhaps better a faith which implies knowledge, a *fides quaerens intellectum;* this is demonstrated both by the New Testament and by the church fathers. Christianity cannot view itself as a mystically esoteric religion without abandoning its true self. History, truth and faith belong together. Therefore, history and dogmatics are closely related. Paul puts *logos* and *gnosis* together. Preaching takes place by

means of clear, intelligible human words. Is it, therefore, true when
Ratzinger says that Christianity opted for the God *of the philosophers?* Did not the apologists try to interpret Christianity as a sort of
perfection of Greek philosophy, as the perfect divine philosophy for
which Greek philosophy was only a forerunner? In the following
chapter Ratzinger, in fact, points out that the God of the philosophers was radically changed in Christianity.[19] In my opinion, on this
point Ratzinger should have emphasised more strongly the difference
between philosophy and faith, for is this not, in a nutshell, the
whole problem of the historicity of Christianity? Did not the historicity of Christianity become most problematic in the following
centuries precisely because philosophy came to play an increasingly
large part in the interpretation of faith? Almost imperceptibly the
biblical, *historical* knowledge of God was transformed into a theology strongly influenced by a metaphysical speculation about God, in
which the knowledge of the living God of Abraham, Isaac and Jacob
and of the Father of Jesus Christ, who reveals himself yesterday and
today in concrete words and events, was most inadequately present.
Do we not here face quite simply one of the main problems of Western Christianity as a whole, both in the Roman Catholic and in the
Protestant churches? The christology of many theologians and theological schools has often been marked by docetism.[20]

In essence the Reformation was the breakthrough of a genuine,
historical, theological insight,[21] but this was soon obscured again by
unhistorical, metaphysical thinking.

A gigantic effort to see history and philosophy together—and this
within the framework of faith in the triune God—was made by
Hegel. He sees and evaluates history as *one* great epistomological
process. Here Lessing's ugly chasms are completely bridged. History,
including the history of Jesus, becomes necessary. It gives final insight to those who have the ability to see it. Hegel is the ingenious
perfecter of the ultimate desires of Greek philosophy, for he *totally*
surmounts the fundamental estrangement of the "Greeks" from history with its "chance events." History has become philosophy and
philosophy history.

One of the most important tasks for contemporary dogmatics is to
rethink the problem of historicity which is being discussed everywhere today. But at the same time this demands a rethinking of the
problem of *metaphysics and history.*[22] The usual distinction or
rather division between "metaphysical" and "historical" must be re-

vised, for the sake both of the "metaphysical" and of the "historical." The term "metaphysics" should not be limited to an outdated, time-bound terminology relating to the old proofs of the existence of God. So-called "Christian Western metaphysics" with its harmony between reason and revelation, faith and knowledge, collapsed with the development of modern science. Since then, metaphysics and modern thinking as historical thinking have become stark opposites. The basis of metaphysics, as we should understand the term today, is the historicity of everything human, and it depends on the temporal-material reality of human existence and, thus, of historical thinking. "History and metaphysics are so closely related that one must say: 'To assert the metaphysical nature of man is to assert the historical man.' "[23] But in metaphysics, thinking "goes beyond" its temporality when man reflects on his personalness which is itself a condition for man's historicity. Without a final effort of the human mind to reflect on its own specific character the word "historicity" also loses its meaning. Material factors like "living space," economics, and other socio-cultural institutions are not all that constitutes history although they are a necessary part of man's existentiality. But they become *history* only when man as a person transcends and freely uses these various factors despite his existential dependence upon them. Only then does history come about.[24] Man's nature is not a given factor from the very beginning that can be defined exactly, as metaphysics believed in the past; man is a being who finds himself in history. Historicity means "having a responsible situation in time, the way of being which is appropriate to man alone and which most distinguishes him from everything which is merely 'ontic.' " "Placed in the course of history he has at any time to appropriate it. By his attitude and participation he enters into a responsible relationship with the 'world,' changes physical time into the moment of decision and thus becomes aware of his 'existence.' "[25]

Personal freedom and responsibility are related to the concept of historicity, but these do not exist as "pure," abstract, human attributes; they are always closely connected with man's temporality, that is his physical, psychological and sociological conditioning. In man there is a dialectical relationship between bondage and freedom which is not transparent for man *per se* but which has to be taken into account if we do not wish to become subject to an all-embracing relativism.

In what we have said immediately above, we have presented the concept of historicity in a more philosophical, or rather existential-philosophical, way. Theology does not automatically reject a philosophical understanding of man. It is aware that philosophy and psychology have many genuine and true insights to say about man that it, too, must seriously consider. But theology cannot tackle the problem of man without man's relationship to God. The historicity of man is a mystery which we shall never be able to explain. Why? Precisely because man's secret is to be found in his relationship to God, and this in two ways: First, because man was created to be related to God. The purpose of man's life is to exercise lordship over the earth as "a son" of God, i.e., to be both a freeman and obedient at the same time. This lordship is not, primarily, merely a matter of doing, whereby a product would be made as a consequence of some human ability, although this is also necessary. His lordship is not primarily a matter of making or producing things but a creative activity which does not exist in the first place for any particular use but which creates new life in others and for others. What is meant by the image of God we only know finally from Jesus, the free and obedient one, whose freedom was his obedience. According to theology, without this relationship to God there can be no true understanding of man.

Second, because man is a sinful being. The word "hamartia" refers to a profound disturbance of the relationship between God and man. Man misses his goal, he follows the wrong direction. *Sicut Deus eritis*, "you shall be as God," was what man was told. However this mysterious expression should be understood, it is certainly said that man questions God's authority, that he wants to be "independent," that he wants to have his freedom without God and that—*horribile dictu*—he succeeds in becoming independent. He stands on his own feet without finally being able to do so. The "fall," as Bauhofer puts it, is "from man's point of view the end of pure access to God. Pure access to God is now only a *divine* possibility."[26] Man is a being estranged from God and yet without having fallen from God's hand. In his ungenuineness, that is, in his subjection to sin, he belongs to God. This is the mystery of man and at the same time his historicity.

This man is the man of history. Among all the beings that exist he is the only one that is "historical." The shifts of the mountainous masses of the earth, the development of a species of animals or an epidemic which causes thousands of people to die are not what we call history. History is the *human* drama of existence, just as the world is "the stage of the history of the human race." Obscure reference is made to this by mythology, legends, poetry, and great dramas. Philosophical man philosophizes about it and the psychologist concerns himself with it. Theology is involved in the endeavour to understand man. Nothing human should be unknown to it but its form of knowledge is primarily theological, i.e., it tries at every moment to understand man in the light of the biblical witness to revelation. But, as we have said, it cannot do this without cooperating with other attempts to understand.

Nor can theology avoid concerning itself with a theology of history, for this is merely a further step in its endeavors to understand man as a son of God and as alienated from God. Theology must reject the attempt to try to understand history on the basis of a closed historical system. It is precisely man's attempt to understand himself and his history while radically denying his transcendental relationship to God which witnesses to man's false autonomy.

This brings us to the heart of our subject: the church and history. God enters this history of man who was created to have a relationship with him and who rebels against him; it is here that he makes himself known, here that he acts for man, judging, healing, opening up the future, and making things new until the fulfillment. This is the witness of the Bible. If the source of philosophy is wonder then this is all the more true of theology.

In what way does the church of Jesus Christ exist in the ambiguous historicity of man? This is the problem with which we must now deal directly.

III
Unity and Division

The church of the disciples of Jesus lives with a promise: despite all inner and outer opposition, the church will be preserved until the last day. This is the only way in which one can understand the last sentence of the command to baptize (Mt. 28:19-20). This statement should not be understood in a "banal" way, that is, the way in which Christ preserves his church is not accessible to reason, not even to pious reason; it is not immediately visible. The promise is fulfilled *sub contraria specie*, i.e., in a way different from that which is seen, that is visible only to *faith*. Faith always takes place in darkness, *in quadam obscuritate* as the Thomists say,[27] a point of view which was later further expounded and made more radical by Martin

Luther, "Thus faith is a sort of knowlegde or darkness that nothing can see."[28] The fulfillment does not take place in full view on a main road but on a narrow path which is often totally hidden. The walker proceeds blindly, often unable to see anything, and what he sees in fact can often be dazzling. He hears a voice which keeps him upright, which gives him the command to go further *or* to change his direction radically.

The history of the church is an extremely ambigous phenomenon. Criticism of the church often is voiced in an uncontrolled way and without genuine understanding, and the same is true of idealizing the church. Both criticism and idealization are based on a common presupposition, namely, that the church is an unambiguous phenomenon which is identical with its visible expression. Here, too, the Reformation recognized something essential which was naturally quickly forgotten.

Today (as always) it must be the task of theology to reflect anew on the nature of the church both as a fellowship willed by God and founded on Christ and as a human, historical, and, therefore, threatened and erring entity, which constantly misunderstands and resists its calling, sometimes even to the point of completely distorting its true nature. It is important to present these two sides of the church. Every dogmatic concept of the church undoubtedly rarely succeeds in expressing this realistically, honestly, and relevantly.

It is necessary to keep two statements together: *ecclesia perpetuo mansura est*, "the church continues forever," and *ecclesia semper reformanda est*, "the church must always be reformed." Both sentences have to be understood in a radical way: the church *is* God's, it *is* his people which cannot perish, chosen for the sake of the world, the beginning of the kingdom of God. At the same time it is always tempted to emancipate itself from God, to become its own Lord, to follow the antichrist. The church can fall into apostasy, become guilty of high treason. In the second sentence the word *reformare* does not (only) mean a "freshening up," an "aggiornamento," but a rethinking, penitence, radical recognition, and corresponding action. This also means that the church can only be preserved if Christ himself preserves it, intervening, chastising, recreating, and strengthening. Martin Luther had a striking word to say on this: "It is not we who can preserve the Church, nor were our forefathers able to do so and nor will our descendants be able to; rather it was, still is and will be the one who says: I am with you until the end of the world,

JESUS CHRIST."[29] Everything depends on the interpretation of this statement, namely, whether it is understood to be harmless, "pious," and undialectical or whether it is taken literally and, thus, seen to be impenetrable and paradoxical.

In the following I shall try to explain this situation by discussing the significance of discontinuity or of the break within the church. If we use the words "discontinuity" or "division" in connection with the church we become uneasy. After all, the church is *one*. And unity means continuity, without division, *semper eadem*, "always the same." "Division" clearly means that the unity has been destroyed, that the truth is divided, that the promise is no longer true. Discontinuity and division are signs of untruth, of falsehood. But where there is continuity and harmonious development, there is truth because truth is indivisible. If the church enters into dispute with itself this is a sign of the fact that it does not represent the truth. This is surely one of the simplest rules of logic. Discontinuity and division give rise to untrustworthiness. This is a very tricky question because the unity of the church is absolutely fundamental. The whole New Testament witnesses to this. But from the point of view of the Bible the term "unity" is not merely a philosophical word. One could say, rather, that it is a historical word, i.e., a word which derives its meaning from history. What does the Bible itself mean by the terms "unity," "division," "new beginning," and, thus, also "truth" and "untrustworthiness"?

First, an often neglected fact must be pointed out: the part just played by division, by schism in Biblical history, both in the Old and in the New Testaments. There we learn of divisions which were willed by God himself, not in order to divide his people, to obscure the truth, but the opposite: in order to establish true unity, so that truth may shine forth.

Let us look at tradition as understood by the Bible. In the Old Testament: the people of Israel was eminently a people of tradition, namely, of a divine tradition to which this people believed it belonged and from which it derived its identity. In the Old Testament, however, we come up against something very shocking and striking. In this tradition there is a conflict between a religious tradition and a sovereign *counterpart* which is *never* identified with this tradition and which, on the contrary, often appears to be critical and even destructive of the religious tradition of this people. In Israel there is a tradition of faithfulness and obedience, but this tradition of

faith was often threatened by apostasy, despised, not in the name of
evil but in the name of a "living" tradition which adapted itself to
the religious situation of the surrounding world. In the Old Testament we meet a God who breaks and punishes the religious tradition of the people. The unheard of fact about the Old Testament is
that here, in the midst of the religious institutions, in the religious
and national life of the nation, in the midst of the ancient traditions,
people rose up who dared to say what kings, priests and high priests,
theologians and pious members of the people did not want to hear.
A word rang out that was directed against the tradition, that
preached the wrath of God and proclaimed God's unconditional,
irrevocable "No." When, after settling down, Israel adopted large
parts of the social and religious style of life of the Canaanites, this
was done with the conviction that they could be reconciled with the
faith in Yahweh. If the Israelites had been familiar with our modern
language they would certainly have referred to a "living" tradition,
to the beneficial development of religious ideas and concepts: here
there was continuity and harmonious unity.

But it was precisely against this living tradition that the merciless
"No" of the prophets was directed. God revoked the earlier covenant
and promised another new one (Jer. 31:31). This means: something
new took place, not in a harmonious development but with a break
which was a break in the tradition brought about by the unfaithfulness of the people. But this did not mean a break in God's faithfulness to his people. God does not leave his people with its tradition
alone, he does not leave it in peace; rather, through his judgment
which is always an expression of his mercy, in a most hidden way
the tradition of God's relationship with his people continues. God
speaks, God judges, God kills and leads through death to the resurrection. The Old Testament with its understanding of the history
of this people and of its religious tradition is a source of theological
insight for the tradition of the church as well. Rightly understood,
the Old Testament is a book which exemplifies a true doctrine of
tradition.

Let us now look at the New Testament. Here it is made clear that
the church was the product of a major break. Paul described this
fact which was shattering for him in the letter to the Romans,
chapters 9–11. For a time God had rejected his old people and had
made his promises applicable to a new people until the moment of
reunion. When the church came into existence the people of God

was divided. For Paul this division is a cause of great concern and of serious doubt which captivates his attention and to which he can find no answer. He is faced with a mystery which he cannot unravel. His thoughts roam around in this darkness without being able to find a reliable support until he finally ends with a doxology to God's unfathomable wisdom. Two things are clear: first, that the matter is hidden in God. "God has placed this matter in a sphere about which neither your rhetoric nor your philosophy knows anything, namely the sphere of faith to which everything belongs which is not visible and clearly revealed. . . . The Lord has promised to live in darkness and he makes darkness his garment."[30]

Second, this division is not to be eternal; it will end one day in God's good time. When and how is his concern. But Paul's clearsightedness enables him to recognize that the new people of God should reflect on the fact that it also might one day be rejected if it came to see its calling as a privilege and not as a calling for the sake of the world. The church has no guarantee of its election and it is warned not to be proud, because the new people is not more protected and safe than the old one was.

But if we look closer we can see that this break had already taken place earlier. The schism in the people of God had already been caused by Jesus of Nazareth. He, the promised Savior, entered the history of the established Jewish church in the political, social, religious, and theological form of the time. The established Jewish congregation lived according to the tradition of the Fathers or of the Elders and was aware of this. This was what constituted its certainty and authority, its promise and salvation. The Mosaic Torah was handed down both in writing and orally, and the oral tradition had the same value as the written one, if not a higher one.

We have to recognize clearly the situation of this established religious community with its guarantors and spiritual bases, with its tradition, wisdom, and clever application of power, in order to understand "this matter concerning Jesus."

This is not the place to go into the details of the relationship between Jesus and the tradition, the law, and the temple with its worship; but it is a fact that Jesus, to whom all things had been given by his Father (Mt. 11:27), and who was, thus, to transmit "God's tradition," made a radical break with the tradition of the people of Israel in the form in which it was living and active at the time. The Gospels give a clear impression of the powerful way in which the words of Jesus upset the Jewish rabbinical tradition. They were like sticks of dynamite in a quarry, even where textually they were a repetition of what had been said before. One quotation of the words of Jesus describes this situation: "No one sews a patch of unshrunk cloth on to an old coat; if he does, the patch tears away from it, the new from the old, and leaves a bigger hole. No one puts new wine into old wine-skins; if he does, the wine will burst the skins, and then wine and skins are both lost. Fresh skins for new wine!" (Mk. 2:21-22).

Jesus was critical of the tradition not only in his words but also in his deeds. He protested against what was laid down as holy, against the inherited and the unquestionable. Thus, he put into practice a word from his childhood, "What made you search? Did you not know that I was bound to be in my Father's house" (Luke 2:49). He did all this not out of hatred for the inherited but because God so willed it and had called him to do it. *He* was to change the old water in the stone water pots into the strong new wine of the kingdom of God (Jn. 2:6 ff).

Was Jesus a revolutionary?[31] This question is not clear. The time in which Jesus lived was full of revolutionary movements of a social, political, and religious nature but in such a way that these three elements were interrelated. In the course of time there was an expression of an often very impatient hope that everything would soon change: the people was to be saved, i.e., be set free from enemies and from those who hated them (Lk. 1:71). Salvation was to be quite a concrete event, political, social, and religious, all in one. This great hope gripped both the broad masses of the people as well as, to a much higher degree, the small groups which were prepared to help and to intervene themselves when the right man, the Messiah, came. Hence, the many extreme groups, like the radical group of priests by the Dead Sea and the many underground movements which were only waiting for the decisive moment. And in the midst of this there was the established Jewish church with its attempts to keep the balance, in order not to displease the Romans or King Herod and thereby to incite them.

What was Jesus' position in this religious and political jungle? Was he a revolutionary? To put it briefly: he was revolutionary in a much deeper and more radical sense than the people of the time or of today recognized. He had to say "no" to the many demands of the time and of the people around him. But his "no" caused him to suffer. After all, he wanted to be the Savior of his people. This burning desire of his people and also of his disciples is related to the temptation in the wilderness. But his "no" was irrevocable.

In quite another way, he was clearly revolutionary in that he consciously set himself up in clear opposition to the religious, established church tradition of his people. The Gospel tradition makes this very clear. His interpretation of the law, his parables, his self-understanding, his attitude to the unimportant people and outcasts, to children and women point unmistakably in this direction. His anger with the rich and the secure and his relentless opposition to the religious leaders were a complete break with tradition. Behind these there was his absolute solidarity with men. He was the servant of God who was to exist for others. His vicarious activity and his revolution belonged together, indeed they were identical: vicariousness was his revolution. Both led to his death. Both were rooted in his unconditional obedience to God. He was simultaneously radically open to God and radically open to man, totally filled with God and totally filled with man. This human life which was lived *totally* for God and *totally* for man, which demanded *nothing* for itself, was in itself a radical break. The old tradition and its bearers (and fellow travelers) *had* to demand his death because his life was an extremely dangerous challenge. It is better "that *one* man should die for the people, than that the whole nation should be destroyed" (Jn. 11:50). The High Priest did not know how great was the truth expressed in this judgment.

IV
The Tradition of Adam and the Tradition of Christ

Jesus' greatest break with tradition was his death, or rather his obedience to death on the cross. In order to understand this, it is helpful to compare the story of the temptation in Gen. 3 with the hymn to Christ in Phil. 2:5-11. In the "hymn of Adam" man is stretching upwards in order to become like God. There a "robbery of God" took place, the result of which was man"s estrangement from God. When Ernst Bloch interprets the expression *eritis sicut Deus,* "you shall be like God," as the true gospel of the Bible which was then later debased as a sin, this interpretation shows its fantastic consequences in his understanding of man's autonomy which can allow no conception of man's subordination to God.[32] In the Christian tradition this phrase (Gen. 3) is the most telling description of man's nature as the creation which lost its freedom *for* God because it understood this freedom as a freedom *from* God. Freedom *for* God means freedom in obedience, freedom from God means emancipation and thus a false deification of man.

In the hymn to Christ the movement is clearly in the opposite direction.[33] Here an emptying (kenosis) takes place, an exposure of oneself or a self-giving. The Son of God lets his likeness to God go in order to become man. He did not become like a man, he became a man. "He became what I am," said Luther. He became the obedient one by becoming like man even to death on the cross. *Ecce Homo*, "Behold the man!"

In his certainly textually incorrect exegesis of this passage, Luther was right when he saw this downward movement in the earthly life of Jesus as reaching to the deepest levels of human existence. "He did not act like the Pharisee who said, 'I thank God that I am not like the rest of men' (Luke 18:11) and was glad that the others were wretched and never wanted them to be like himself. And that is the 'robbery' in which a man concerns himself with, no, keeps to himself what he has and does not give it back willingly to God to whom it belongs. And to want to be like God, self-sufficient, glorifying oneself, owing nothing to anyone, etc. But that was not Christ's way; rather he gave that form back to God the Father, emptied himself, did not want to use that title against us and did not want to be unlike to us. For he indeed became like one of us for us and took the form of a servant, i.e., he made himself subject to all evils, and although he was free he made himself the servant of all and did not act otherwise than as if all the evils that are ours were his."[34]

I have given this quotation in full because it can help us to understand the words "tradition of Adam" and "tradition of Christ."

The word "tradition" is rich in meaning but it is not unambiguous. On the one hand, it means the spiritual movement in which man constantly receives what is true in order to make it his own in freedom and to pass it on to others. In a little book by Josef Pieper, *Tradition, Concept and Claim*[35] there is a convincing reference to this tradition which is necessary to man: tradition is something different from discussion, it is authority, binding. Traditon has nothing to do with conservatism or stagnation. There is a genuine understanding of tradition which makes one free and independent of "conservatism." It is certainly right and necessary to speak of tradition in this way and one might ask whether one should not stick to this interpretation of the word "tradition" in order not to confuse the terms. The counter question, however, would be whether it is not essential to introduce a "lack of clarity" at this point precisely because the matter itself is not clear and simple. By speaking of tradition as clearly as Pieper does, one is subject to the danger of oversimplifying the matter despite one's profoundness and, thus, of minimizing it involuntarily. Man, in whom tradition takes place and whose agent he is, is not a neutral being. He is not only a being which is subject to God but also a being estranged from God. Therefore "tradition" is not a "pure" word, not a simple word for communication, and certainly not a neutral, functional word. The function of tradition has been determined *before* the movement. Man is the recipient of tradition but at the same time the one controlling tradition. He "supervises" the movement of tradition. Since Adam, as the one who is subject to God, continually hears the voice, *eris sicut Deus*, he is a danger to the purity of the tradition. Tradition does not discuss, says Pieper. No, but man does discuss. And discussion means questioning, unnoticeably changing the things which he receives *proprio sensu*, according to his own understanding. Man is the great "hermeneutist" who works on what he has received, understands it and hands it on understood in one way or another. Freedom and responsibility are part of tradition but this tradition has a bias, a certain tendency, which is a threat to its purity. Tradition shares in man's ambiguity. By speaking in this way we are not rejecting the great word "tradition," on the contrary. This gives a dialectical clarity to the concept of tradition which is more appropriate to the reality and vitality of this existential human factor.

It is this tendency which we have tried to describe with the symbol "tradition of Adam."[36] There is a conflict between the tradition of Adam and the tradition of Christ which is part of human existence and is fully expressed in the church. The Christian view of existence is not dualistic in a Marcionite sense, but it is anything but monistic since it is aware of the great tension and division within our existence. At the Assembly of the World Council of Churches in Uppsala, 1968, Metropolitan Ignatios Hazim described this tension appropriately in three terms, "dialogical," "diabolical," and "parousian."[37]

In the death of Jesus the tradition of Adam is taken to its final, negative extreme, to its "extreme case," where to all appearances it triumphs over Christ. But the paradox is that, precisely here where man—and it is religious man—conquers Christ, Christ is the victor. The death of the suffering servant of God is God's victory over the tradition of Adam, the resurrection is the mighty proclamation of this victory. This fact is the foundation for the Gospel and every-thing relating to it, this is what gives validity to the promise to the church, "And the gates of hell shall never overpower it."

Since the life, death, and resurrection of Jesus and through the power of the Holy Spirit, man's life has become "parousian." This expression means two things. First, in the midst of powerlessness and lack of cogent proof for the cause of Jesus, in faith the victory of Christ is certain. The church voices this faith in its creed, its praise, and its preaching. Second, until the parousia the church lives in the tension between these two "traditions" which are character-ized by Adam and by Christ. This tension is not basically a harmless matter which affects only the external affairs of the church. The ex-pression "the pilgrim Church," *ecclesia peregrinans*, can be used sentimentally and without seriousness: the church suffers under the pressure of the world and under its own imperfections. In the midst of its suffering it yearns to be united with its lord and bridegroom. But the tension goes far deeper because it is a fight between Christ and the antichrist in the church itself, between the two "traditions" which go right through the whole church. Luther's idea of the king-dom of the devil and the kingdom of Christ, which are constantly opposed to one another across new fronts in the visible church, must be taken very seriously, because otherwise ecclesiology becomes harmless and untrustworthy.

In order to describe the situation of the church in history, we should like to point out a strange linguistic usage in the New Testa-ment. The word "paradosis" occurs here in two diametrically op-posite senses. First, the term means "tradition" in the sense of the faithful handling of something which was received. Paul refers to receiving and accurately transmitting the Gospel (1 Cor. 15:1 ff) and to the equally accurate transmission of the words of institution (1 Cor. 11:23). Tradition means a movement within which Christ is constantly received in the church and transmitted for the salvation of the world.

Second, the word means "betrayal," the delivering of someone into the hands of the enemy, the act of denouncing a friend and thus making him subject to death. Thus it is often used in the story of Jesus' passion. Third, one could indicate a further meaning which in a sense includes the first two: Jesus surrenders himself, he exposes himself to death for the sake of man (Rom. 8:32, Gal. 2:20 and Eph. 5:25).

Here we shall look only at the first two meanings. One could say that this linguistic identity of two quite different meanings of a word was quite coincidental and meaningless. Linguistically this may be so. But this identity could also be the paradoxical expression of a truth which is constantly confirmed by history. The striking thing is that these two actions can be combined in *one* act: the church can *believe* it is proclaiming Christ while in *reality* it is betraying him; it can *believe* it is handing on the tradition of Christ while in *reality* it is a servant of the tradition of Adam. Theology must take account of this real possibility, indeed, it must be aware that this possibility often has become and does become a reality. The church can crucify Christ again *today*. No church can or may escape from this "mystery of iniquity." It is a feature of the nature of the church "in this age."

V
The Temptation of the Church and the Kingdom of God

In what has been said above the word "temptation" has already been used. We shall take it up again here because temptation is part of the problem of "the church in history."

Temptation is an existential factor of all human existence. Man can miss his mark, animals cannot. The higher the destiny is, the greater the force of the temptation to withdraw from this destiny.

At the beginning of the Bible there is a story about the temptation of man; at the beginning of the Gospels there is reference to the temptation of Jesus. Can we know what constituted this temptation? Only a spiritual interpretation which understands the whole situation of Jesus in the midst of the Jewish people can approach this question and the answer to it. Jesus knew the burning desire of the nation, to which he himself belonged with body and soul, to be saved "from our enemies, out of the hands of all who hate us" (Lk. 1:71), the desire for the fulfillment of the promises made to their fathers, starting with Abraham. The Messiah-king was impatiently awaited, the one who was to establish Israel again or, in a broader perspective, who was to initiate the new age. He saw the suffering of the nation to which he belonged. In the passage about the temptations the devil appears as the skillful interpreter of the pressing, sometimes enthusiastic, sometimes accusing shouts of the people to Jesus to bring about the kingdom of God. He alone had the power and thus the possibility to bring about the promised ful-fillment. The devil represented the people, the disciples, the crowds which gathered round him. The temptation was genuine and real. Jesus was exposed to a devilish temptation; if this is denied it im-plies denial of the genuine humanity of Jesus and the whole story of the temptations becomes a meaningless game. For christology, the relationship to the temptation account is a touchstone of its biblical fidelity and credibility.

Dostoevsky gives a fantastic interpretation of this story, entering into all the details, in his story "The Great Inquisitor" in his novel *The Brothers Karamazov*. Dostoevsky does not tell the story from the point of view of the biblical situation. He is not concerned with a correct historical exegesis; he wishes to understand this event on the basis of *his own* presuppositions. It is a matter of explaining modern history and he sets Jesus and the church in that history. Jesus appears in medieval Spain, but it is not a question of the Middle Ages but of *our* time. The Great Inquisitor represents the voice of the unhappy, disturbed people of his time who are torn between faith and doubt and wish for peace and quiet. He accuses Jesus because he did not listen to the demands and advice of the spirit of the wilderness because of his pride. For in this way he has made himself guilty of man's misfortune.

The three temptations sum up the whole painful history of man-kind. Temptation is not only a private, inner, personal affair; it affects all men and their salvation. Because Jesus said "no" then, man was not "saved"! The three offers made by the man-loving devil incorporate the innermost desire and endeavour of man: give us bread, solve our problems of which the most painful one is the prob-lem of freedom, create peace—both external and in our consciences, order, authority, liberation from the necessity of decision which is beyond our strength. After having tried to find happiness and equilibrium by revolution and bloodshed, men now come to the church, pleading for protection, voluntarily surrendering their in-dividual freedom in order to be happy at last.

Jesus had said "no" and it is this "no" which is the basis for the Great Inquisitor's accusation. The mystery of this man is that, having followed Jesus passionately in his youth, he had now recognized that Jesus was *wrong* when he rejected the clever, man-loving spirit of the wilderness. The church which he now represents has had to improve the matter and, therefore, it is not with Jesus but with him. With his humble-proud "no" Jesus had betrayed the overwhelming majority of people and left them in the lurch. The church had to choose whether to follow Jesus with his "yes" and his little band of strong men or whether, for the sake of the happiness of mankind, it would take leave of Jesus and follow the tempter. It chose the latter. Man's happiness is more important to him than the radiant, unblemished but inhuman attitude of Jesus to life and to his disciples. It changed Jesus' "no" into "yes."

Here the church is set directly in the temptation story. The striking thing in Dostoevsky is that he puts the atheist, Ivan Karamazov, who tells the story, together with the pious starets and disciple of Jesus, Sozima, without any transition. There are two churches: the one which denies Jesus, the great church of authority and education, incorporated by the Great Inquisitor, and the church of Sozima which follows Jesus whose all-embracing love includes all men in order to call them in freedom to a brotherhood which embraces the whole earth. There are the church of compulsion and the church of invitation. In the latter there is authority, too, but in the form of a brotherly exhortation which allows something to grow which will encourage life.

Who is the Great Inquisitor?[38] No doubt Dostoevsky was thinking primarily of the Roman Catholic church in its "Jesuit" form, as seen by the slavophile Orthodox Christian, Dostoevsky. This church betrayed Christ by setting itself in God's place. By means of its influence, its totalitarian power and its desire to rule, it had turned brotherhood into a barracks with a yard in which people could now play together like children while everything was determined by the church. The torments of freedom have been removed and in doing so the church has shown that it is man's true friend. The church is the great, man-loving benefactor because it makes life easy for men (although they have to work hard!) and promises them eternal blessedness and joy after death as a reward for their "confidence" and obedience. The church is presented as the victor but at the same time as the one who has succumbed totally to the temptations of the devil. It overcomes temptation by succumbing to it!

But if one looks more closely one can see behind the Great Inquisitor the image of any absolutistic, politically authoritarian power which robs man of his freedom on the pretext of making him free. The Great Inquisitor has the features of all dictators and of all dictatorial systems which make all men equal in the name of a genuine humanism.

Thus, for Dostoevsky the Great Inquisitor follows the *same* line as the great positivist or socialist dictatorships in which the problem of man is not solved *with* God but *without* God. For him this means without *Christ*. And without Christ inevitably means finally destroying man as man.

In this connection one cannot help thinking of Auguste Comte's third sociological stage in which everyone lived together in *one* closed space under the leadership of the new priesthood of the experts, where the individual gave up his individuality "voluntarily" for the sake of the whole and of order. There is no room for individual freedom. Men have to be educated for "the whole" from earliest childhood. One sees Huxley's *Brave New World* clearly before one's eyes.

It is characteristic and not coincidental that Comte sees Jesus as a revolutionary, destructive individualist and, therefore, totally rejects him. From his point of view Comte agrees with the Great Inquisitor. Jesus was an irresponsible charlatan who would only have caused harmful confusion if more intelligent people had not taken the matter into their own hands. Although he rejected Catholicism as outdated theism, he still thought that elements of this church, namely, the authoritarian hierarchy, were necessary as a model for this third stage.[39]

In Dostoevsky's eyes the Roman church was thus associated with the major anti-Christian movements of the time. The Great Inquisitor knows what he is doing; he has to lie and this lie constitutes his suffering. But he takes it upon himself because he loves men. In the name of Jesus he, i.e., the church, denies Jesus.

This example of a terrible temptation of the church is taken from great literature. In his book on Dostoevsky, Eduard Thurneysen interpreted the story of the Great Inquisitor as the attempt by religion and the church, "to escape from that deep problem of life in which the God of the beyond finds the only way of showing himself to man, by making the unknown God of the beyond into a known God of the here and now."[40]

This discussion leads into the problem of the relationship between the church and the kingdom of God. In the two expressions "church" and "kingdom of God" we find the tension which is described by our main subject: the church in history. For in the history of man with its struggle between the tradition of Adam and the tradition of Christ the church and the kingdom of God have their place. We must now go into this problem in more detail.

Karl Barth made the two following paradoxical statements: the kingdom of God is the church. The church is not the kingdom of God.[41]

The kingdom of God is the church: where Christ is, there is the kingdom of God. He himself is the church or *autobasileia*, as Origen says. "Here on this earth and in time, and therefore in the immediate context of all human kingdoms both small and great, and in the sphere of Satan who rules and torments fallen man, God has irrevocably and indissolubly set up the kingdom of His grace, the throne of His glory, the kingdom which as such is superior to all other powers. . . ."[42]

The lordship of God will only be directly, universally, and visibly recognized at the end and fulfillment of all history. But here already the Kingdom of God "in the guise of the new and obedient humanity . . . is provisionally and very imperfectly but genuinely actualized where in virtue of the mighty work of the Holy Ghost there is an awareness of its incursion and therefore the communion of saints."[43]

In these sentences Barth describes and takes further the definition of the church in the Barmen Declaration of 1934: "The Christian Church is the congregation of brothers in which Jesus Christ is present and acts as Lord in the Word and Sacraments through the Holy Spirit."

This document is a fortunate rewording and expansion of the words of Article 7 of the Augsburg Confession. "It is also taught that there must always be and remain one holy Christian Church, which is the assembly of all believers among whom the Gospel is preached in its purity and the holy sacraments are administered according to the Gospel."

Where this is done the coming kingdom of God is present among us. Christianity is the future in the present.[44] Preaching is not only a discussion *about* the kingdom of God; rather *in* preaching the kingdom of God becomes a reality among us as it is accepted by believing hearts. The sacraments are not some sort of mysteriously religious actions but eschatological actions of the kingdom of God in which the One who is to come becomes present among us through the Holy Spirit. The church has to be understood in this eschatological view of the kingdom of God. The Bible is not the book of a mystery religion which shows us the way from this world to a "superior" religious world; rather, it is the witness to the kingdom of God in the history of the people of God intended for the whole world. The Biblical dimension is the historical dimension; in the Bible, history means the place where God struggles with Satan in order to save his creatures from alienation and banishment. The dimension of the kingdom is the prophetical, eschatological approach to history and nature where it is a matter of the whole world and not only of individual souls.

In terms of the kingdom of God, creation and redemption belong together. The cross and resurrection of Jesus, reconciliation and redemption are included in God's act of creation. They are understood on the basis of the creation, as the creation is understood on the basis of these acts of God.

God's activity in the world is *one* act. In this universal activity of God, the church has its place as the first fruits of the new creation. In the church the new, as the "beginning of the new creation," is already present, invisible, hidden, but it is a certainty for faith which is "faith" and not "sight" (2 Cor. 5:7). This certainty is not based on something which is humanly empirical and given but on the gospel which is preached to us and which is handed to us in the symbols of the sacraments. Preaching and the sacramental acts contain that "which is beyond our seeing, beyond our hearing and beyond our imagining" (1 Cor. 2:9), the renewing reality which is summed up in the word "gospel." All that the church constitutes, it is by virtue of the kingdom of God which is made present by the Holy Spirit. And this is all in a most provisional form and in "thorough incompleteness" because the people, which is the bearer of this reality, is a gathering of those who have already entered into the kingdom of the Son but still remain sinners and subject to the temptations of the evil powers.

The sentence "the kingdom of God is the church" is a statement of faith and trust: God's work continues. The tradition of Adam can never overcome the tradition of Christ. The church will never be destroyed by the flow of history. It will continually rediscover its identity. The truth of this promise must be upheld but it must be supplemented by Karl Barth's following statement of the opposite, which is a safeguard against all misunderstanding: the church is not the kingdom of God but it exists for the sake of the kingdom of God. When the kingdom comes the time of the church will be over.

These two sentences of Karl Barth have to be pronounced at the same time and kept together with their marked dialectic. They refer to the human and the divine elements of the church which cannot be separated or confused.

The church lives in history; it bears the marks of ambiguity which attach to everything historical. Where the church does not recognize and confess its servanthood, it ceases to be the church of God.

One must reject the intermediate solution of an idealistic theology —of both Catholic and Protestant type—which would maintain that the two entities stand in a "relationship of organic extension" to one another, as if the church were the germinal beginning of the kingdom of God which gradually, *gradatim*, grows into the fullness of the kingdom of God. Here the dividing line between the two has been obscured and the church has unnoticeably become the central concept. That is church romanticism which cannot be justified either on the basis of Scripture or in terms of the nature of things.

The kingdom of God is the center and the goal of everything which happens in the church. By nature the church is a function of the kingdom of God on earth, in history; it can only be defined in terms of the dimension of the kingdom of God because it is radically subject to the kingdom of God as its servant and guardian until the final fulfillment.

This, then, also means that the kingdom of God is the critical limit of the church, namely, where the church is no longer a function of the kingdom of God and has gone beyond its bounds it is no longer the church of Jesus Christ; then it loses itself and becomes something else. Then the kingdom of God will find for itself other servants.

The church can exceed its limits in a number of different ways. In this connection I should like to draw attention only to one way: the church substitutes religion for the kingdom of God. When I say "religion" here I am aware that I am being one-sided by using the word in a critical sense. "Religion" is not a straightforward word. It can describe something profoundly human, a longing for God which is expressed in many ways and is derived from man's transcendental relationship. The man who is beginning to understand himself as a person asks questions about God. In this questioning about

God he has already been touched by the ultimate truth. In this sense religion can be seen as an existential facet of man which was expressed in the words of Augustine, ". . . thou hast made us for thyself and restless is our heart until it comes to rest in thee."[45] Man as man is touched by God, he is always affected by the ultimate truth. Let us imagine that the word "God" could completely disappear from human consciousness, "without its being replaced by another word which speaks to us in the same way! Man would no longer be man. He would have crossed himself back to a resourceful animal."[46] This is the way in which one can and must speak.

In history, where human life has its place, life is not lived in a pure form. We have already seen this. Time and again in human history there are traces of genuine religion, but there is also false religion, namely, where man ultimately seeks not God but himself, where man honors not God but idols. A mistake takes place which changes religion into unbelief. Man has a tendency to bend everything toward himself, to exploit it for his own benefit, including God. This is the *hybris* which hides itself in religion. Religion can be a cover for the human will for self-preservation and then everything is perverted. This false religion is related to the church in history and to the temptation by the devil.

It was along these lines that Dietrich Bonhoeffer understood the term "religion" when he described religion as a betrayal of true, this-worldly, created human life. For Bonhoeffer, religion is inwardness, that is, it exists only deep within a person, individualism, alienation from the world, and a sense of other-worldliness. To present this religion as the gospel is "un-Christian, because for Christ himself is being substituted one particular stage in the religiousness of man, i.e., a human law."[47] That which has developed historically, that is that which has been added to the Christian faith as a consequence of certain, perhaps non-Christian, influences of a religious, cultural, or philosophical nature, is considered without hesitation to be essential and, thus, unrelinquishable.

According to Bonhoeffer, religion alienates a man from life and places him in an unreal area where God is no longer Lord but has become the servant of life. This is why Bonhoeffer believes that we are approaching a religionless age because history does not stand still.[48] The history of the last few centuries has been getting further and further away from this religiosity, and since the churches have identified themselves to a large degree with this "religious" view of

Christianity they are involved in a steadily growing crisis. If the churches do not radically reflect on this, they will simply have to perish, and, thus, at the same time a judgment of God upon churches which have betrayed their cause will be realized. Bonhoeffer refers to a nonreligious interpretation of Christianity; this means that the great Christian words have to be interpreted anew in a completely different historical situation.[49] Bonhoeffer is aware how difficult this is. He feels he is "being driven back to first principles. Atonement and redemption, regeneration, the Holy Ghost, the love of our enemies, the cross and resurrection, life in Christ and Christian discipleship—all these things have become so problematic and so remote that we hardly dare any more to speak of them."[50]

We referred earlier to the perspective of the kingdom of God. We shall outline very briefly and roughly the perspective of religion and it should not be forgotten that, while we are speaking in a one-sided way, there is some truth in it. From the point of view of religion, God and the world are seen as two entities which have a this world-other world relationship to one another. This world and the other world contrast with one another as metaphysically defined forms of existence, separated from each other as secular and sacred. Within the framework of the view of religion, piety is determined by mysticism and psychology because its main concern is to save individual souls from the world. The religious approach emphasizes an inner piety, a piety of the soul, often of a very moralistic type. Its concept of sin is casuistic. Thus, the religious approach is basically anthropological and not theocentric. The real encounter, between the true God who has revealed himself in history and man as he really is, does not take place. Instead of a real encounter there is the functioning of a perhaps very impressive system of piety. Religion is the essential thing, the kingdom of God becomes insignificant. The church is in danger of disintegrating even though the external appearance of the church can be powerful and most effective from the point of view of religion.

The church in history faces the constant temptation to settle down, to build fixed houses. History witnesses to this. The image of the church in the course of the ages is often embarrassing and sometimes shattering for someone who looks at it more closely. The church of the kingdom of God has almost always lived under pressing circumstances; often it was persecuted by the false church. History's list of martyrs contains many who fell victim to a large and

62 THE MISSION OF THE CHURCH

authoritarian church. The so-called history of heresy can be seen in a new light; for the heretics were often only heretics in the eyes of the big church. They were frequently people who were called to protest against a false church but who were persecuted and even killed by the big church as false, obstinate Christians. The spiritual tyranny of a hierarchical church or of a confessional church or of a relatively undogmatic free church can be just as terrible as the tyranny of an authoritarian state. The church in history can become associated with a particular social class, often in a favorable economic position; it can set itself up as a confederate of nationalistic, hyperconservative national groups; it can enter into an alliance with the state, sometimes known as a concordat; it can take the form of an established, democratic national church. Wherever this happens the church is tempted to become established and to consolidate itself in a worldly way and to forget the essential. One can indeed see the shadow of the Great Inquisitor! Every effort is made to protect the church from disturbance.

The church in history is repeatedly led to the way of the cross where the two opponents, religion and the kingdom of God, meet. Each exists simultaneously in close proximity to the other. This dialectic in the concept of the church is constantly coming up in theology and should never be neglected. It was quite clear to Martin Luther that the true church of God was not identical with the empirical church. *Abscondita est ecclesia, latent sancti,*[51] the church is hidden, the saints live unnoticed." This ecclesiology which is related to the *theologia crucis* was already present—according to Luther —in the Old Testament. "Who knows whether it has not always been so in the course of the world's history from the very beginning as far as the Church of God is concerned, that some people were called the people of God and saints who should not have been, but that there were others among them like a remnant who were not called people of God or saints."[52]

The paradox of the concept of the church reached a climax in the distinction of the young Barth between the Church of Jacob and the Church of Esau in the second edition of his commentary on the Letter to the Romans. The Church of Jacob is the church "in which the miracle takes place that the truth of God is made visible over and above men's lies." The Church of Esau is the church "in which the miracle does not happen and in which, therefore, everything that is heard and said about God can only reveal that every man is a liar." "The two churches do not, of course, stand over against one another as two things. The Church of Esau alone is the observable, knowable, and possible Church—comprising Jerusalem, Rome, Wittenberg, Geneva and all the past and future and holy places. . . . But the Church of Jacob is likewise in principle the unobservable, unknowable and impossible Church, capable neither of expansion nor limitation; it has neither place nor name nor history . . . in it is simply the free Grace of God, His Calling and Election; it is both Beginning and End."[53]

Here the tension within the concept of the church has become so Kantian and dialectical that the true church is relegated to a completely inaccessible *noumenon*-world with the consequence that the earthly, visible church is entirely left to this world and its form. The tremendous dialectic is transformed into an almost undialectical simplicity. Here a fantastic division is posited; it will remain as an exaggerated witness to the tension between the church in history and the kingdom of God.

In order to shed light on the question of kingdom of God – church I should like finally to include a document which expresses the same problem from another angle, that of the tension between an authoritarian church and a free and brotherly church or between a church of the law and a church of the Spirit.

The passionate untheological language is derived from that of the Roman Catholic Church long before the Second Vatican Council and can be translated without difficulty into the language of any other church of today.

VI
Whitsun Prayer in Time of Trouble

"*Spirit of God,* I found a new name for You somewhere: 'God's effervescence.' They called You God's stormy effervescence! And then I remembered, yes, the storm is Your sign, the rushing wind, Your symbol, with which You 'filled the whole house where they were sitting' (Acts 2:2). 'Blood and fire and columns of smoke' (Acts 2:19; Joel 2:30) these harsh signs of the weather are Your companions! And my heart began to rejoice, to go out to You, Holy Spirit: *the stormy effervescence of the Lord fills the whole earth, Alleluia!*"

But where are You here on earth? They say that Your Church is full of You! And yet it's so calm, so quiet—almost a bit dead! "Two-thirds a corpse" was the judgement of a Communist from the Soviet Union. When I hear about a storm it is somewhere else! . . . We have to believe that You are only in the Catholic church. Where it's so calm and quiet!

Holy Spirit, You give us a heavy burden! For, after all, we don't want a storm at all. We fight against it. As soon as it begins to be more stormy and effervescent somewhere in Your Church, storm spirit of the Lord, we are immediately afraid! Gently! Quiet! The pious people might be offended! And as for our opponents! How anxious we immediately become! . . .

Everyday I have to pray—Your Church lays it down for me—now in Whitsun week: You will renew the face of the earth, Alleluia! And again my heart leaps! Make new, make young again—so that is Your way! O how I love You for that, You Spirit of the eternally young and new divine love!

But, but in *Your Church,* Lord, there *everything is so old!* The old is so very important to it, much, much more than the new! "Innovator"—that means the same as heretic for us! Where anything new tries to develop among us then how the voices are raised: Careful! Stick to the old! It's always been like that! Why suddenly change it? In Your Church, which prays for You to make everything new, the new always meet with great distrust and astonishment! . . .

Whereas the old, how important that is! I have lost count of how many anniversaries of old things and objects have been celebrated in Your Church! 1500 years, 1100 years, 700 years, 300 years and even the most recent is already 40 years old ("Rerum Novarum"). That is not young and new any more for our quickly passing lives. And I ask in horror, *what is happening in Your Church that is really new?* . . .

Spirit of the Lord, who love the new, when will You renew the face of Your Church? When will you show us how much of the old in her may and must disappear so that her face can again become new and beautiful and young? If You will it, the old will disappear before the raging of Your storm and everything will become new! If You will—in the distance I can already hear the many thousands of voices of unbelieving people shouting out again overwhelmed in the amazement of faith: "The old order has gone, and a new order has already begun!" (II Cor. 5:17). But often it is still hard to believe in You, Holy Spirit, and it is painful to add another 'Alleluia' to the prayer that You will renew the face of the earth! . . .

Holy Spirit! The people of today have become the slaves of many things. They have become the slaves of money, the slaves of mammon! They have to perform feudal services for the rich and are themselves as hungry as slaves, hungry for bread, hungry for justice, hungry for freedom! What would they give if only Your Church were suddenly to proclaim *freedom* to them loud and clear! Show us how to become free from slavery to the letter, free to love these many enslaved people! Let the storm of Your love blow again! Yes, let it be *stormy* in Your Church again! Make her face *new!* Let the banner of *freedom* wave again over the children of God! Then they will again believe in You, holy effervescent storm of the Lord, renewer of mankind, Spirit of love and freedom! Amen."[54]

NOTES

1. Walter Kasper, *Die Methoden der Dogmatik*, Munich, 1967, p. 74. (Our translation.)
2. a) *ibid.*, p. 51. b) *ibid.*, p. 52.
3. Max Picard, *Die Flucht vor Gott*, Freiburg, 1955, p. 9 f. English translation: *The Flight from God*, 1951.
4. Garrigou-Lagrange, *De Revelatione per Ecclesiam Catholicam proposita*, Rome, 1929, Vol. I, p. 139.
5. Walter Bodenstein, *Neige des Historismus—Ernst Troeltschs Entwicklungsgang*, Gütersloh, 1959, p. 146.
6. Quoted by Hermann Diem, *Dogmatik. Ihr Weg zwischen Historismus und Existentialismus*, Munich, 1964, pp. 9 and 11.
7. *Warum bleibe ich in der Kirche?* ed. Walter Dirks and Eberhard Stammler, Stuttgart, 1971.
8. Cf. e.g., Jürgen Habermas, *Technik und Wissenschaft als "Ideologie"*, 1969; English translation in: Jürgen Habermas, *Toward a Rational Society*, trans. Jeremy J. Shapiro, Heineman, London, 1971, and Hans Rudolf Müller-Schwefe, *Technik und Glaube. Eine permanente Herausforderung*, Göttingen, 1971.
9. Some help in understanding the problem of hermeneutics today is given by Eduard Schillebeeckx, *Glaubensinterpretation. Beiträge zu einer hermeneutischen und kritischen Theologie*, Mainz, 1971, and Henri Cazelles, *Ecriture, Parole et Esprit*, Paris, 1970. Cf. also Helmuth Thielicke, *Der Evangelische Glaube*, Tübingen, 1968, and *"Parole et Dogmatique. Hommage à Jean Bosc,"* Paris, 1971.
10. Cf. Josef Pieper, *Uberlieferung, Begriff und Anspruch*, Munich, 1970, p. 42 f.
11. "The essence of the Biblical concept of truth is thus its relationship to time; it is always a matter of something which has happened and which will happen, not of something which is and must be natural. Thus truth is a historical phenomenon and basically an element of eschatological promise." Walter Kasper, *op. cit.*, p. 71. Cf. also *Dogma unter dem Wort Gottes*, Mainz, 1965, p. 58 f and his most recent book *Glaube und Geschichte*, Mainz, 1970.
12. Cf. Helmuth Gollwitzer, *Krummes Holz—Aufrechter Gang. Zur Frage nach dem Sinn des Lebens*, Munich, 1970, pp. 213 f and 222 f.
13. Cf. e.g., Gerhard von Rad, *Old Testament Theology*, Vol. 1, New York, 1962, pp. 121-123.
14. Norbert Lohfink, "Un exemple de théologie de l'histoire dans l'ancien Israël Deut. 26, 5-9," in *Révélation et l'Histoire*, ed. Enrico Castelli, 1971, p. 193: "The creed in Deut. 26, 5-9 therefore does not simply refer to some events selected from sacred history; rather its aim is to point out all that can be recalled as being the history of Israel, from the beginning up to its climax, the reign of David and of Solomon."
15. Norbert Lohfink, *Das Siegeslied am Schilfmeer; Christliche Auseinandersetzungen mit dem Alten Testament*, 1964, pp. 102-128.
16. Paul Ricœur, *Histoire et Vérité*, Paris, 1955, p. 85.
17. Joseph Ratzinger, *Introduction to Christianity*, trans. by J. R. Foster, New York, Herder and Herder, 1970, p. 94.
18. Concerning the word "symbol," see C. Eichenseer, *Das Symbolum Apostolicum beim hl. Augustinus*, St. Ottilien, 1960, pp. 9-133 and J. D. N. Kelly, *Early Christian Creeds*, Longmans, Green, London, 1950, p. 52 f.

19. Joseph Ratzinger, *op. cit.*, p. 99: ". . . the Christian faith gave a completely new significance to the God of the philosophers . . . thus profoundly transforming him."

20. Note, e.g., the question directed by Karl Rahner to the Christology of the Council of Chalcedon: "Chalkedon—Ende oder Anfang?" In *"Das Konzil von chalkedon III,"* Würzburg, 1954, pp. 3-49.

21. Cf., among others, Wilhelm Link, *Das Ringen Luthers um die Freiheit der Theologie von der Philosophie,* Munich, 1954.

22. Cf. Walter Kasper, *Die Methoden der Dogmatik,* Munich, 1967, p. 76.

23. Oskar Bauhofer, *Das Geheimnis der Zeiten, Christliche Sinndeutung der Geschichte,* 1935, p. 32.

24. On the question of the temporality of the human person and thus of man's personal existence, see: Oskar Bauhofer, *Mensch in Wahrheit; Uber das personale Sein,* Einsiedeln, 1970, pp. 46-76.

25. Herders *Kleines philosophisches Wörterbuch,* Freiburg, 1959, p. 62.

26. Oskar Bauhofer, *Das Geheimnis der Zeiten,* 1935, p. 42.

27. "In darkness" because the object of faith is not "transparent" but based on the authority of God through the church.

28. From the Commentary on the Letter to the Galatians, 1531. *WA* 40, I, 229, 15.; *Luther's Works,* American Edition, vol. 26, p. 129 f.

29. *WA* 54, 470, 8 f.

30. The quotation is from Luther in a letter to Melanchton of June 29, 1530. *WA* Briefe 5, 406, 54 f.

31. Cf. Gerhard Gloege, *Aller Tage Tag. Unsere Zeit im Neuen Testament,* 1960, p. 190 f, and Oscar Cullman, *Jesus und die Revolutionäre seiner Zeit,* Tübingen, 1970.

32. Cf. Helmuth Gollwitzer, *Krummes Holz—Aufrechter Gang,* Munich, p. 268.

33. Cf., among others, Ernst Lohmeyer, *Kyrios Jesus,* Sitz. Ber. der Heidelberger Akademie der Wissenschaften, Heidelberg, 1928, Vol. 4.

34. *Sermo de duplici iustitia,* 1519. *WA* 2, 148, 6 f. German translation by E. Hirsch in *Hilfsbuch zum Studium der Dogmatik,* Berlin, 1957, p. 28 ff.

35. Josef Pieper, *Uberlieferung, Begriff und Anspruch,* Munich, 1970, p. 23.

36. Cf. my article "Tradition comme problème anthropologique et christologique" in *Ecriture et Tradition, Journées œcuméniques de 1968,* Chevetogne, 1970, p. 105.

37. This excellent address is published in *Uppsala Report,* ed. Norman Goodall, Geneva, 1968, p. 29 f.

38. Cf., among others, Nicolas Berdyaev, *Die Weltanschauung Dostojevskijs,* Munich, 1925: English translation made from French edition by Donald Attwater, *The World-Outlook of Dostoevsky,* London and New York, 1934. A. Maceina, *Der Grossinquisitor. Geschichtsphilosophische Deutung der Legende Dostojewskijs,* Heidelberg, 1952, and René Girard, *Dostoïevski, du double à l'unité,* Paris, 1963.

39. Cf. Henri de Lubac, *Le Drame de l'humanisme athée,* Paris, 1945, p. 163 ff.

40. E. Thurneysen, *Dostojewskij,* Munich, 1922, p. 45.

41. Karl Barth, *Church Dogmatics,* Vol. IV/2, ed. G. W. Bromiley and T. F. Torrance, Edinburgh, 1958, p. 656.

42. *Ibid.,* II/2, p. 688.

43. *Ibid.,* IV/2, p. 656.

44. Few people have presented the point of view of the kingdom of God as clearly as the older and the younger Blumhardt. Cf. Gerhard Sauter, *Die*

Theologie des Reiches Gottes beim älteren und jüngeren Blumhardt, 1962, and Christoph Blumhardt, *Heute schauen wir vorwärts*. Ein Blumhardt-Brevier, ed. Otto Bruder, Zurich/Stuttgart, 1966.
45. Augustine, *Libri Tredecim Confessionum* I, 1. *Library of Christian Classics*, London, vol. VII, p. 31.
46. Karl Rahner, Meditation über das Wort "Gott" in *Wer ist das eigentlich GOTT?* ed. Hans Jürgen Schultz, Munich, 1969, pp. 17-18.
47. Dietrich Bonhoeffer, *Prisoner for God: Letters and Papers from Prison*, ed. Eberhard Bethge, trans. R. H. Fuller, New York, 1954, p. 147.
48. *Ibid.*, pp. 122 and 145-146.
49. *Ibid.*, p. 125 f.
50. *Ibid.*, p. 140.
51. *WA* 18, 652, 23.
52. *WA* 18, 650, 27. On the whole problem see, among others, Paul Althaus, "Der Heilige Geist und die Kirchengeschichte" in *Die Theologie Martin Luthers*, Gütersloh, 1962, p. 294 f.
53. a) Karl Barth, *Der Römerbrief*, 2nd. edition, Munich, 1967, p. 326.
b) Karl Barth, *The Epistle to the Romans*, tr. from 6th edition by Edwyn C. Haskyns, London, 1933, pp. 341-342. (O. tr.)
54. The author of this prayer, abridged here, is an Austrian professor of New Testament, Dr. Josef Dillersberger, who published "Ein Pfingstgebet aus Zeitnot" in the "Katholische Kirchenzeitung" in 1931. This prayer to the Holy Ghost earned him numerous black marks with the Roman clergy, and he was obliged to withdraw from his academic teaching. He was not fully rehabilitated until the time of the Second Vatican Council. His last public lecture, in 1967, bore the title: *Der Geist meint es anders*, "The Spirit intends otherwise."

Chapter 3

Missiones Dei

A Contribution to the Discussion on the Concept of Mission

I
Mission as Confrontation

"I appeal to you therefore, brethren, by the mercies of God, to present your bodies as a living sacrifice, holy and acceptable to God, which is your spiritual worship. Do not be conformed to this world but be transformed by the renewal of your mind, that you may prove what is the will of God, what is good and acceptable and perfect" (Rom. 12:1–2).

With these exhortations Paul begins the instruction of the congregation which concludes the Letter to the Romans. But before he says anything about the style of life appropriate to the Christians' eschatological existence, he emphasizes that the basis of the parenesis is in God's eschatological action. "I appeal to you . . . by the mercies of God. . . ." Since God has been merciful the church which confesses its faith in this mercy must act in accord with God's grace.

By referring to God's mercy, Paul recapitulates briefly everything which he has written to the church about the resurrection of Christ and about the Holy Spirit who gives the life in Christ to men so that they can "walk in the Spirit."

Since God has shown himself merciful, a life in faith and hope is not merely a possibility but the only way of living in the world which does justice to the content of the faith and of the hope.[1]

Just as Paul begins his parenesis with a reference to God and his acts, so he also concludes with an expression of his conviction that the God of hope will give the church joy and peace in the Spirit (Rom. 15:13).

Since Paul with his faith in the God of hope is convinced that God will give the church joy and peace which constitute the eschatological kingdom of God (Rom. 14:17), it is significant to him to exhort the church to persevere in difficulties until the kingdom of God finally comes. It makes sense to exhort people to lead a life in accordance with the content of their hope of the kingdom of God, because God himself has begun to establish this kingdom and, as God the Holy Spirit, to introduce this eschatological kingdom into the history of the world. Sin and death still contradict God's lordship but, in the faith that God's lordship will one day be unchallenged, the church is called to make this hope a reality in its life.[2] The parenesis becomes meaningful on the basis of faith and hope: it can be expressed because human history does not depend on the hopelessness of sin and death.

On the contrary, in the hope of the coming kingdom of God men can create something "new" and thus make true history.[3] The hope of the kingdom to come with "righteousness and peace and joy in the Holy Spirit" (Rom. 14:17) also includes the faithful expectation that the history made by men *en pneumati* will one day prove to be the history of the kingdom of God in the world.

This is the faith and the hope which is based on God's mercy. It relies on Christ's promise that the Holy Spirit is sent to man as a guarantee of the kingdom of God (2 Cor. 1:22; 5:5), and faith expects the kingdom of God to be part of the world's history whenever and wherever the Holy Spirit makes history in the form of expressions of righteousness, peace, and joy.

God's eschatological activity has begun; now the Holy Spirit acts in man and through man. *Therefore* Paul can exhort the Romans to create a history which is not in conflict with the mercy of God but, on the contrary, is the *praxis* of the charismata: one worship alone in which all that belongs only to the old world is confronted with the *praxis* of the kingdom to come.

Paul says concretely that church members should present their bodies as a gift which is pleasing to God, that is that they should serve God with all that they have and are. This constitutes their worship (Rom. 12:1). This worship means nothing less than that men in their bodilyness, i.e., in their whole existence, allow the world and their own lives to take the form of love and of sacrifice.

The opposite of such a life of worship is to "be conformed to this world." *me syschematizesthe to aioni touto* (Rom. 12:2) : do not be conformed to this world but think of yourselves with sober judgment (*sophronein*—Rom. 12:3) according to the measure of your faith. Instead of being reconciled to the present situation, the church has the task of acting in accordance with its share of the faith which the Holy Spirit gives to each one as his eschatological existence.

Paul is saying that the church should act according to the measure of its faith, that is, *it should act according to its share in the gifts of the Holy Spirit.* The gifts of grace or *"charisma* signifies technically in Paul the specific participation of the individual Christian in grace, in the Spirit or, as here, in faith—a participation which as such expresses itself correspondingly in a specific *praxis* of the member in and for the body of Christ."[4] That the Holy Spirit dwells in men is demonstrated by many forms of service; but this activity always is a confrontation of the old world with the new. Do not be conformed to this world but transform the world and history which are subject to sin and death by means of the many services of love.

These texts from the Letter to the Romans are certainly not those which are most quoted by the theology of mission when considering the nature of mission, but nevertheless something quite central is expressed here about the way in which the apostle of the Gentiles understood the people of God as a *communio* in service, in mission.

First, Paul states that faith in the presence of the Holy Spirit in and with the gifts of grace constitutes a church whose *praxis* must be a manifestation of faith in acts of faith and hope.

This means that the acts of faith and hope must contradict everything in the old world which constitutes a negation of the expectation of the righteousness of the kingdom to come. This way of living in faith and hope is worship (service of God) in history where the old world is confronted with the new. The function of the church in the world is to bring about a confrontation between that which must perish and a *praxis* which corresponds to the hope of that which is to come.

Second, concerning the service which each individual is to render in accordance with the gifts of grace given to him, Paul says that this service is indeed the service of each individual but that, when men confront the world of sin with the will of God (Rom. 12:2) , they do this as members of a fellowship. Indeed, this confrontation takes place only because the many have received the same Holy Spirit.

The service of the individual cannot be played off against the service of the community. Accordingly, the way of life to which the community is called in the Holy Spirit can never be less than an effort to realize the form of existence which is a manifestation of the presence of the Spirit. The daily service of the church in a world which is full of suffering, persecution, weeping, hatred, and lovelessness (Rom. 12:9–13:10) must be the negation of the negative, so that the world can become a world in which no wrong is done to a neighbor (Rom. 13:10).

Third, Paul speaks of the life of faith and hope as a mission in the world. This is fundamental.

What Paul says is that mission is a joint mission of the Holy Spirit and of men in the world. *All mission is the mission of the Holy Spirit.* Without the Holy Spirit being sent to each individual person there can be no share in the faith and hope which create the opposite to present circumstances and allow a new world to become a reality.

But exactly like this sending—the sending of the Holy Spirit to men—mission is at the same time the sending of men: a *praxis* not in contrast to but in harmony with the presence of the Holy Spirit.

In other words, in the concrete history of the charismata in the world the history of the Holy Spirit coincides with that of man. This common history is mission, sending into the world.

The mission of the congregation is entirely determined by eschatology. As the common history of the Holy Spirit and of man, mission consists of the practice of faith and hope in the world, and this mission is determined by the will of God to establish his unchallenged lordship over this world and to enable the whole creation to share in the freedom from the powers of evil which faith and hope in the Holy Spirit already enjoy (Rom. 8:18-23).

This understanding of mission means, *one the one hand,* that all acts of faith and hope are of a missionary character. As acts of faith and hope they exist only in so far as they are the *praxis* which manifests the sending of the Holy Spirit. However, *on the other hand,* this does not mean that, because mission is determined by all that the congregation is and does, it loses its specific content.

Since mission entails a confrontation between the old world and a way of life with eschatological hope, the whole practice of the church must be evidence of a conflict with everything in man and about man which is in opposition to the hope of the kingdom of God. A church which can live in peace with the old aeon in its life and varied activities is a contradiction in itself.

The church of the faith in Christ and the hope in Christ with its variety of charismatic services must always be a part of the history of peace, righteousness, and joy in a world of war, oppression, and torture. The basis of its existence is the presence of the Holy Spirit which manifests itself in the history of faith and hope (the *praxis* of the charismata) as the guarantee of the eschatological kingdom of God in the world.

II
The Mission of the Holy Spirit

"But when the time had fully come, God sent forth his Son, born of woman, born under the law, to redeem those who were under the law, so that we might receive adoption as sons. And because you are sons, God has sent the Spirit of his Son into our hearts, crying, 'Abba! Father!' " (Gal. 4:4-6) .

God sent his son *exapesteilen* in order to redeem man from sin and death under the law, and God sent the Spirit of his son *exapesteilen* in order to make sinful men into sons.

The word *exapostellein* is found in Paul only in these two verses, Gal. 4:4 and 4:6.[5] There is nothing to indicate a shift in meaning between v. 4 and 6. Therefore we must assume that Paul means the same thing in both cases, namely, that God is sent into the world: as God, the Son, in one person, Jesus of Nazareth, and as God, the Holy Spirit, in many persons, namely, in the men who share the charismata of the Holy Spirit.[6]

In both Gal. 4:4 and 4:6 God, the Father, *ho theos*, is the origin of the sending,[7] and this text indicates that both the sending of the Son and the sending of the Holy Spirit are the beginning of an economy of salvation. Both forms of sending are totally unique. In the one it is a question of God's presence in the world, to initiate God's eschatological activity with his creation. Using the language which the church adopted in its theology of the trinity, Paul calls this sending the sending of the Son of God. In the other it is a question of God's presence in the world in order to continue what began with the death and resurrection of Jesus, so that human life can be lived in a world of sin and death in the hope that life in Christ will finally overcome evil and death. Paul calls this presence of God the Holy Spirit, sent into the world.

Not only other Pauline epistles but also other New Testament writings understand the sending of the Son in a similar way as a sending which is totally different from the sending of the Holy Spirit.[8] God acts in history in different ways but these ways of acting speak of a God with a will which aims at establishing his eschatological kingdom, a God who is fully present in the one, Jesus, and in many men. Thus, the one God of sending must be confessed as God —Father, Son, and Holy Spirit.

The proclamation of the sending of the Son accepts that the God of the promises to Israel is really present in Jesus of Nazareth. The proclamation of the sending of the Holy Spirit expresses the belief that the God of the promises fulfilled in Christ is really present in the history of man as God, the Holy Spirit: the God of the as-yet-unfulfilled promises of Christ, the guarantee of the coming kingdom of God.

The sending of the Holy Spirit is a consequence of the sending of the Son. Therefore, the New Testament also proclaims that the Holy Spirit is the Spirit of Christ.[9] Both forms of sending are equally necessary in the history of salvation. Without the sending of the Holy Spirit the history of Christ remains part of the past only: a presence of God which took place only once at a particular time and in a particular place, and, as a consequence, the confession of the church that the death and resurrection of Jesus apply to all men in all times becomes empty and incredible. Only with the presence of the Holy Spirit can the death which took place for all and the hope of life for all be made accessible to the many.

And consequently it can be said that, without accepting the sending of the Holy Spirit, the history of Christ is deprived of its historical nature. Thus incarnation should not be understood as a unique event in history, "born of Mary," but must be understood as the revelation of an eternal presence of God. Accordingly, the cross and resurrection are no longer to be seen as acts in history which are accessible only to faith. The events become facts—and as such are *either* superstition *or* they are written off and their historicity is identified with the significance of the proclamation of the cross and resurrection for faith.

Only the maintenance of the New Testament confession of God's

74

presence in history as the Holy Spirit makes it possible to proclaim the Christ-event *both* as the unique coming of the kingdom of God in a particular history *and* as God's saving act in Christ for all men in all times. Between the risen Lord and his saving act and man's salvation there is the sending of the Holy Spirit: God's new act of revelation in history.[10]

A theology of the sending of the Holy Spirit as God's new act of revelation in history does not in any way lead to triteism, but rather takes up in its own way the teaching of the early church "that one and the same God from beginning to end comes to the help of the human race in various economies."[11] The confession of a new presence of God in the world—*missio Spiritus Sancti*—does not imply a faith in three gods but *a confession of the one God with a history of love.*

We know God only as the God who creates history—the God of love who "from that fountain of love or charity within God the Father" (*Ad Gentes*, No. 2) makes history in the sending of the Son and who, as a consequence of this history of Christ, creates the now-history of love in the sending of the Holy Spirit.

In the history of man, God has made known his love of his creation. He has shown that, as love, he not only entered history once in Jesus of Nazareth, but also in this Jesus God promised that he himself and his kingdom would constantly take historical shape whenever and wherever love becomes a reality in the world. In the sending of the Holy Spirit God begins to fulfill his promise that the time between the resurrection and the second coming will not merely be the unfolding of an eternal "now" so that the end of time will be identical with the beginning of time. The sending of the love of God in the sending of the Holy Spirit means that the history of man becomes the common history of God and man and not just a theater of the glory of God which at the most can point to a God whose history in the world was concluded 2000 years ago in Palestine.

The confession of faith in the triune God is the confession of a God with a history: a God who, as God the Holy Spirit, himself receives a history when human history becomes a manifestation of the new presence of the love of God in the world.

The confession of faith in the sending of the Holy Spirit is a confession of the common history of God and man. It is a confession that the love which is expressed in the world is the same as the love which was uniquely expressed in Jesus, and which will reign in the kingdom of God when everything which is opposed to God has been overcome (1 Cor. 13:8) .[12] The confession of the sending of the Holy Spirit as the new presence of God in the world is the only thing which makes possible the prevention of the division of love into human and Christian love without it being necessary to secularize all love.

The sending of the Holy Spirit makes it possible to state that the same love which defied death in Jesus is a reality in the world although evil and death contradict it. Here we are confronted with *that which is unique in the sending of the Spirit in comparison with the sending of the Son.* The special characteristic of God's new saving activity between the resurrection and the second coming is that God himself and his kingdom take shape in history *in the world of sinful men.*

In the sending of his Son God identifies himself with one man. And it is precisely this Jesus who makes death the place of the presence of God, of the kingdom of God and of life (cf. 2 Cor. 5:21) . The consequence of this is that the world/history of sinful men can become the place of the presence of the love of God—and that this happens through the sending of the Holy Spirit. It is love, mercy, trust, and joy which have to die the death of sin, which now make the divine-human history of the kingdom of God in the world.

We should not look for the history of the kingdom of God beyond human history; rather, the history of love, joy, and peace *in* the world is the history of the Holy Spirit in and with the world. It is *this* which makes known the sending of the Holy Spirit.

The Acts of the Apostles refers to the sending on the day of Pentecost as a sending in time and space, a sending of a historical nature. There is nothing invisible or a-historical about it. The promised presence of God in the Holy Spirit has come to us, says Peter in his sermon at Pentecost: "Which you (both) see and hear" (Acts 2:33) . There is nothing which is just left to the imagination of his listeners. Rather, they are to believe that the signs which they see and hear are the signs of the presence of the Holy Spirit as promised.

Paul speaks in a similar way about the sending of the Holy Spirit to each individual person. This sending is also manifest in history—in the charismata of the Spirit.

"Service is not merely the consequence but the outward form of the realization of grace."[13] In 1 Cor. 12 Paul refers to the charismata as the *phanerosis* of the Spirit. These signs of the presence of the Spirit take various forms. Each individual person has his own specific way of sharing in the presence of God, but it is the same Holy Spirit, the same Lord and God who takes historical shape in the world in so many different ways.

Indeed, the charismata are not merely signs which point to a generalized presence of the Spirit in the world. The charismata are *he phanerosis tou pneumatos* (1 Cor. 12:7) : the revelation of the Spirit in concrete human history. The word *phanerosis* occurs in the Pauline writings only here and in 2 Cor. 4:2 (cf. 2 Cor. 4:10), but the context and the root of the word exclude any doubt about its meaning. It means "outward manifestation," really "public manifestation." Thus Paul explains to the Corinthians that the one Holy Spirit cannot be separated from its many gifts. The charismata are manifestations of the sending of the Holy Spirit to men. Where the charismata are, there is the Holy Spirit. Where the Holy Spirit is, there are the charismata: the concrete history of the Spirit in and with the world.

This means that faith need have no doubt about where the Holy Spirit is present or where the history of the kingdom of God in the world is taking place. Love, joy, peace, patience, kindness, goodness, and faithfulness are fruits of the Spirit (Gal. 5:22). It is not only the service of apostle, prophet, and church administrator but also the history of love, joy, and peace which are evidence of the kingdom of God because, being the common history of man and the Holy Spirit, they are a *praxis* of the hidden sending of the Holy Spirit to men.[14]

The unique sending at Pentecost was the sending of the Holy Spirit to the Apostles, the witnesses of the resurrection (Acts 1:21-22; 2:32). The coming of the Holy Spirit was the fulfillment of the promise that the history of the eschatological kingdom of God would continue even after the cross and resurrection until a new creation, unchallenged by sin and death, came to reveal the salvation of Christ.

With the sending of the Holy Spirit at Pentecost the history of Christ became history in the world.

It was only at Pentecost that the new People of God, which unites in history the risen Lord and sinful men in one community, came into being. Only after the sending of Pentecost did the common witness of the Holy Spirit and the confession of Christ begin. In this witness, where the Holy Spirit witnesses to our spirit that we are accepted as sons in the Son (cf. Rom. 8:16), the Holy Spirit reveals his presence in the world (1 Cor. 12:3, 7).

The sending of Pentecost establishes the church which confesses Christ as a separate people in history with its own history and with a specific task: to be the instrument of the fellowship of men with God through Christ in the Holy Spirit: "Repent, and be baptized every one of you in the name of Jesus Christ for the forgiveness of your sins; and you shall receive the gift of the Holy Spirit" (Acts 2:38).

Another aspect of the proclamation of the event of Pentecost is that in and with the presence of the Holy Spirit the church receives special charismata. The presence of the Holy Spirit manifests itself not only in the acceptance of Christ but at the same time in the services and functions of the church which make the church an effective sign of the unity between men and the risen Lord in the Spirit, i.e., an instrument of the saving presence of the Holy Spirit in the world.[15]

One cannot define the church as the people to whom salvation has come. By virtue of the specific presence of the Holy Spirit in specific charismata in the community which confesses Christ, the main characteristic of this community is that it is a people which is to be the instrument of salvation in the world. The confession of Christ, the sacraments and the various services which arise in the church on the basis of Christ's institution are seen in the preaching of the New Testament as specific gifts which the Holy Spirit gives to the church. Thus the church receives a special task: to be an effective sign of the sending of the Holy Spirit to men. The church is constituted by the presence of the Holy Spirit, a presence which is made known in and with specific gifts to the church of the resurrection faith. And these specific gifts (offices, sacraments) have one thing in common: they are instruments of the sending of the Holy Spirit to men.

In addition to these charismata which equip a congregation for service and mission, the New Testament recognizes another type of charismata. These are charismata by means of which not particular services or functions but particular expressions of human life become a *phanerosis* of the new presence of the Holy Spirit in the world—of the Spirit which enables the kingdom of God to take historical shape in the world after the cross and resurrection. Paul speaks of love, joy, and gentleness, etc., as charismata of the Holy Spirit (Gal. 5:22; Rom. 12–15; 1 Cor. 12–13).

All these phenomena are expressions of human life which make love manifest—the presence of the Holy Spirit in man. Where joy, peace, goodness, patience, and hope are to be found, there the history of love takes place in the world. The Christian faith proclaims about this history of love that it is not made "by man alone."

Love is not created by the will of man. Love belongs to the life which is given us by God; it is a factor of our human existence which comes before our will. Therefore the history which is made by men takes place in the tension between our will and the concrete reality with which we are confronted.

The reality which exists before we act is determined in two different ways. On the one hand it is the given—the history which has been made—and on the other it is determined by the fact that as history it is always a history which either fulfills or denies the love in our lives.

Christian faith implies that our life takes a particular form, namely, that of a love which is given by God to man and which, therefore, has to be realized as our way of life in history.

The life of love does not become a reality by ignoring or going against our will. This is the mystery of the doctrine of creation: that the history of God's love is subject to the will of man. But deeds of love will never be able to be *our* fulfillment of the history of love. For this the impossible would have to happen; our will would have to *want* to realize the history of love.

Only there where our will is created anew by the Holy Spirit can the love of the life which is given become history—a history which is always the history of the Holy Spirit and of man.[16] There is only one love, that of the Creator. And there is only one history of love in the world: the history which presupposes the sending of the Holy Spirit to man.

The New Testament knows nothing of a special type of acts of love which would be the *praxis* of the sending of the Holy Spirit, and of another type of merely secular love. The New Testament states that, when the love which men experience governs our will and thus makes history, it is that love which is the history of the kingdom of God in the world.

In this way one can understand what the Second Vatican Council meant in the following sentences: "For, since Christ died for all men, and since the ultimate vocation of man is in fact one, and divine, we ought to believe that the Holy Spirit in a manner known only to God offers to every man the possibility of being associated with the paschal mystery." (*Gaudium et Spes*, No. 22, cf. fn. 12, *ibid*. pp. 221-222.)

Seen against the background of the relationship between the sending of the Holy Spirit, the charismata and the manifestations of the presence of the Holy Spirit in the world, the sentence quoted above does not constitute a statement which refers to an a-historical presence of God everywhere in the world. Rather this sentence becomes a statement which, on the basis of a confession of the *phanerosis* of the Holy Spirit in and with the charismata, expresses the certainty of faith that the hidden presence of the Holy Spirit unites men with the crucified and risen one *and* that faith must confess this presence wherever it recognizes the history of love.

Love, which can never be the achievement of the creation itself, is always a gift of the Holy Spirit whenever and wherever it becomes a reality in the world of the transitory, of evil, and of death.

With the unique event of the sending of the Holy Spirit at Pentecost the gifts of the Spirit, which are indivisibly bound up with the presence of the Spirit, become the gifts of the Spirit sent by Christ. This is what constitutes "the new." In the sending of the Son and of the Spirit, God himself has received a history which cannot be undone. Whenever and wherever the Holy Spirit comes to dwell in man so that love takes place in the world, he comes as the saving Spirit of Christ.

Faith knows that the presence of the Holy Spirit in the world as the Spirit of salvation is mediated by preaching and the sacraments. This is how the communion of saints knows that its life is a life in mission. But, in addition to this, faith knows from the witness of the Apostles that, although the church has been chosen to serve as an instrument for the Holy Spirit with his specific gifts of grace, God's saving presence in history in the form of the Spirit of Christ extends beyond the people of God which confesses Christ. In the charismata of the Holy Spirit—in love, goodness, and mercy—faith confesses the presence of the Holy Spirit who, with the unique sending of the Spirit at Pentecost, has linked all his activity in history with the act of salvation in Christ.

Just as in sending his Son the triune God has limited himself so that his lordship has become a lordship through Christ, so in sending the Holy Spirit God has bound himself to acting in a new way: to lead his creation to the goal (salvation) through the Spirit of Christ.

"We may believe," said Augustine, "that God gives no gift inferior to himself" (De fide et symbolo, 19).

The God who sends himself in and through his gifts to man, and thus makes manifest his presence in the world, *is* the triune God who, after sending the Spirit at Pentecost, takes historical shape in the world in a new way—as the saving Spirit of Christ.

III
Missiones Dei

The term "mission" can be applied only to the participation in God's own sending to man. This is a confirmation of the "gradual change in missionary thinking . . . where the term *missio* is less and less equated with the activities of missionaries and missionary societies, while more and more attention is given to historical developments, to questions about history and eschatology, and to the acts of God, the *missio Dei* in history."[17]

Against the background of what has been said above about the understanding of the "sending of God," we have to adopt a different approach from the main emphases in the ecumenical study on mission between the Assemblies of New Delhi 1961 and Uppsala 1968. This also gives us a different view of the relationship between the *missio dei* and the mission of man.

God is *missio*. In the ecumenical study this means that God is a God of mission. This is taken to mean that God himself is mission, that God is a living God who is constantly coming to man and to the whole creation in order to be "present in the actual life situation of every man."[18] "God in his mission is at work in this world. . . . He is paving the way for his Kingdom through world history."[19] The witness of the Bible—centering around the presence of God in Christ—speaks of a God whose mission to the world cannot cease without God's ceasing to be God.

"God is not a dead God . . . He manifests Himself today, as He did in the days of our fathers, as the One who Himself carries on the missionary enterprise."[20] When God sends the prophets, the Son, the Holy Spirit, the apostles and the church,[21] all of these acts of sending are to be understood as sending in history by means of which God reveals who he is and how he works eternally. The acts of sending which God brings about because he himself is mission are all signs of this mission but not instruments of it.

Man's mission is called upon to point to God's acts in history and to commit itself to the signs of the presence of the "God of mission" which he himself establishes.

In this conception of the *missio dei, missio* is understood as an overall term which embraces the sending of the Son, the Holy Spirit, and of man. The mission which is God cannot be identified with the sending of the Son and of the Holy Spirit in history; it is a feature of the nature and activity of God.

The many sendings (missions)—including those of the Son and the Spirit—*are signs which God uses to demonstrate the identity of his acts with his nature.* That God is the God of mission, therefore, means that mission is the determining factor of God's nature and acts. In God being and acting cannot be separated. God acts according to his nature; *esse et velle* are identical.

In contrast to this we must remember that *missio dei* is not *a description of God's nature but of a triune God with a history.* Since God as the triune God is God the Father, God the Son—sent into the world—and God the Holy Spirit—sent into the world—all theology of mission must have a trinitarian basis. *Missio* is a theological concept which refers to the fact that in Jesus of Nazareth God took a historical form on one occasion and that after the cross and the resurrection he continually takes historical form in a new personal presence as God the Holy Spirit.

According to the missionary thinking expressed in the theology of mission of the introductory chapter to the decree on mission of the Second Vatical Council, *"Ad Gentes,"* missio dei should be understood as a statement about God's personal acts in the Son and the Holy Spirit. Against this background the participation of the church in the *missio dei* means that it shares in the presence of the Holy Spirit in the world and receives the gifts of this presence so that the Holy Spirit itself takes historical form in the world in and through men. Where the confrontation between the various different charismata of the new creation and "this old world" takes place, there God makes history in the world for himself and his kingdom.

Where this confrontation is a confrontation between the world and the specific charismata of the congregation people are called to repentence and baptism. There the world is called upon to become the church which believes in Christ and to be a special instrument for the history of the Holy Spirit in the world.

Where there is a confrontation between love and the world of hatred, it is not the church but the kingdom of God which takes historical shape in the world. There the Holy Spirit—present in and through love—becomes history in the world as the guarantee of this kingdom of God.

"Reference to the Spirit is the way in which the Christian faith speaks about God as the one who is present in our world creating new things."[22] The distinction between the activity of the Holy Spirit in the church and in the world is that it is *not* the prerogative of the Holy Spirit to determine where the common history of God and man for the sake of the kingdom of God is to take place.

"The Spirit blows where it will." But, by means of the presence of the Spirit in and through the specific institutions and functions of the congregation which mediate the presence of the Spirit, the congregation can cause the common history of God and of man to come about.

The history of salvation does not only take place *modo deo cognito*, "in a way known to God," where love and goodness are made real in this world as a *praxis* of the presence of the Spirit. Just as salvation acquires real history in the world where "the new," i.e., the history of the kingdom of God, is brought about by love, so salvation also acquires history in the world where the *congregatio sanctorum* allows the history of the new creation to become a reality.

That all mission is missio Dei *does not, therefore, mean,* as was understood almost everywhere in Protestant missionary theology in the sixties, *that God alone is the agent of all mission.* It does not mean that the distance between God and man is so emphasized that human mission can never be anything other than a sharing in the signs of God's own *missio* which God himself establishes.

On the contrary, that all mission is missio Dei *means that* mission as the history of the new creation is the *common* history of the Holy Spirit who is sent and of man, a *common* history of God and man which can take place *both* when and where the Holy Spirit wills *and* when and where the people of God which confesses Christ takes seriously its mission.

The term "mission" can only be applied to that which is the common history of God and man, the history of the new creation.

This point of departure implies a rejection of a certain way of linking ontology and history which is characteristic of some Catholic thinking about the relationship between the church, salvation and history.

Under Pius XII in a document from the Holy Office about the question of heresy in Boston,[23] the axiom *extra ecclesiam nulla salus* was interpreted in the following way: salvation can exist outside of the visible Catholic church but never without any relationship to it. As the *ecclesia militans* the church is one and visible, but it is possible to have both visible and invisible membership *in voto* in the one, visible, undivided, and concrete church. Thus, an attempt was made to give an ecclesiological answer to the question of salvation outside of the church. By means of a complicated discussion between 1940 and 1960 the concept of the church was so watered down that all men of good will were included in one way or another within the salvation of the Catholic Church.

Over against such an attempt to solve the problem of *Heilsgeschichte* it must be stated that it is theologically illegitimate to speak of a church outside of the church. The idea of a church outside of the church is untenable for many reasons but above all because it conflicts with the ecclesiology of the New Testament. In the New Testament the church always has a historical dimension: in the world it is the fellowship of those who believe in and confess Christ.[24] Moreover it is church imperialism to claim that the church embraces people who confess to be Moslems or Buddhists.

Since the Second Vatican Council the Catholic Church has also officially ceased trying to solve the question of salvation outside of the church by means of reflecting on a church outside the church. *Lumen Gentium*, No. 16 states: "Those also can attain to everlasting salvation who through no fault of their own do not know the Gospel of Christ or His Church, yet sincerely seek God and, moved by grace, strive by their deeds to do His will as it is known to them through the dictates of conscience. Nor does divine Providence deny the help necessary for salvation to those who, without blame on their part, have not arrived at an explicit knowledge of God, but who strive to live a good life, thanks to His grace." In Hans Küng's terms this can be interpreted in the following way: one can ask what is there outside of the *church* but the question cannot be answered. However, one cannot ask what is there outside of *God* and his plan of salvation. There is no such thing as *extra* but only *intra* because God wills all men to be saved and to come to the knowledge of the truth.[25]

But there is another way of ending up in an ecclesiological cul-de-sac. It can be maintained that there is certainly no church outside of the

church but that, since all grace is the grace of Christ, all grace is by
nature ecclesial and thus salvation always comes through the church.
*The center of interest for such reflections is the sacramental—
ecclesial grace—as a category. From there one can proceed to ecclesiology* (as for example Karl Rahner, E. Schillebeeckx, O. Semmelroth).

If one considers grace, which is ecclesial by nature, as a possible
condition of every true existence then one has the theological basis
for calling all mankind the people of God and for describing the
church as the "social manifestation" of grace in history (Rahner).

Thus, the church is understood as a sign of the grace of Christ
which is active everywhere in the world and makes all men of goodwill not only into anonymous theists but "anonymous Christians"
(Rahner).[26] *This combination of history and an ontology of grace*
is characteristic of this and other attempts[27] to keep history as the
"history of mankind's deeds and thoughts" (Rahner) and at the
same time to understand this history as the history of salvation. The
history of salvation is coextensive with history precisely because
there is an *ontological* presupposition for this—that God's saving
grace is a condition of every true existence.[28]

But this ontological presupposition itself has a *historical* presupposition: the incarnation. In Rahner"s terms, the transcendental
a priori openness of man to the grace of God "is necessarily accomplished in the history of the action and thought of mankind, and
may be so in a very explicit or in a quite anonymous way. Consequently there is never a history of transcendental revelation in isolation. History in the concrete, both individually and collectively, is
the history of God's transcendental revelation."[29] By means of such
a theological combination of metaphysics of being and history, in
which the transcendental and the historical constitute a whole and
are mutually interdependent, history is deprived of its capacity to
produce anything really new.[30] The element which constitutes history (the supernatural existential—God's self-giving through grace)
lies outside of history, but, since human transcendence is expressed
in history, history necessarily becomes the "history categorical self-
interpretation" of the transcendental, supernatural existential.

This all means that salvation has no real history. The church has
no real history and mission has no real history because there cannot
be more in the special *Heilsgeschichte* of the church than in the

general *Heilsgeschichte* of the world. Nothing "new" happens where the fellowship which confesses Christ develops in the world. Karl Rahner's teaching about "anonymous Christians" and what E. Schillebeeckx has said about "implicit Christianity" has had a marked influence on the discussion in missionary theology of the relationship between salvation—world—history—church and continues to exert that influence today.

The terminology which is used in this discussion would be considerably improved if the urgently necessary recognition took place that it is meaningful to adopt the statements of Rahner and Schillebeeckx about salvation outside of the church only if one is prepared at the same time to adopt the *same* theological view of history.

In the theology of mission, which tries to create a theological platform for a meaningful dialogue between Christianity and other religions, use is often made of the concept of "the hidden Christ of the religions." The discussion about the relationship between mission and dialogue which was conducted during the sixties is still far from having reached a consensus and there are very different theological starting points for talking about the hidden presence of Christ in the religions.

When George Khodr uses the expression "God hidden in the world of religions"[31] and understands by mission "to name him whom others have already recognized as the Beloved—to awaken the Christ who sleeps in the night of the religions" he does so on the basis of a theology of the presence of the Holy Spirit everywhere in the world.

With the sending of the Spirit at Pentecost the economy of salvation of the Holy Spirit began: "The Spirit is present everywhere and fills everything by virtue of an economy distinct from that of the Son. . . . The Spirit fashions Christ within us. And since Pentecost it makes Christ present. It interiorizes Christ in the here and now . . . the Spirit operates through its energies according to its own economy, and we could, from this angle, consider the non-Christian religions as places where his inspiration is at work."

In addition to this distinction (not separation!) between the economy of the Son and that of the Holy Spirit which has been maintained above all by Orthodox theologians, George Khodr emphasizes that salvation means that man becomes through grace what

God is by nature. The latter is presented in the following way: salvation is a mystery. What constitutes salvation is that men come to share in God's own life through the economy of Christ and of the Holy Spirit. This dual economy of salvation is not limited to a "historical unfolding in a linear history"; rather, just as the incarnation means that the whole of mankind can potentially share in true existence and the resurrection means that the whole creation is filled with the fullness of Christ, so the sending of the Holy Spirit signifies "a universal Pentecost."

As the Holy Spirit of the salvation which has taken place in Christ, the Spirit is present everywhere and fills everything by virtue of His economy. Until the second coming, the church which confesses Christ and celebrates the Eucharist is the first fruit of mankind which is called to be the unique and glorious body of the Savior. The church should be understood as the Sacrament of this future unity—the *communio* of the kingdom of God between God and man—which will be made up *both* of people who have been incorporated into the church through Baptism *and* of people who have been made members of the body of *Christ* by the hidden presence of the Holy Spirit in the world.

If one does not wish to end in an untrinitarian Christ-monism and either maintain that the risen Christ is directly present everywhere in the world, thereby avoiding asking the question of the "how" of this presence, or make church structures (the ministry, preaching) into a *sine qua non* for the presence of the Crucified and Risen one in history, then one has to take seriously in one's theology that the sending of the Holy Spirit stands between the history of Christ and our history.

"Without His work (the work of the Paraclete) nothing can exist in history, neither the reality of the Incarnation and reconciliation in Christ, nor personal commitment to him in his community of faith."[32] It is the sending of the Spirit at Pentecost which is the *conditio sine qua non* by which the history of Christ enters the history of the world. Without a theology of the sending of the Holy Spirit theology either becomes a false spiritualism or an equally false institutionalization of the history of Christ.[33] Together with George Khodr, any attempt to come to terms with salvation through Christ in our history must find its point of departure in the acceptance of the specific economy of salvation of the Holy Spirit. Over against George Khodr's unhistorical conception of the economy of the Holy Spirit one must emphasize that the triune God acts historically as God the Holy Spirit.

Mission and history are indivisibly related to one another: "God sent his Son, born of a woman, subject to the law": God took historical form in Jesus Christ and "God has sent the Spirit of his Son into our hearts, crying, 'Abba! Father!' ": God the Holy Spirit takes historical form in the history of human beings. As we have already stated, the *missio* of the Holy Spirit is not invisible and his action is not a-historical. In his sermon at Pentecost, Peter does not call upon the crowds to see the invisible and to hear the inaudible; rather he calls upon them *to see* what they can see and *to hear* what they can hear, i.e., to keep faith and history, facts and their significance together and to confess the presence of the Holy Spirit in history.[34] The sending of the Spirit at Pentecost means that the Holy Spirit has thus begun to work in the world in a specific way, by being present in specific persons.

It is not all places and all people and all times that are filled with the presence of the Holy Spirit; rather particular people at particular times and in particular places become the place of the presence of the Holy Spirit. The expression *Missiones Spiritus Sancti* underlines this historical dimension of the presence of the Holy Spirit in the world. It emphasizes that salvation acquires a history which is made by people who "walk in the Spirit."

If we examine the preaching of the New Testament about the presence of Christ in the world, it can be seen that the early church was aware that this presence takes various forms. The Christian faith confesses a presence which is realized through Christ's institution: "He who hears you hears me" (Lk. 10:16) , "This is my body which is given for you."—"This cup is the new covenant in my blood" (Lk. 22:19 f) .

In addition, in the preaching which it has received, the church confesses an equally real presence of salvation which comes through the exercise of love, goodness, and mercy: "You gave *me* food . . . and you gave *me* drink, . . . you clothed *me* and visited *me* when you concerned yourselves with the hungry and the thirsty, the naked and the persecuted" (Matthew 25:35 ff) . In this parable it is not hunger and thirst, the lack of clothes and persecution—all that constitutes a destruction of creation—which become the place of the presence of

Christ. Rather it is love, goodness, and mercy overcoming evil and its negative consequences which are recognized as the place of the presence of Christ.

This preaching throws light on the New Testament message about the presence of the Holy Spirit in the world. On the one hand, the church confesses that something new has happened—that salvation takes place where people are baptized and the Gospel is heard. The aim of the preaching is that the presence of the Holy Spirit—and thereby Christ's salvation—should be mediated by preaching, sacraments, and offices, i.e., by the gifts of the Spirit to the congregation.

On the other hand, the church confesses that something new is happening—that salvation takes place—where love, goodness, and mercy overcome evil and destruction in the world. Indeed what is preached is that the Holy Spirit—and therefore Christ and his salvation—are present where the fruits of the Spirit are to be found. Whenever and wherever people allow love, goodness, and mercy to take place the world is changed. There history of salvation is made because "the new" comes about with the overcoming of the world which is turned in on itself.

There is nothing invisible or a-historical about this form of the presence of the Holy Spirit in the world. *Missiones Spiritus Sancti* does refer to an immediate presence of God among men but this does not imply that this presence has no manifestation, no specific *phanerosis* nor specific history which faith can and must confess. Not all changes and all history constitute a *phanerosis* of the Spirit without distinction. History is not another term for the living God who acts.

But faith knows where salvation becomes history in the world. In faith in the Risen One the church knows that the presence of the Holy Spirit is made manifest in the history of love. And the church knows the love of Christ and is aware what can and must be called love. Salvation and the new creation have a *history* in the world beyond the community of those who believe in Christ, namely, the history of the love which "renews the face of the earth," because this history is the common history of the Holy Spirit and of man.

Where the community which believes in Christ recognizes signs of *this* history, its mission or sending is not to quench the Spirit (1 Th. 5:19) but "to recognize what happens before our eyes, confessing its meaning and participating in its fulfillment."[35]

NOTES

1. E. Käsemann, "Worship and Everyday Life, A Note on Romans 12," *New Testament Questions of Today*, tr. by W. J. Montagne, Philadelphia: Fortress, 1969, pp. 188-195. Cf. "Principles of the Interpretation of Romans 13," *ibid.*, pp. 196-216. Otto Merk, *Handeln und Glauben*, Marburg, 1968, p. 169, tries without success to disprove Käsemann's view that Paul is also speaking about the charismata in Rom. 12:9.
2. E. Käsemann, "An Apologia for Primitive Christian Eschatology," *Essays on New Testament Themes*, tr. by W. J. Montagne (Studies in Biblical Theology, 41, London, SCM, 1964), pp. 169-195. "It is . . . unthinkable for Paul that Christian existence should remain permanently in that state of conflict between flesh and spirit which determines it today. Such a redemption would not be total redemption, it would not be *redemptio mundi*. Certainly, in the tribulation of the Christian the possibility of the new obedience is given. But it proves that God's sovereignty is still being contested. Pauline eschatology, like that of the Apocalypse and of the whole of primitive Christianity, centres round the question whether God is indeed God and when he will fully assert himself as such."
3. J. B. Metz, "An Eschatological View of the Church and the World," part II, chap. II, pp. 81-100; attached to it is "Appendix II," "On the Hiddenness of the Problem of the Future in Metaphysics," pp. 98-100, *Theology of the World*, tr. by W. Glen-Doepel, New York, Herder & Herder.
4. E. Käsemann, "Worship and Everyday Life," *ibid.*, p. 192.
5. *apostellō* by K. H. Rengstorf, vol. 1, p. 406, *Theological Dictionary of the New Testament*, ed. by G. Kettel and G. Friedrich, tr. by G. W. Bromiley, Grand Rapids: Eerdmans, vol. 1, 1964.
6. H. Mühlen was the first to point out that these verses from the Letter to the Galatians must have dogmatic consequences. *Der Heilige Geist als Person*, 1967[2], pp. 198-206.
7. K. Rahner, "Theos in the New Testament," *Theological Investigations*, vol. 1, *God, Christ, Mary and Grace*, transl. by C. Ernst, O.P. (Baltimore, 1961, Helican Press), pp. 79-148.
8. E.g., Rom. 8; Acts 2; Jn 15.
9. Cf. Vl. Lossky, *Théologie Mystique de l'Eglise d'Orient*, 1944, p. 156.
10. Cf. N. A. Nissiotis, *"Pneumatological Christology as a Presupposition of Ecclesiology,"* *Oecumenica 1967*, pp. 235-252.
11. Irenaeus, *Against Heresies*, III, 12, 16.
12. *Gaudium et Spes*, No. 39, "Pastoral Constitution on the Church in the Modern World," p. 237: "As deformed by sin, the shape of this world will pass away. . . . What was sown in weakness and corruption, will be clothed with incorruptibility. While charity and its fruits endure, all that creation which God made on man's account will be unchained from the bondage of vanity."
13. E. Käsemann, "Ministry and Community in the New Testament," *Essays on New Testament Themes*, p. 65.
14. E. Käsemann, "Worship and Everyday Life," *op. cit.*, p. 194, on the relationship between Rom. 12: 5-8, 9 ff: "For he who walks 'in Christ' or 'in the Spirit' lives by the power of grace and his activity is a manifestation of it. Even his 'ethical" existence is understood eschatologically in Paul and the concept of *charisma* is intended to demonstrate this as clearly as possible."

Cf. A. Greiner, "l'Esprit-Saint dans le Noveau Testament," *Le Mystère de l'Esprit-Saint*, 1968, p. 62. On the term *"karpos,"* D. F. Hauch, vol. 3, pp. 614-616, *Theological Dictionary of the New Testament*, ed. by Kittel and G. Friedrich, tr. by G. W. Bromiley, Grand Rapids: Eerdmans, vol. 3, 1965.

15. N. A. Nissiotis, "L'Eglise monde transfiguré," *L'Eglise dans le monde, églises en dialogue*, 1968, p. 39: "Its (the Church's) essence is divine grace through the work of the Paraclete. The institutions of the Church are the expression of this absolutely transcendent, theonomous, divine essence, different from all that is characteristic of other human institutions. . . . Its members [of the community of faith] are called to holiness specially incarnate in the charismatics who have a service, a separate, personal diaconate which makes them instruments of the transmission of divine grace. The institutional aspect is the charisma of greatest value which the Holy Spirit gives to the Church."

16. H. Schlier, *Der Brief an die Galater*, 1949, p. 181, "In the case of the desires of the flesh and of the Spirit it is a matter of the *poiein* [of] man in which man himself is called into question. . . . There is no reference here to a cooperation between the Spirit and man in the sense that by *their* acts each contributes something to the overcoming of the flesh but rather in the sense that the Spirit only prevails over the flesh of man when man, that is the Christian, allows himself to be led by the Spirit having opened himself to him and decided to receive him."

17. M. A. Thung, *Concept*, June, 1970. Cf. *The Church for Others*, Geneva, 1967, *Drafts for Sections*, WCC o.j. Th. Wieser, [ed.]: *Planning for Mission*, 1967. On the debate on the theology of mission since Uppsala, 1968 – J. Aagaard, *Mission after Uppsala*, 1968. "Major trends in the field of missions and ecumenism," Paper read to the Society of Missiologists, Oslo, 1970.

18. *Drafts for Sections*, WCC, p. 33, quoting *The Church for Others*, Geneva, 1967, p. 13.

19. J. Verkuyl, *Secular Man and Christian Mission*, P. Löffler, ed., WCC 1968, p. 28.

20. W. Andersen, *Towards a Theology of Mission*, 1955, p. 47 f.

21. *Drafts for Sections*, WCC, Geneva, p. 33 quoting *The Church for Others*, Geneva, 1967, p. 13.

22. P. E. Persson, "Kyrka får världen – Missionens målsättning? *Nordisk Missionstidskrift*, 1969, p. 122.

23. Published, October, 1952, in *American Ecclesiastical Review*.

24. H. Küng, *Christenheit als Minderheit*, Einsiedel, 1965.

25. *Ibid.*, p. 36.

26. W. W. Kantzenbach, "Die ekklesiologische Begründung des Heils der Nichtchristen. Problematische und verheissungsvolle Wege und Tendenzen in der neuesten romisch-katholischen Theologie." *Oecumenica 1976*, pp. 210-233. B. A. Willems, O.P., "Who Belongs to the Church?" *The Church and Mankind, Concilium, Dogma*, vol. 1, New York, 1965, Paulist Press, pp. 131-151. K. Lehman, "Karl Rahner," *Bilanz der Theologie im 20. Jahrhundert, Bahnbrechende Theologen*, 1970, pp. 143-180.

27. In the difference between Rahner and Schillebeeckx in their concept of the grace of Christ in the world, cf. H. Nys, O.P., *Le salut sans l'Evangile*, 1966.

28. In Rahner's writings this ontological presupposition is called "the supernatural existential" and in Schillebeeckx "the openness of man for the whole of reality and thus for grace as the *finis* of all reality."

29. K. Rahner, J. Ratzinger, *Revelation and Tradition*, tr. by W. J. O'Hara, Questiones Disputatae, 17, New York, 1966, Herder & Herder, p. 17.

30. Cf. J. B. Metz's disagreement with such positions. See fn. 3, pp. 98-100.

31. Christianity in a Pluralistic World—The Work of the Holy Spirit, WCC, Addis Ababa, Jan., 1971, The Ecumenical Review, vol. XXIII, Geneva, 1971, pp. 118 ff, esp. p. 123, 125 f, and 128.

32. N. A. Nissiotis, Pneumatological Christology as a Presupposition of Ecclesiology, *Oecumenica 1967*, pp. 235-251.

33. *Ibid.*

34. On this point, cf. many important considerations in P. Frostin, *Politik och hermeneutik*, Lund, 1970.

35. Cf. J. Aagaard, *Mission After Uppsala*, fn. 17.

Chapter 4

Fides ex auditu and the Salvation of Non-Christians:

Contemporary Catholic and Protestant Positions

I
Extra Ecclesiam Salus Est

What is the relation of the salvation of non-Christians to the church and to the explicitly Christian faith which comes through hearing the gospel *(fides ex auditu)*? This is one of the more critical questions confronting theology today even though it has been neglected in most Protestant circles and has chiefly been discussed by Roman Catholics. Our concern in this chapter is to see why the problem is urgent, review Protestant and Catholic positions on it, ask where they disagree and what they can learn from each other, and propose a Protestant approach.

The problem is important, not only in a theoretical way, but also on the pastoral level. Churches and Christians are confused. They do not know what attitudes and policies to adopt in reference to non-Christians and to their religions and secular quasi-religions. A major reason for this is to be found in the gigantic theological reversal which has taken place in recent generations on the salvation of non-Christians. Formerly it was almost universally agreed that salvation is rare or impossible apart from explicit faith or outside the visible church *(extra ecclesiam non salus est)*. Now, however, it is widely assumed that the contrary is the case—*extra ecclesiam salus est*. Yet the old attitudes toward pastoral problems, evangelism, and missionary work still linger on. It is thought to be invariably good when someone embraces Christianity and enters the church. It is invariably bad when someone leaves. Evangelism at home and on mission fields abroad should have as its primary objective converting as many people as possible; anything which might hinder this, such as cordial cooperation and mutually appreciative dialogue with other religions or ideologies, should be discouraged. However, these attitudes and policies are also widely attacked, so that in some circles the very idea of evangelism, of preaching the gospel to all men, has been entirely replaced by secular *diakonia*, by the social action and philanthropic service of the nonreligious needs of men. In large part, neither the defenders nor the attackers of these various views have much clarity on the question of salvation. This problem, especially on the Protestant side, is generally bracketed and passed over in embarrassed silence.

The results are often painful. The attackers of the old policies give the impression, sometimes against their will, that they are totally this-worldly and quite indifferent to the problem of ultimate human destiny. The defenders of these same policies are caught in an equally difficult dilemma, for they themselves no longer really believe that damnation is the fate of unbelievers or that non-Christian religions should always be viewed primarily as instruments of perdition. Yet their actions and psychological attitudes suggest that they think this. In the absence of the old beliefs, the old policies become perhaps even more objectionable than they were in the past because they are no longer expressions of genuine conviction. Consequently, although not now pursued with their ancient rigor, they are to a greater extent than formerly simply manifestations of communal or institutional self-assertion and defensiveness. This becomes the real though hidden motive for seeking to increase or at least maintain the membership of the church, and it contributes to that preoccupation with quantity rather than quality, with numbers of converts and amounts of money rather than living faith, which is so characteristic of both laity and leadership among Protestants and Catholics in America and perhaps elsewhere also. Thus the real reasons for seeking to maintain and increase the size of the church are masked under pallid versions of the rhetoric of "saving souls" (and sometimes also of "service," of course).

This situation is, to be sure, understandable. It is the perhaps inescapable consequence of the transition now taking place from mass Christianity to a minority position in an increasingly de-Chris-

tianized society. The attitudes towards non-Christians exemplified
by the *extra ecclesiam nulla salus* and the modern missionary movements developed during fifteen centuries when all of the West was
nominally Christian and during the last two hundred years of imperialistic Western expansion. That situation is now rapidly and
radically changing. It will take time for a new and more appropriate
understanding of the relation of Christianity to the salvation of
mankind to be articulated and established. We shall later examine
what has so far been done in this direction and ask about new approaches. In this section, however, we must first say something about
the change of views on the salvation of non-Christians which has
now become so widespread.

Both Roman Catholics and Protestants have in the past affirmed
that "outside the visible church there is no salvation," although they
interpreted this in different ways. The Catholic understanding of
the church was in terms of a hierarchical institution headed by the
Pope. The most extreme form of the affirmation that this is the *sole
locus* of salvation is to be found in the bull *Unam Sanctam* promulgated by Boniface VIII in 1302: "We declare, state and define that it
is absolutely necessary for the salvation of all men that they submit
to the Roman pontiff" (D.S. 875). On the Reformation side, the
emphasis fell on the preaching of the Word and the response of
faith. Thus Luther says in the Large Catechism, "For where Christ
is not preached, there is no Holy Spirit to create, call and gather the
Christian church, and outside it no one can come to the Lord. . . .
But outside the Christian church (that is, where the Gospel is not)
there is no forgiveness, and hence no holiness."[1] The Second Helvetic
Confession of 1566 states flatly that "none can live before God who
do not communicate with the true Church of God,"[2] while the Westminster Confession of 1646 qualifies this only slightly by saying that
outside "the visible church . . . there is no ordinary possibility of
salvation."[3] Thus despite the difference in formulations, there was
agreement on the normal impossibility of salvation outside the explicitly Christian domain. Non-Christians who lived in the period
after Christ were with few exceptions doomed to perdition, and the
religions or philosophies which they espoused in preference to Christianity, however admirable in a purely human way, must still be
condemned as the work of Satan.

This is not the place to describe why this view developed in the
patristic period and during the middle ages in opposition to the

wide diversity and, in part, much greater generosity of early Christian attitudes.[4] What is important for our purposes is to see how and why it has been so widely abandoned. On the Catholic side, it was already officially condemned in 1949 (D.S. 3866 ff), and now Vatican II has affirmed that even atheists may be saved (LG 16),[5] given a highly positive evaluation of non-Christian religions (*Nostra aetate*),[6] and led to the establishment of a Secretariat for Non-Believers which has as a major purpose the promotion of dialogue with other religions and ideologies.

Protestant churches have not officially acted either singly or collectively on this question, and the so-called "conservative evangelical" groups which exist in most of them continue, by and large, to speak in terms of "no salvation outside the church" in the sense of "no salvation apart from explicit decision of faith in Christ during this life." These groups are a minority, but in proportion to their numbers they do far more missionary work in traditionally non-Christian lands than do the major denominations. A leading spokesman for this outlook, H. Lindsell, editor of *Christianity Today*, says: "God does not reveal himself redemptively through other means than those presently indicated in the Word of God: i.e., through His children's missionary activity in a lost world"; or, alternatively phrased, by "the message which has come through men . . . and which the man must accept to be saved." From this it follows that "there are no real values in the non-Christian religions."[7] A similar position was taken in a declaration on "Mission—and Neo-Universalism" made by the Congress on the Church's Worldwide Mission, held in Wheaton, Illinois, in 1966, organized by agencies representing 13,000 missionaries.[8]

Among Catholics, the position of so sizable a minority would provoke extensive debate in the rest of the church, including the professional theologians; but in Protestantism, organizational patterns and divisions make it possible for this conservative evangelical view to go undiscussed by the majority. The majority holds that there is salvation outside the church, and this position has become so thoroughly dominant that it is generally not even articulated. This is true even among theologians who are usually thought of as confessionally conservative. Writing as early as 1923, Paul Althaus was able to say that "The more recent dogmatics has virtually unanimously broken through the limits of the old Protestantism which wanted to confine God's saving revelation strictly to earthly his-

tory."[9] The great majority of Protestant exegetes[10] since the middle
of the nineteenth century have held that the obscure passage in which
Christ is said to have preached to the spirits in prison (1 Pt. 3:19,
cf. 4:6) reflects a belief in the early church that those who die in sin
will still, in the mercy of God, have a chance to respond to the
gospel. Similar interpretations are sometimes advanced by Catholic
biblical scholars.[11] In addition to exegetical considerations of this
and other kinds, as well as other theological and nontheological factors, the great majority of even conservative Catholic and Protestant
academic theologians now appear to accept what might be called
"quasi-universalism."

This quasi-universalist view is different from the universalism
(*apokatastasis*) espoused by Origen and condemned at Constanti-
nople in 543 (D.S. 781). It insists that there can be no dogmatic or
objective certainty of the salvation of everyone (especially not of
oneself) for that would be to deny the real peril of the human situation. (This lack of certainty even about oneself does not contradict
the Reformation doctrine of the assurance of salvation (*Heilsgewiss-
heit*) because that is a matter of trusting God and his mercy, not
of objective certainty regarding one's own perseverance).[12] Nevertheless, one must hope, really hope, for the salvation of all. The
more exclusive sounding New Testament passages (e.g., Lk. 16:16)
must be interpreted in the light of the more universalist ones (e.g.,
Col. 1:20; Eph. 1:9, 10; Phil. 2:10, 11; 1 Cor. 15:28; 1 Jn. 2:2; Acts
3:21). It is clearly wrong, so the argument goes, to follow the tradition in making the exclusivist texts primary and distorting the
others in order to make them conform. That is to go against the
fundamental thrust of the biblical message according to which God
wills the salvation of all (1 Tim. 2:4). The Christian believes that
God's mercy and power are infinite, and he therefore has every
reason to hope that God's goodness will ultimately triumph everywhere and in everyone. To be sure, the exclusivist passages must be
taken seriously as warnings against the genuine dangers of rejecting
the good news; but these dangers are greatest, not outside, but inside the church, for here it is that men are confronted most fully
with the gospel and are thus in a position to decide with apparent
definitiveness against Christ (cf. Heb. 12:25, 2 Pt. 2:21).[13] Even in
such cases, however, the Christian must hope. To deny this, to affirm
dogmatically that it is necessary to believe that in some cases the
possibility of eternal separation from God is actualized, is nothing

short of blasphemous. This is to corrupt the gospel by making bad news part of the good news.[14]

Such a position, it should be observed, seeks to remain within the historic mainstream of Christian orthodoxy by vigorously maintaining that salvation is only through Christ. There are, of course, many theologians who consider themselves Christian who doubt or deny this, but in this essay we shall not deal at any length with them. Our concern is with those who, while "quasi-universalist," insist that God's redemptive action in human history is only through the *gratia Christi*, that "there is no other name under heaven given among men whereby we must be saved." They hold, however, that the redemptive power of this name, of Jesus' life, death, and resurrection, cannot be confined to what is explicitly Christian or to the visible church.

There is another limitation of our discussion which must be mentioned. The possibility of salvation outside the church of which we are speaking has to do with its personal or individual aspects. We shall not discuss the role which the church may have in the redemption of mankind in some collective or cosmic sense. This means, among other things, that we shall not deal with the suggestion that the large-scale historical changes which can in one way or another be traced back to Christianity's influence may play a part in God's redemptive purposes. It may well be true, as many historians believe, that the de-divinization of nature and the state by biblical faith and the injection of eschatological hopes into the stream of history have done much to produce the Western civilization which is now becoming world civilization with all its wondrous yet terrifying scientific, technological, political, social, cultural, and moral dynamism. It may be, as a certain eschatological interpretation of history would hold, that this is one of the ways in which God is preparing the world for that final judgment and restoration of all things (Acts 3:21) without which individual salvation would be meaningless.[15] Be that as it may, our concern here is with the relation of explicitly Christian faith and of the visible church to the personal dimensions of the salvation of non-Christians, not to its broad, social, historical, or cosmic aspects.

Finally, in concluding this section on the belief that there is salvation outside the church, it will be well to remind ourselves of the nontheological reasons why it is now so widely affirmed. Why have Catholics and Protestants who are as deeply concerned as their predecessors with faithfulness to Scripture and tradition now reversed the "orthodox" position on this point? Karl Rahner answers this question by saying that "The man and Christian of today cannot think otherwise, and this for a very simple reason which was not present previously. In previous ages . . . someone of a 'different Creed' or an unbeliever was looked on simply as a stranger . . . and one was quite prepared to assume without any qualms that he lacked true faith on account of some guilt on his part and . . . that he would be lost through a just judgment. . . . Today the 'unbeliever' is the neighbor, the relative, the human person on whose honesty, reliability, and decency one must rely just as much as on the corresponding qualities of one's fellow believers (in which process one sometimes gets the staggering impression that one can rely much more on the former than on the latter) ."[16] H. Ott comments on this passage: "In view of the contemporary human situation and the experiences all of us have, only a sectarian sensibility could manage to consider all men who do not explicitly confess Christ as automatically lost and excluded from the realm of God's saving actions . . . if we have heard the kerygma, we cannot otherwise construe the historical context which is now ours, nor draw any other conclusion than this. It is precisely out of the spirit of the gospel that this interpretation comes."[17]

In short, when the whole of Western society was professedly Christian, it was easy to make harsh judgments about the distant and unknown adherents of other religions; but now that the world is becoming smaller and more unified and the non-Christians are our neighbors and our kinsmen, this is impossible. It is impossible, so the secular observer would say, for social-psychological reasons, and to this the Christian need only add that these social-psychological factors must also be understood as God's gift enabling the church to see that the gospel itself is opposed to such harshness.

II
The Salvation of Unbelievers and Non-Christian Religions

What are the implications of this now widespread view that God saves apart from explicitly Christian faith, apart from membership in the visible church? We must first say something about the many answers which are given to this question before trying to evaluate them.

Symmachus, the fourth century defender of ancient paganism against Christianity, once said: "It is impossible that so great a mystery should be approached by one road alone." This is one of Arnold Toynbee's favorite quotations.[18] He argues that it expresses a conviction which Christians also must now adopt. It represents the only possible road to that tolerance and mutual appreciation among men of different faiths which is increasingly necessary in a constantly smaller and more unified world.[19]

Toynbee is, of course, not the first professed Christian to agree with Symmachus. He is actually a twentieth century representative of the Protestant theological liberalism which developed in the nineteenth century. Influenced by historicist and philosophical relativism, many thinkers in this tradition surrendered the claim that Christianity is the absolute religion. Ernst Troeltsch, for example, thought of it as in a sense absolute for its adherents or absolute for Western culture, but not for all men.[20] A similar, though perhaps somewhat less relativistic, position was adopted by another devout churchman, W. E. Hocking, who was the editor and guiding spirit behind the Laymen's Report of 1932, *Rethinking Missions*, commissioned by six American Protestant denominations.[21] Even today probably most educated and sensitive Christians, both Catholic and Protestant, find such an approach persuasive.

Yet there are not only theological, but also nontheological difficulties with it. From the point of view of the objective scholarly study of religion, there is a great deal of evidence against the notion that the various religions of the world are simply different paths to the same goal or multiform manifestations of a common essence. It has so far proved quite impossible to formulate a description of the single goal or common essence which is not clearly marked by its origins in a particular religious or philosophical position (even though the author is often quite unaware of this). Those who formulate these descriptions propose as many goals and essences of all religions as there are different religions. If, in despair, one adopts a relativistic position by saying that, despite the irreducible pluralism of moral and religious options, they are all equally true and good, then one has no basis for preferring one to another, or for opposing, for example, Nazism or diabolistic shamanism.[22]

The intrinsic difficulties of the liberal approach no doubt help to explain the triumph within Protestant theology after World War I of the radically different position represented most notably by Karl

Barth.[23] Even if he is not altogether consistent, his general view is that all religions, including Christianity in so far as it also is religious, are simply manifestations of the sinful effort of human beings to save themselves, to justify themselves, to refuse to allow God in Jesus Christ to do all and be all. This position leaves no room for Christian pride or self-congratulation. Christians and the church are no less sinful than other communities and men; and, furthermore, other men are saved by God in and through Jesus Christ no less than is the Christian. Christians are simply those who know that this is true and therefore have the commission to communicate this good news; but they have no reason to think of themselves as morally, religiously, or in any other way better than non-Christians. The only thing that is distinctive about them is their knowledge of what is true of all men and their election thereby to the joyful task of proclamation.

Hendrik Kraemer has followed a modified version of this Barthian view, and he has written more—and in mission circles more influentially—than any other recent Protestant on the theological interpretation of non-Christian religions.[24] The Barthian condemnation of religion has also contributed to that extraordinarily high theological evaluation of secularism and secularization which one finds presented in A. van Leeuwen,[25] in popular form in Harvey Cox's *Secular City*[26] and, from a more existentialist point of view, in F. Gogarten.[27]

The result of this Protestant reaction against religion is that, rather paradoxically, Roman Catholic theologians are now the ones who most often express high appreciation of the faiths of other men. This development was long delayed, but it is Catholic views of non-Christian religions which now most often resemble those of nineteenth century liberalism. Karl Rahner, more than anyone else, has supplied the systematic framework for the new interpretations.[28] He has met with opposition,[29] but views deriving from him, or at least similar to his, seem to have become overwhelmingly dominant.[30] They agree with some varieties of the old Protestant liberalism that God is present in the transcendental depths of the religious questings and experiences of all men, and that this general revelation or presence of God is articulated with varying degrees of adequacy in the rituals, ethics, communal structures and world views of the various religions. They disagree most emphatically with the old liberalism, however, in maintaining that this universal awareness of the divine is not simply a part of man's endowments, but must be understood from the Christian point of view as the gift of grace, as a "supernatural existential," as the presence of Christ himself. It is Christ who saves in and through other religions, and to the degree that men become conscious of the essential meaning of their faiths, they will be led to explicit knowledge and confession of Jesus Christ as the adequate articulation and express fulfillment of what they already implicitly believe or are searching for. Non-Christians, however, need not only learn from Christianity; they can also teach. They may have discovered much in hidden ways about God and the *gratia Christi* which the church does not yet know and which it needs for the enrichment, and in a sense completion, of its own faith. The door to such an outlook was opened by the Second Vatican Council's Declaration on Non-Christian Religions *(Nostra aetate)* ,[31] but it is by no means entirely new. In a way it is a contemporary form of the cosmic logos Christologies of some of the early fathers, beginning already with Justin Martyr in the second century,[32] which built on such biblical themes as the Johannine view of Christ as "the real light which enlightens every man" (John 1:9) .

With the waning of Barthian influence or, more precisely, of dialectical and kerygmatic theology, similar approaches have begun to gain strength in the last few years among non-Catholic theologians.[33] The need for dialogue in view of the increasing challenge of pluralism and the revival of non-Christian religions has led some Christians, especially in India, to emphasize the motif of the cosmic Christ at work in all mankind. Perhaps only the Chicago Lutheran theologian, Joseph Sittler, in his now famous speech at New Delhi in 1960, has given a clearly defined theological basis for this approach.[34] As far as systematic theology is concerned, the contribution of Paul Tillich has been more important.[35] His philosophy of religion is in some respects structurally similar to the Catholic position we have mentioned. He views all religions as different symbolic articulations of the transcendental ontological relation to God present in the depths of human experience. While he relates this to the logos doctrine of the early fathers, he does not give it a Christocentric interpretation: he does not say, as would Karl Rahner, that it is Jesus Christ, the incarnate Lord of Christian faith, which is at work in other religions.

Wolfhart Pannenberg, in what is perhaps the intellectually most impressive recent speculative effort in this area by a Protestant theologian, combines insights drawn from Tillich's philosophical interpretation of religion with his own highly futuristic eschatological view of salvation history in such a way as to see biblical religion as the center of a universal process of the integration of all religions.[36] Tillich's emphasis on the transcendental knowledge of God has also influenced the recent confessionally oriented Lutheran interpretations of religion by C. H. Ratschow and P. Beyerhaus.[37] Nevertheless, these Protestant appreciations of non-Christian religions tend to be consistently more reserved than their Catholic parallels. This is also evident in the current exploration by the World Council of Churches of the possibilities of dialogue with other faiths. In contrast to what was said by the Second Vatican Council in 1965, the Addis Ababa statement of 1971 specifically refrains from affirming that God or the grace of Christ are redemptively at work in non-Christian religions.[38] Thus despite the insistence that Christians have no cause to feel superior, because God saves others no less than themselves, the impression is left that Protestants are now the ones who come closest to maintaining the spirit, though not the letter, of the old dogmatic axiom, *extra ecclesiam non salus est.* God, it would seem, saves non-Christians despite the errors of their ways, rather than in and through the truths and values they contain.

The reasons for this reversal of positions are, of course, more important than the fact that it has occurred. Catholics seem more concerned than most Protestants to maintain the importance of explicitly Christian faith for all men. To be sure, the bond between the salvation of non-Christians and explicit Christianity is an invisible one. There is often no empirically evident relation between the way God acts to save outside and inside the church. Yet, so the argument goes, there must be a connection. Otherwise the incarnation and the visible church would be irrelevant to the personal salvation of most mankind. Consequently one must not only affirm that God saves non-Christians, but also try to explain how (something which, as we shall see, Protestants are reluctant to do). One must show how their religious and perhaps also secular faiths are means which God uses to help communicate the very grace of Christ. These religions, in the now famous phrase of H. Schlette, are the "ordinary ways of salvation" in contrast to Christianity, which is the "extraordinary way."[39] One must develop theories explaining how nonbelievers can be regarded as "implicit" (Schillenbeeckx)[40] or "anonymous" (Rahner) Christians. They must be described as having made a "fundamental option" for Christ,[41] even though not a thematically conscious one, and as therefore being basically oriented toward explicit faith in him and participation in the Christian community which that involves. In short, the major Roman Catholic tendency is to give an "ecclesiological grounding" to the salvation of non-believers,[42] and this leads to extensive inquiries into how God saves and to more positive evaluations of non-Christian religions than are commonly found on the Protestant side.

III
The Issues

As we have seen, it is chiefly Roman Catholics who are now investigating the question of the salvation of nonbelievers and what this implies regarding the redemptive import of the religious and secular faiths by which they live. The Barthians and the secularizing theologians have been negative in their evaluation of these faiths, and those Protestants who have been more positive, such as Tillich and those influenced by him, have generally not looked at the problem from the point of view of individual or personal salvation. The few Protestant contributions so far have been largely prompted by the Catholic discussion and have been mostly critical. Roman Catholics have not, as far as I know, responded to these criticisms. They have limited themselves to expressing regret that Protestants have done so little in the area. H. Vorgrimler says: "No help can be expected from recent evangelical theology on this question because in view of its general pessimism regarding the ultimate fate of [non-Christians] and its general refusal of a futuristic eschatology, it has not touched upon this theme."[43] J. Neuner comments more accurately that if Protestants are confronted with this question of the salvation of non-Christians, "they will generally answer that we do not know: it is God"s concern, and not ours; revelation speaks only about salvation in Jesus Christ."[44]

In trying to define the issues, therefore, we cannot draw on a history of interconfessional controversy. Actually as we shall see, the disagreements within the confessions are probably greater than those between them. We shall, however, start with the objections which Protestants have so far formulated against positions such as Rahner's, and in this way seek to discover where the crucial problems lie.

The first issue is one which, as far as I am aware, U. Kuhn has discussed at greatest length.[45] He points out that it is hard to see how the importance which both Scripture and the Reformation attribute to the *fides ex auditu*, the faith which is an explicit response to the gospel, can be maintained in combination with notions of implicit saving faith. It is not that the answer is simple. Salvation is experienced, Rahner suggests, when "man experiences himself as inescapably grounded in the abyss of irremovable mystery, and accepts and experiences this mystery in the depths of his conscience and the concreteness of his history (for both are constituents of his existence), not as consuming judgment, but as fulfilling nearness (for this is what we call faith)."[46] If this, we may ask, abundantly occurs quite apart from explicit awareness of God, much less of Jesus, what happens to the cruciality of the gospel, of the *fides ex auditu*, of decision for or against Christ?

The second objection is directed against the christological and ecclesiological grounding of "anonymous Christianity." The grace which is the source of this implicit faith is the *gratia Christi*. Further, its goal is explicit faith in Christ and therefore also membership in the visible church. It is oriented towards explicit Christianity as its fulfillment, appropriate articulation, adequate expression or "objective correlate,"[47] and this is true even in the case of those who are not in the least aware of this and think of themselves as opposed to Christ and his church. According to some writers, such views are reminiscent of the unwarranted claims Roman Catholics have traditionally made for the church.[48] They smack of ecclesiological triumphalism.

The third Protestant criticism, which we have already seen mentioned by the Catholic author Neuner,[49] is that it is wrong even to discuss how non-Christians might be saved. This should simply be affirmed "doxologically" rather than by making "dogmatic" statements and constructing speculative explanations.[50]

The first and second of these objections are not consistent with each other. One is based on a Reformation, and especially Lutheran, view of faith, and the other on a Barthian understanding of the church. A Lutheran emphasis on the *fides ex auditu* has an ecclesiological dimension, because explicit faith in Christ normally leads to baptism and to membership in the visible church. If then the concept of salvation is linked to the *fides ex auditu*, it must also be closely related to the church, to communities which profess Jesus Christ as Lord. These are both the product of explicit faith and also its source, for it is in and through them that the gospel is proclaimed. To deny an intimate connection between the church and salvation is therefore equivalent to minimizing the importance of the *fides ex auditu*. Karl Barth, however, in his view of the church does deny such a connection. He summarizes his thought on this point by saying, "1. the world would be lost without Jesus Christ . . .; 2. the world would not necessarily be lost if there were no Church; and 3. the Church would be lost if it had no counterpart in the world. . . . What is to prevent Christ from going his own direct way to man?"[51] As an expression of abstract possibilities, of what late medieval scholasticism called the *potentia absoluta dei*, this is no doubt defensible, but Barth quite rightly insists that theology must have some reference to the concrete order which God has ordained. His ecclesiological minimalism therefore involves, as we have already noted in connection with his discussion of religion, a devaluation of the significance of explicit faith for salvation.

Indeed, in his respect—though obviously not in others—one might say that Barth is ultra-Catholic. Explicit Christianity is considerably less important for him than in a position such as Rahner's. He can even speak of "implicit" expressions or "coming-to-speech" of the whole of Christian truth.[52] He does not say, as Rahner does, that the church's mission, its proclamation of the gospel, "improves the salvation situation and the chance of salvation of the individual,"[53] but rather appears to hold that Christians should engage in mission and proclamation, not in the hope of helping anyone, but simply because they have been commissioned to do so.[54] The Barthian inversion of law and gospel is at work here, contributing to the impression that for him the gospel makes a purely noetic difference, informing "potential Christians" that they are already saved, telling *christiani designati* of their actual status.[55] It is hard to see how this can be reconciled with the Reformation understanding of the Gospel and the response of faith as deliverance from servitude to the law and from the dominion of sin, death, and the devil.

What is true of Barth in this area applies even more strongly to most other contemporary Protestants. They do not even raise the question of the salvation of non-Christians, either because they assume it is so evident that it is not worthy of discussion, or else because they are not interested in the problem of what personal or individual salvation might mean outside the Christian sphere. This holds also of Paul Tillich and, following him, Dorothee Sölle, who in the notion of the "latent church" have a concept somewhat similar to that of "anonymous Christianity."[56] They never ask how this might be related to the ultimate destiny of human beings. Much less are they concerned with comparing its ultimate saving import to that of manifest Christianity.

It is therefore no exaggeration to say that many contemporary Roman Catholics, despite their talk of implicit or anonymous Christianity, actually stand closer in this area to the Reformation, at least in its Lutheran form, than do most present-day Protestant theologians. They say that there is no salvation apart from faith, that saving faith is oriented toward explicit faith and is fulfilled in the overt confession of Christ as Lord, and that it makes a real, more-than-noetic, ontological or empirical difference even in its anonymous, but much more in its explicit, form. The question therefore arises whether they succeed in sufficiently expressing in this conceptuality the reality of the transition from death to life pointed to by the law-gospel distinction and by the correlated emphasis on the *fides ex auditu*. From a Lutheran perspective, there is here a greater common basis of discussion than with most Protestants. And this is true, not only of the avowedly confessional Lutherans, but also of such men as Bultmann, Ebeling, or Käsemann.[57] They put great stress on the *fides ex auditu* even when their "existentialist" or "anti-objectivizing" systematic presuppositions make it impossible for them to go on and ask what this means for the salvation of non-Christians.

The basic issue, then, is that of the *fides ex auditu*, not of ecclesiological triumphalism. It is, to be sure, objectionable to use such phrases as "implicit" or "anonymous" Christianity (or, for that matter, Paul Tillich's or Dorothee Söelle's "latent church"), for they appear to reflect an arrogant claim that whatever is true, good and beautiful in non-Christians is "really" Christian. This objection applies even more strongly against the *extra ecclesiam nulla salus* even when one means by this, as Rahner does, simply that saving grace wherever found is dynamically oriented towards "sacramental visibility in the dimension of the church."[58] Nevertheless, even when this triumphalistic rhetoric is eliminated, as Hans Küng[59] has done in his presentation of a position which depends heavily on Rahner, the basic problem still remains. It is a problem, furthermore, not only in reference to Roman Catholics but, as we have seen, at least equally in reference to views such as Barth's. How should one evaluate the concepts—not simply the words—of "implicit saving faith" (Rahner) or of "potential" Christians or *christiani designati?* And if we reject them, what alternative description or explanation of the salvation of non-Christians should be proposed?

For reasons already indicated, this is a question which we shall discuss chiefly in reference to Rahner. His is the most important work in the area, and it is also more challenging than that of Barth from a Lutheran perspective. But before attempting to assess it, we must say a word about the third objection earlier mentioned, the view that the salvation of non-Christians is a problem about which we can say nothing. We must also ask why it has been so widespread in Protestant circles.

One of the reasons for Protestant silence is no doubt the traditional suspicion, grounded in the *sola scriptura,* of speculative efforts to answer questions which are not directly dealt with in the Bible. It may be doubted, however, that this is a sufficient explanation. From the time that Luther developed his theory of ubiquity, through the era of Orthodoxy and down into the modern period, Protestants have not been averse to discussing problems which go much beyond anything which Scripture says. It could be replied that what the Reformation is concerned with is the avoidance of useless speculation. Clearly many new questions have arisen in the course of history of which the biblical authors knew nothing, but these should be discussed only if they are important for the concrete life of faith. This consideration, however, would seem to demand serious attention to our theme. What is thought about the salvation of non-Christians helps shape practical attitudes toward them and influences the form and urgency of missionary activity both at home, in traditionally Christian lands, and abroad. Other objections arise from the influence of Buber's personalism and Heidegger's existentialism on much recent theology, but are themselves highly technical and speculative. Although their theoretical foundations are not the same as that of Troeltsch's relativism, they lead to similar conclusions. Theological affirmations are true only *pro me* or for the confessing faith community of which one is a part. Any attempt to state in general terms what is true regarding the condition of outsiders or unbelievers is irrationally mythological, or illegitimately metaphysical or inauthentically objectivizing. At its worst it is an attempt to escape from the question of one's own personal relation to God, and at best it is idle curiosity.

Following popular usage, this might be called the existentialist position, even though it is shared to one degree or other by many people who are not in any formal sense adherents of that philosophy. Its warnings must, of course, be taken seriously. Concern about the salvation of others, particularly of "mankind in general," has often been associated with neglect of one's own salvation—with personal inauthenticity and all kinds of psychological, moral, social and religious pathologies. Nevertheless, these are reasons for caution about real dangers, rather than for prohibitions against the investigation which we are pursuing. When interpreted as prohibitions, they lead to a now-centered privatism, a lack of interest in the church and its pastoral and missionary policies, and an indifference to the ultimate destiny of individuals, not to mention mankind and God's whole creation, which ill accords with the structure of Christian faith as we find it expressed in the Bible.

Existentialism, however, is not the major cause of the present neglect of our question. The most recent theological developments focus, not on the individual, but on questions of broad social or even cosmic scope. Certain versions of the theologies of hope, of secularization, and of evolutionary process are not in the least wary of universal statements which are "objectivizing" or "metaphysical" in the sense of purporting to describe the nature of history or of things in general. And yet they also avoid the theme of individual salvation—this time, it would seem, of believers no less than of unbelievers.

The explanation for the contrast between Catholic and Protestant thought on this point would seem to be social-psychological rather than theological. Protestant theolgy is more university-oriented even in America where much of it is done outside of universities. It is therefore less closely related to the interest either of the institutional church or of ordinary Christians. While this does confer on it a freedom from ecclesiastical interference which has at times been of great practical importance for the pursuit of truth, it also means that it is constantly tempted to fall into another kind of servitude— servitude to what ever is fashionable or respectable in the intellectual milieu of which it is a part. The question of individual salvation clearly is not one of the themes which is either fashionable or intellectually respectable among the students and the academic and nonacademic intelligentsia who constitute a major part of its audience. Thus at least among Protestants in America, only the conservative evangelicals show much interest in the problem, and their attitude is usually negative and polemical. This troubles a great many people in the churches, but the professional theologians of the major denominations are either unaware of this or do not take it seriously. It would appear that Protestant theology in Europe suffers from much the same social-psychological inhibitions, with the result that the great bulk of the academically competent theological discussion of the matter is Roman Catholic. In this area it is the Catholics who have the greatest sense of what is of practical importance to the concrete life of faith as it is lived by the Christian community and who are therefore pastorally most relevant. It would be irresponsible of Protestants either to ignore this development or simply to criticize it. If we have objections, the only proper response is to seek for alternative approaches.

IV
New Approaches

Our question in this concluding section is whether a Reformation approach which holds that salvation is by explicit faith in Christ alone, *sola fide ex auditu,* can meet contemporary practical and pastoral concerns in reference to non-Christians as well as or better than the currently popular Catholic theory of anonymous Christianity which teaches that salvation is by implicit as well as explicit faith, i.e., *fide explicita* (or *ex auditu*) *et implicita.*

It is, of course, impossible in the space available here to do more than indicate the various factors which support and oppose these two positions. It shall begin with the preliminary point that neither the arguments from tradition nor from Scripture are decisive. It will next be suggested that the advantage of the second position in satisfying contemporary pastoral concerns is more apparent than real. The first position can also be interpreted in such a way as to meet this need. Third, however, it appears that such an interpretation would seem excessively eschatological and perhaps also "mythological" from the point of view of Rahner (as well as of much Protestant theology). Especially the second of these objections raises nontheological questions regarding the empirical and philosophical adequacy of the two positions. Here we shall note that the *sola fide ex auditu* view seems preferable both from the point of view of the empirical study of religion and from the perspective represented by linguistic

analysis or ordinary language philosophy.[60] In contrast to the philo-
sophical trends which have been dominant in Europe, this Anglo-
American movement appears to favor a "Reformation" rather than
"Roman Catholic" theological interpretation of the status of non-
Christians.

Before proceeding with these points, however, it should be observed that the problem with which we are dealing is of secondary
importance for the concrete life of faith. As has already been pointed
out, the issue is not whether salvation is through Christ, or faith is
necessary, or explicit faith is important, or unbelievers are saved.
On the level of the properly religious or Christian use of language in
worship, preaching, and action, it is possible, so we shall suggest, to
make all these affirmations no matter which position one chooses.
Our question is a second-order theoretical one in systematic theology
regarding the best way to organize faith affirmations and relate them
to each other and to other statements of both a theological and nontheological character. To be sure, failure to do this properly does
have adverse consequences. An inadequate theological system (or
conceptuality or language) can make it difficult, and at worst impossible, to express what needs to be said for the sake of faith, and
a more adequate one can at times be of considerable help. Nevertheless, the history of theology is replete with examples of truths expressed in a poor theological idiom (e.g., in medieval scholasticism)
and falsehoods in a good one (e.g., in confessional Lutheranism).
Similarly, it is possible that in our contemporary situation, Catholics
may be making the fundamentally right affirmations of faith about
non-Christians in terms of a questionable doctrine of implicit faith,
while Protestants fail to make these same affirmations even though
they could be expressed in a more fully Christian way if they were
related to salvation *sola fide ex auditu.*

This question of how to understand the salvation of unbelievers
cannot be decided simply by reference to tradition. It is true that
there is a history of Catholic, but not of Protestant reflection on the
problem,[61] and that this makes use of the concept of implicit faith
(though not in the same way as is done by such contemporary Catholics as Rahner). Even more important are centuries of Catholic
discussion about the relation of grace to the sacraments even when
these are not used (as in the *votum baptismi* and the forgiveness of
sins before sacramental penance). Thus once the analogy between
word and sacrament is introduced, Catholics have categories which

they can use in constructing a theory of the salvation of non-Christians by means of an implicit faith which is "anonymously" Christian because it does have a real though hidden connection with the *fides ex auditu* which comes from the preaching of the gospel.[62] Thus Rahner's theory has roots in the Catholic tradition, but this obviously does not mean that Protestants should automatically reject it. Nor, for that matter, do these traditional origins imply that Catholics should accept it. Urs Hans von Balthasar, for one, has bitterly charged that it produces neglect of decision, cross, and proclamation.[63] Rahner replies that it need not do so,[64] and the debate could go on forever. Some criterion other than tradition is needed to decide the issue both for Catholics and Protestants.

The obvious alternative is to turn to Scripture, but this appeal also is indecisive. It is true, as we have already noted, that the Bible normally speaks in terms of the *sola fide ex auditu*,[65] but only a highly literalistic exegesis would say that this excludes the possibility of the kind of saving implicit faith or fundamental option which the Catholic authors postulate. If the grace of Christ does operate anonymously in the depths of human existence in such a way that men are enabled to experience and eccept the mysterious abyss in which they are grounded, "not as consuming judgment, but as fulfilling nearness,"[66] then it is hard to see how one can deny from either a Christian or Reformation point of view that this is indeed saving faith. The question is whether this is an appropriate way to speak, not only about those who have never heard the gospel, but (as we shall see) even about those who are believing Christians. The answer to that question depends, in turn, not on exegesis, but on the systematic and historical framework within which one interprets the biblical data. In Rahner's case, the framework consists of a certain vision of man in relation to God which he has articulated in terms of a complex and comprehensive set of partly philosophical and partly theological theories about grace and salvation and about human nature, experience, knowledge, and language.[67] It would be difficult to show that this Thomistic-idealist-existentialist anthropology is incompatible with Scripture, and to the degree that one finds it plausible, it becomes difficult to refute as unbiblical its somewhat —but by no means entirely!—minimizing interpretation of the *fides ex auditu*. In brief, exegesis in the strict sense cannot settle the issue because, in the language of continental hermeneutics, interpretation is dependent on one's preunderstanding (Vorverständnis).

The same must be said, it seems to me, if one appeals, not to the letter of Scripture, but to the fundamental spirit or attitude of the early church towards unbelievers. It does not seem, however, that this tells against the kind of Catholic position we are considering. Primitive Christians appear from later perspectives to have had an extraordinary combination of relaxation and urgency in their attitude toward those outside the church. On the one hand, they do not seem to have worried a great deal about the ultimate fate of the vast majority of the non-Christians among whom they lived. We hear of no crises of conscience resulting from the necessity they were often under to conceal the fact that they were believers even from close friends or kindred. The ordinary Christian, at any rate, does not seem to have viewed himself as a watchman who would be held guilty of the blood of those he failed to warn (Ezek. 3:18). Yet, on the other hand, missionary proclamation was urgent and faith and baptism were to them life from death, the passage from the old age into the new. From the point of view of most subsequent theologies, the tensions involved in this combination of attitudes seem insupportable; and so it is at least plausible to suppose that the early Christians had certain unrecorded convictions about how God saves unbelievers and how this is related to belief in Christ and membership in the community of faith. One of these convictions, as we have already mentioned, is perhaps reflected in 1 Pet. 3:19, and others (about which we shall say a bit more later) can be uncovered by careful exegesis. By and large, however, it would appear that these views never became a problem and so remained unarticulated or unwritten. Perhaps we could say that, in terms of the basic New Testament eschatological pictures, the "non-Christians" (gentiles) are not headed toward either heaven or hell. They as yet have no future. They are still trapped in the past, in the darkness of the old age. Only through the message of the coming Kingdom, of God's Messiah, does the new age, the true future of the world, become real for them, and only then do either redemption or damnation become possible. In any case, whether one accepts this view or not, the scriptural mandate to the theologian in regard to our question is to try to develop an understanding of God's redemptive action outside the church which helps present-day Christians, like those in the early period, to be both relaxed and urgent in bringing the gospel to others. This, however, is exactly what Rahner and his associates are attempting to do.

If appeals to Scripture and tradition are indecisive, then we must turn to present pastoral concerns, to the requirements of the contemporary situation. Among Catholics and Protestants who are concerned about our problem, there is a wide though often only tacit agreement regarding the practical conditions which should be met by a theological treatment of the status of non-Christians. First, it must describe the relations between Christians and non-Christians in such a way as to exclude boasting. Christians have no cause for thinking themselves personally or communally superior because of their Christianity. A second point is in a way a necessary corollary of this, but carries it much farther. The believer should be trustful about the salvation of non-Christians. He should not be upset just because they show no interest in religion or Christianity, or even if they turn away after having appeared interested. This attitude should apply also to those who leave the church, even to friends, relatives or children. Our churches, after all, are very different from those of the early centuries. If men and women leave, not because of the offense of the cross (and who but God can judge that?), but because the church has become personally meaningless to them, then one should regret their departure for what this indicates about the inadequacies of the church rather than for their own sakes. Sometimes, to be sure, Christianity is rejected for reasons which are clearly harmful or destructive to the person involved, and in that case one may have the responsibility to plead, warn, and beseech; but apart from this, no social or psychological pressure, no withdrawal of love or suggestions of retribution, are allowable. God deals in his own ways with each human being, and even if we agree with a man like Rahner that in general it is better to be a Christian than not to be,[68] this does not mean we have any knowledge of the point at which this is true in the history of any given individual or society.[69]

Third, this opens the way to genuine dialogue with men of other faiths. One can speak with them about one's own and their deepest convictions without the inhibitions induced by the belief that one has the duty to convert, refute, or persuade. Such inhibitions have greatly harmed the missionary enterprise because they have made the missionary pharisaically defensive about Christianity and unfairly aggressive and critical toward non-Christian positions. One must therefore converse and cooperate with nonbelievers simply because they are fellow human beings whom the Christian needs at least as much as they need him. God does not only speak to the world through the church, but also to the church through the world. Dialogue is a part of the *theologia crucis*. The old man must be put to death in the mutual and often painful effort to discover the realities of anguish, confidence, and longing which lie beneath the surfaces of each one of us.

In the fourth place, however, and in apparent tension with these first three principles, Christians must proclaim the gospel. They must be eager to confront all men with the claims of Christ, they must be concerned to give everyone the chance to decide. There are some whom God has prepared, and who are needy, ready, or eager for explicit faith in Christ. Other men cannot know who are, and they themselves often have great difficulty in recognizing God's call. This is why the proclamation of the gospel requires a seeking and a wrestling, a going into the highways and byways in order to compel them to come in (Lk. 14:23). The very freedom which must be granted to refuse the gospel or leave the church also demands that everyone be given the opportunity to accept and enter.

These four principles may be viewed as a specification in terms of the contemporary situation of that strange fusion of urgency and relaxed trustfulness which we earlier suggested characterizes the bewildering variety of scriptural statements regarding non-Christians. Not everyone would agree. A certain kind of progressive would question the fourth point, and many conservatives have difficulties with the second and third. Nevertheless, it would be easy to show that theologians as diverse as Kraemer and Rahner think of each of these elements as imperative and as therefore constituting conditions which must be satisfied by a theological interpretation of the situation of non-Christians.

It is here, of course, that the challenge to the *sola fide ex auditu* becomes acute. Does not the denial of implicit saving faith imply that all non-Christians are damned? How then can one avoid thinking of true believers as superior beings (through grace, of course!) who must bend every effort to save souls from hell and cannot possibly engage in open and equal dialogue apart from any intention to convert? These seem to be the views of the conservative evangelicals who at present are the ones who chiefly insist that salvation is only through explicit faith.

This need not be the case, however. We have already noted that a part generation of dogmaticians such as Haring, Schlatter, R. Seeber, and, most recently, Althaus, basing themselves on such possible hints as 1 Pt. 3:19, broke through the limits of the old Protestant orthodoxy by no longer confining saving revelation to this life.[70] Perhaps intellectual fashions rather than theological reasons led to the abandonment of such solutions but, for whatever reasons, the question has since been neglected by Protestants and the field left to the rigorists. The Roman Catholics have in this respect done better. To be sure, the dogma that judgment of the unjustified takes place immediately after death (D.S. 858, 1002) has made it impossible to speak of the possibility of salvation beyond the confines of this life, but numerous theologians, including Rahner,[71] have overcome this problem by suggesting that, in effect, dying itself is the point at which every human being is ultimately and expressly confronted by the gospel, i.e., by the crucified and risen Lord. It is only then that the final decision is made for or against Christ, and this is true, not only of unbelievers but also of believers. All previous decisions whether of faith or unfaith are preliminary. The final die is cast beyond our space and time, beyond empirical observation, beyond all idle speculation about "good" or "bad" deaths, when a person loses his rootage in this world and passes into the inexpressible transcendence surpassing all words, images, and thoughts. We must trust and hope, though not know, that in this dreadful yet wondrous end and climax of life no one will be lost. And here, even if not before, salvation is explicit, indeed vastly more so than in the *fides ex auditu*. Thus the second of the pastoral exigencies is satisfied. It is possible to be hopeful and trusting about the ultimate salvation of non-Christians no less than Christians even if one does not think of justifying grace as already at work apart from explicit faith.

Further, this outlook can be developed in such way as to meet the first condition, that is, oppose boasting and a sense of Christian superiority. One must say, for example, as we already noted in the first section, that the situation of the Christian is in one sense more, not less perilous than that of the non-Christian. Judgment begins in the house of the Lord (1 Pt. 4:19), and many of the first shall be last and the last first (Mt. 19:30). Further, a refusal to accept the church's invitation to believe is not to be equated with a refusal to accept God's invitation; and even when it is—as the story of Joseph's brothers (Gen. 37–50) and unbelieving Israel (Rom. 9–11) remind us—God can turn the evil men do into salvation both for themselves and for others (Gen. 50:20).

Perhaps the most important barrier to Christian boasting within this perspective, however, is that the *sola fide ex auditu* suggests, even if it does not demand, an eschatological understanding of salvation which contrasts with the ontological interpretation required by the concept of implicit saving faith. Ontologically interpreted, salvation is primarly an inward grace which is articulated and strengthened by explicit faith. If saving faith comes only through hearing, however, then the process is reversed. Explicit faith in Christ is understood, not as expressing or articulating the existential depths, but rather as producing and forming them. For the Christian, even the mature Christian, this process has just begun. He has only begun to confess Jesus as Lord, to speak the Christian language, the language of the coming kingdom. His thoughts, volitions and affections are just beginning to be conformed to the One who is the express image of the Father (Heb. 1:3). The Holy Spirit which is in him is the pledge, not the participation in future glory. He has not yet learned to love God above all things and his neighbor as himself, for this is what comes at the end of the road in the eschatological fulfillment. What distinguishes his love from that of the non-Christian is not its present subjective quality, but rather the fact that it is beginning to be shaped by the message of Jesus' cross and resurrection.

Only at the end of the road, only in the eschatological fulfillment, will the Christian have truly learned to love God above all things and his neighbor as himself. In this perspective, the description we have seen Rahner give of implicit faith is far too glorious even for the *fides ex auditu* and must rather be applied to ultimate completion when faith passes into the beatific vision. Only then, in the murky and untamed depths of his being, will the Christian experience and accept the abysmal mystery on which he is grounded, "not as consuming judgment, but as fulfilling nearness." In short, every aspect of the new life exists in the modality of hope. This is why the believer is *simul justus et peccator*, and why, as Luther put it, "we do not yet have our goodness *in re*, but *in fide et spe*."[72] This also is why pride in being a Christian is excluded. He has by grace just begun to learn of the one in whom alone is salvation, but in moral and religious quality he is like other men, worse than some and better than others.

In answer to objections that this makes salvation merely fictive or imaginary, not ontologically real, it can be said, to use a simile, that the man who has changed directions may be only a step removed from his neighbors and yet be living in light rather than darkness, dawn rather than night, the beginning of the new age, not the end of the old. Speaking in more complex terms, the metaphor of a child learning a language is useful. The content of what is said by toddlers is very much the same whether they speak a primitive or a modern tongue. In both cases they express the same elementary needs and reactions in basically the same world of objects to be enjoyed or avoided and of persons to be trusted or feared. But one language may open up all the riches of human history and of a vastly promising though ominous future, while the other, the better a child learns it, imprisons him more tightly in his little tribe or village. At two years of age, the primitive might still be a potential Plato, Newton, or Beethoven; at twenty, never. In terms of this analogy, all human beings are toodlers, whether St. Peter, St. Paul, or the veriest infant in Christ. Eschatologically the decisive question regarding them is whether the language they have begun to learn *ex auditu* is that of Jesus Christ, is that of true humanity, or something else. Is, for example, the love about which they feebly stutter and are just beginning to understand and hope to attain, is this love defined by Jesus' life, death, and resurrection, or in some other way? In any case it is ridiculous for Christians to boast. They are, as one American Catholic author[73] has put it, like infants mouthing scraps out of Shakespeare or the *Principia Mathematica,* parrotlike, by rote. Only occasionally do they have inklings of the meanings of the words they utter. Thus, there is perhaps even less reason for such boasting in this perspective than when salvation is *fide explicita et implicita.*

Nor is there any reason to suppose that this position need reduce the possibility of dialogue and cooperation with other religions. To hold that the Christian language is the only one which has the words and concepts which can authentically speak of the ground of being, goal of history, and true humanity (for one cannot genuinely speak of these apart from telling and retelling the story of Jesus Christ), is not at all the same as denying that other religions have resources for speaking truths and realities, even highly important truths and realities, of which Christianity as yet knows nothing and by which it could be greatly enriched. Whatever the faults of Hellenization, it must also be seen as a process by which Christians learned much of value from ancient paganism and the cultures and philosophies which were its offspring. Conversely, one way in which Christians can serve their neighbors may be through helping adherents of other religions to purify and enrich their heritages, to make them better speakers of the languages they have. It can be argued that this is a better basis for dialogue than when one seeks to find the grace of Christ at work in non-Christian religions. Then the danger is not so much that of subverting Christian truth (Rahner certainly does not do that), but rather that of failing to do justice to non-Christian truths. One may guess, for example, that the Buddhist concept of Nirvana is much more instructive if one takes it on its own terms, rather than tries to find it in analogies to heaven.

It would seem that the fourth imperative, that of evangelization, is also better served by a *sola fide ex auditu* understanding of salvation. To be sure, the alternative view may be able to supply equally good reasons for bringing the gospel to all who are interested in listening, but the way it does this seems pretentious, perhaps imperialistic. There is something arrogant about supposing that one knows what non-Christians are in the depth of their beings better than they know themselves and that therefore one's task is to increase their self-awareness. Evangelism is not ontological psychotherapy, but rather the offer to teach one's own beloved language, the language which speaks of Jesus Christ, to all those who are interested, and then leave it to them and to God as to whether they choose the new language over the old.

As was suggested at the beginning of this section, perhaps the major difficulty with the approach we are examining is that for many contemporary Protestants and Catholics its futuristic reference seems mythological or unreal. It speaks of the salvation of non-Christians as having no present reality, but as beginning (and consummated) in or after death. This violates even Rahner's rules for the "Hermeneutics of Eschatological Statements,"[74] and is of course flatly contradicted by those Protestants whose existentialism leads them to deny a temporally and objectively future Eschaton.

It would be possible to argue in reply that a futuristic eschatology is one of the mythological elements (in the technical, not pejorative sense of the term) which are indispensible to Christianity, and that the arguments against it are functions of the modern mood rather than of modern knowledge. The human sense of what is real or unreal is socially constructed,[75] and what seems credible or incredible to contemporary intellectuals is much more the product of their social-psychological conditioning than of their science.

While I believe this is true, it is more useful for our purposes to mention in conclusion the points of view from which the concept of implicit faith and the associated theory of religion seems mythological in the bad sense of the word. This is the case, first of all, from the perspective of many empirically oriented theories of religion. These regard each religion as a distinctive symbolic system linking motivation and action and providing an ultimate legitimation for basic patterns of thought, feeling, and behavior uniquely characteristic of a given community or society and its members.[76] Religions are seen, not as expressions of the depths or transcendental heights of human experience, but as systems of ritual, myth, belief, and conduct which constitute, rather than being constituted by, that which is most profound in man, e.g., his existential self-understanding.

As in the case of languages, what religions have in common are formal structures and abstract patterns, not a concrete reality which lies behind their diverse articulations. Religions are thus just as incapable as languages of being understood in those categories of transcendental philosophy or of salvation history which are employed by Rahner, Tillich, Pannenberg, and others. This means in reference to our particular problem that the concept of implicit faith not only lacks evidence but also plausibility. From the point of view of much, perhaps most, contemporary history, phenomenology, sociology, and psychology of religion, the faiths by which men live, whether Christian or non-Christian, are always acquired *ex auditu*.

The reasons which remain for using the concepts of anonymous grace and implicit faith are philosophical rather than properly theological. If one supposes that what is most fundamentally human in man is preconceptual and prelinguistic and that this can be arrived at by means of transcendental deductions or existential analyses, then it makes sense to follow Rahner in using these ideas to account for the salvation of non-Christians. It is doubtful, however, that his theory is persuasive apart from the German philosophical tradition of romanticism, idealism, and existentialism (and perhaps then only when combined with a highly reinterpreted Thomism).

Certainly from the point of view of the currently dominant Anglo-American outlook, this whole construction is more than questionable. Its picture of man is the inversion of the one which Rahner employs.[77] The humanly real, one might say, is not constructed from below upwards or from the inner to the outer, but from the outer to the inner and from above downwards. The acquisition of a language

—necessarily from outside—is a "jump which was the coming into being of man,"[78] and all the heights and depths of human knowledge, faith, hope, and love are the effects, not the causes, of the manner and the skill with which one uses language. Many though not all of those who have formulated this approach have been bitterly antireligious and anti-Christian, but this does not destroy the theological usefulness of their insights.[79] We might say that just as a man becomes human by being taught a language, so he begins to be a new creature through hearing, learning, and internalizing the language which speaks of Christ.

Now at the end of our discussion, however, we should once again remind ourselves not to exaggerate its importance. The emphasis on *fides ex auditu* does not depend on a philosophical position, though it may be helped by some and hindered by others. Nor is it impossible to have the right attitude toward non-Christians if one falters at this point. Despite disagreement in theological theory, we can wholeheartedly share Rahner's hope that the Christian of the future "will not anxiously scan statistics to see whether the Church is really the biggest ideological organization or not, or whether it is growing proportionately quicker or slower than world population. He will indeed go out into the world with missionary zeal and bear witness in the name of Chr ist. He will wish to give his grace to others, for he possesses a grace which the others still lack. But he will know that if his zeal is serene and patient it will have a better chance of success. He will know that he can imitate God's forbearance which, according to St. Paul, is of positive significance for salvation, not condemnation. He knows that God willed this world as it is, for otherwise it would not exist . . . and that what is willed can and must be hoped for, not only as the revelation of God's justice but also as the revelation of his infinite loving kindness to man. Consequently, the Christion will meet boldly and hopefully as brothers those who do not wish to be his brothers. . . ."[80]

NOTES

1. Large Catechism, II, 3, nos. 45 and 56, T. G. Tappert, ed., *The Book of Concord* (Philadelphia, 1959), pp. 416 and 418.
2. In chapter 17 (13). See A. C. Cochrane, *Reformed Confessions of the 16th Century* (Philadelphia, 1966), p. 266. Allowances are of course made for those who are unwillingly separated from the church. The Latin reads: *negemus eos coram Deo vivere posse, qui cum vera Dei ecclesia non communicant sed ab eo separant.*

3. See XXV. 2. Text in P. Schaff, *Creeds of Christendom* (New York, 1919), p. 657.
4. For a brief and easily accessible sketch, see H. Küng, *The Church* (New York, 1967), pp. 313-319.
5. W. M. Abbot, ed., *The Documents of Vatican II* (New York, 1966), p. 35. Cf. K. Rahner's interpretation, "Atheismus und implizites Christentum," *Schriften zur Theologie VIII* (Einsiedeln, 1967), pp. 187-212.
6. *Documents of Vatican II*, pp. 660-668.
7. *An Evangelical Theology of Missions* (Grand Rapids, 1970), pp. 112-113.
8. H. Lindsell, ed., *The Church's Worldwide Mission* (Fort Worth, 1966), pp. 223-226, and republished in part in *Christianity Today XV* (1971), pp. 752-753.
9. *Die Letzten Dinge*, 9e unveränderte Aufl. (Gütersloh, 1964), p. 188, fn. 2.
10. For a list, see Bo Reicke, *The Disobedient Spirits and Christian Baptism* (Copenhagen, 1946), pp. 47-49.
11. W. J. Dalton, *Christ's Proclamation to the Spirits* (Rome, 1965), pp. 22-23. This author does not himself, however, agree with this opinion.
12. S. Pfürtner, *Luther and Aquinas on Salvation* (New York, 1964).
13. So also Althaus, *op. cit.*, p. 187.
14. Representative statements of such views are, in addition to Althaus, E. Brunner, *Eternal Hope* (Philadelphia, 1954), pp. 170-184 (chapter 17), and K. Rahner—H. Vorgrimler, "Hell," *Theological Dictionary* (New York, 1965), pp. 201-202.
15. For Catholic tendencies in this direction, see G. Lindbeck, *The Future of Roman Catholic Theology* (Philadelphia, 1970), pp. 1-50.
16. *Theological Investigations V* (Baltimore, 1966), pp. 355-356.
17. "Existentiale Interpretation und Anonyme Christlichkeit," *Zeit und Geschichte: Festschrift für R. Bultmann*, E. Dinkler, ed., (Tübingen, 1964), p. 375. "In der Tat dürfte bei der heutigen Lage der Menschheit und bei den Erfahrungen, die wir alle machen, nur noch eine sektiererische Gesinnung es fertigbringen, alle Menschen ohne explizites Bekenntnis zu Christus von vorneherein als verloren zu betrachten, sie aus dem Bereich des heilbringenden Handelns Gottes auszuschliessen . . . wenn wir das Kerygma vernommen haben können wir die uns heute vorgegebene geschichtliche Situation nicht anders deuten als so, wir können aus ihr keine anderen Folgerungen ziehen als diese. Gerade aus dem Geiste des Evangeliums folgt diese Deutung."
18. *Christianity Among the Religions of the World* (New York, 1957), pp. 111-112.
19. Cf. also his *An Historian's Approach to Religion* (New York, 1956).
20. The final phase of Troeltsch's thought on this question is to be found in his 1923 Oxford lectures, *Christian Thought: Its History and Application* (New York, 1957).
21. Cf. also his *Living Religions and a World Faith* (New York, 1940) and *The Coming World Civilization* (New York, 1956).
22. Cf. O. C. Thomas, ed., *Attitudes Toward Other Religions* (New York, 1969), pp. 20-22.
23. B. E. Benktson, *Christus und die Religion: Barth, Bonhoeffer und Tillich* (Stuttgart, 1967).
24. Most recently, *World Cultures and World Religions* (Philadelphia, 1960), *Religion and the Christian Faith* (Philadelphia, 1957), and *Why Christianity of all Religions?* (Philadelphia, 1963).

25. *Christianity in World History* (London, 1964).
26. New York, 1966.
27. *Despair and Hope for Our Time* (Philadelphia, 1970).
28. Full documentation is given by K. Riesenhuber, "The Anonymous Christian According to Karl Rahner," in A. Röper, *The Anonymous Christian* (New York, 1966), pp. 145-179. For two of Rahner's later essays, published after this study appeared, see "Anonymous Christians," *Theological Investigations* VI, (Baltimore, 1969), pp. 390-398 and n. 53 *infra*.
29. Especially H. van Straelen, *The Catholic Encounter with World Religions* (London, 1966). See also fn. references in *Theological Investigations* VI, p. 397, and fn. 63 *infra*.
30. E. Fahlbusch, "Theologie der Religionen: Überblick zu einem Thema romisch-katholischer Theologie," *Kerygma und Dogma* XV (1969), pp. 73-86.
31. Cf. n. 6 *supra*.
32. Apologia I, 10, 46.
33. For an excellent survey, see P. Beyerhaus, "Zur Theologie der Religionen im Protestantismus,'" *Kerygma und Dogma* XV (1969), pp. 87-104.
34. Cf. P. Beyerhaus, *ibid.*, p. 91.
35. Besides his three volume *Systematic Theology* (Chicago, 1951-1963), see esp. *The Dynamics of Faith* (New York, 1957) and *Christianity and the Encounter of the World Religions* (New York, 1963).
36. "Erwägung zu neier Theologie der Religionsgeschichte," *Grundfragen Systematischer Theologie* (Göttingen, 1967), pp. 252-295.
37. Cf. the references in P. Beyerhaus, *op. cit.*, p. 98, fn. 37; p. 103, n. 40.
38. J. C. Haughey, "From Proclamation to Dialogue," *America*, May 8, 1971, 483-485.
39. *Towards a Theology of Religions* (New York, 1966), p. 81.
40. "Kirche und Welt," *Weltverständnis im Glauben*, ed. J. B. Metz, 1965; cited in F. W. Kantzenbach, "Die ekklesiologische Begründung des Heils der Nichtchristen," *Oecumenica* 1967, ed. F. W. Kantzenbach and V. Vajta (Minneapolis and Gütersloh, 1967), pp. 219 f. fn. 32.
41. Cf. fn. 28 *supra*.
42. Cf. Kantzenbach, fn. 40 *supra*.
43. *Mysterium Salutis* III, 2 (Einsiedeln, 1965), p. 599.
44. *Christian Revelation and World Religions* (London, 1967), p. 10.
45. "Christentum ausserhalb der Kirche," *Erneuerung der einen Kirche: Festschrift für H. Bornkamm* (Göttingen, 1966), pp. 290-297.
46. My translation. Cf. *Theological Investigations* V (Baltimore, 1966), p. 7: "indem der Mensch sich unentrinnbar als gegründet im Abgrund des unaufhebbaren Geheimnisses erfährt und dieses Geheimnis in der Tiefe seines Gewissens und in der konkretheit seiner Geschichte (beide sind für seine Existenz konstitutiv) als erfüllende Nähe und nicht als verbrennendes Gericht erfährt und annimmt (was man den Glauben nennt)."
47. For the relation between the "transcendental'" revelation common to all men (and therefore all religions) and the "categorical" biblical historical revelation, see especially K. Rahner and J. Ratzinger, *Revelation and Tradition* (London, 1966), pp. 1-23.
48. Especially Fahlbusch, *op. cit.*, but also Kantzenbach, *op. cit.*
49. N. 44, *supra*.
50. Kantzenbach, *op. cit.*, pp. 212-213.

51. *Church Dogmatics* IV.3.2 (Edinburgh, 1952) 72.1, p. 826.
52. *Church Dogmatics* IV.3.1 (Edinburgh, 1961), p. 126.
53. "Anonymous Christianity and the Missionary Task of the Church," *Idoc-International* 1 (4 April, 1970), pp. 70-96, esp. p. 90.
54. E.g., in *op. cit.* IV.3.2, 72.3, p. 528.
55. These phrases are cited by Kuhn, *op. cit.*, p. 294.
56. Kuhn, *op. cit.*, discusses the use of this concept by these two authors.
57. Kuhn, *op. cit.*, pp. 296-297 gives illustrative citations.
58. *Op. cit.*, p. 82.
59. In J. Neuner (ed.), *op. cit.*, pp. 22-66.
60. One of the few short accounts of this movement which can be recommended is that of A. M. Quinton, "Contemporary British Philosophy," *A Critical History of Western Philosophy* (ed. D. J. O'Conner (London, 1964) esp. pp. 535-545 on Wittgenstein.
61. S. Harent, "Infideles," DTC VII/2 (Paris, 1923), col. 1926-1930.
62. K. Rahner, *op. cit.*, p. 86.
63. E.g., *Cordula oder der Ernstfall* (Einsiedeln, 1966), pp. 84-96, 100-109, 124-129.
64. Rahner, *op. cit., passim.*
65. For references, see n. 45 and n. 57 *supra.*
66. Cf. n. 46 *supra.*
67. Most of Rahner's theological writings are relevant, but see especially his *Hörer des Wortes.*
68. Cf. n. 53 *supra.*
69. *Ibid.*, p. 78.
70. For the references, see Althaus, *op. cit.*, p. 188, n. 2.
71. *On the Theology of Death* (New York, 1961).
72. *WA* 4, 147, 23 ff. (Schol. to Ps. 101:3), cited by S. Ozment, *Homo Spiritualis* (Leiden, 1969), p. 121.
73. V. Preller, *Divine Science and the Science of God* (Princeton, 1967), *passim.*
74. *Theological Investigations IV* (Baltimore, 1966), pp. 323-346.
75. P. Berger and T. Luckmann, *The Social Construction of Reality* (New York, 1966).
76. See esp. the articles, with extensive bibliographies, on religion by C. Geertz and R. Bellah, *International Encyclopedia of the Social Sciences* (New York, 1968) XIII, pp. 398-414.
77. S. A. Erickson, *Language and Being: An Analytic Phenomenology* (New Haven, 1970). Even though Rahner is partly dependent on Heidegger, the latter's view of man is perhaps more compatible with that of linguistic analysis.
78. W. Sellars, *Science, Perception and Reality* (New York, 1963), p. 6.
79. P. Holmar, "Language and Theology," *Harvard Theological Review* LVIII (1965), pp. 241-261.
80. *The Christian of the Future* (New York), p. 85.

II.

THE STRUCTURE
OF THE CHURCH

Chapter 5

The Gathering of the Congregation

Worship in the Church and in Everyday Life

I
The Discussion About Worship

Public worship is being discussed again. People are not only discussing it, they are disagreeing and fighting. And that is a good thing. Because this is a sign that people expect something of worship. Where nothing is expected of worship any more it is already dead. The most gratifying aspect of the present discussion about worship is that it reveals the fact that there are expectations, even if these are expressed only in the form of dissatisfaction and criticism. A silence of the grave which left worship services to fade away in insignificance and a disinterest which had come to terms with their irrelevance to everyday life would be worse than the most servere criticism.

A century of silence, accompanied by the scholarly murmuring of experts explaining historical details, has been broken. Suddenly, everyone has joined in the discussion, the church members, especially the young people, the so-called laymen and nonspecialists who are not nonspecialists precisely because they are participants in worship. Indeed, if worship really concerns everyone, then everyone may and must take part in the discussion.

It is maintained that public worship is the point at which the whole congregation comes together. This is pure fiction since in fact well over 90 percent of the congregation do not come to church services, and the minute section of the total congregation which takes part in worship is drawn from a particular sociological and age group which is in no way representative of the whole.[1]

What happens in the service is determined by tradition and by the minority of the total congregation which is accustomed to this tradition. This minority is guided by a minority of the clergy who, for their part, are ruled by a hierarchy which is again heavily dependent on tradition. At least, it is this minority which makes the decisions whereas the majority of those who make up the church is hardly ever consulted. But if the service is really to be the central gathering point of the whole congregation, then it is essential to listen to the opinions of the members of the church, including those who do not attend today's services.

Alongside those who are critical of the present form of worship services and want to introduce new life into them, there are some who have fundamental doubts about worship as a whole. Their question is, "Why worship services at all?" To that question something must first be said about the term "worship service." In normal linguistic usage it is taken to mean a particular meeting which usually takes place at the same time (on Sundays), generally in the same building (a church) and usually according to a set form (service book). Such a worship service is usually—a telling misnomer—"held" by a pastor and usually "attended" (German "besucht"—visited) —another telling misnomer—by the same group of people.

The fact that this special event, which is so different from everyday life, is described as "worship" can only be seen as a disaster and is certainly foreign to the New Testament. Indeed, when the New Testament refers to "worship" it is not in the sense of a special, cultic[2] event limited to a particular time but rather of a continuous attitude which relates to life as a whole both on Sundays and in everyday life (Rom. 12:1).

What we today describe as "worship service" the New Testament modestly calls a "meeting together" (1 Cor. 11:18, 20; 14:23).[3] We should have achieved a lot if we could go back to this sober, purely technical terminology of the New Testament in order to preclude the grotesque misunderstanding that Christian worship is limited to meetings. For as long as this limitation gives credence to the widespread error that worship is synonymous with attendance (!) at a meeting, it will continue to be impossible to see that true worship is something much broader. In other words, we should no longer call our worship services worship services. But since it will not be practicable to alter the use of a term[4] which has been so used throughout the world for centuries, we shall probably have to continue to use the old term, and the comments which follow will also adopt the traditional terminology when there is reference to the gathering of the congregation.

This sort of gathering of the congregation in the name of Jesus will continue to take place in the future for as long as the church exists, because a church as the body of Christ without gathering, without congregation, without *koinonia,* is a contradiction in itself. It is naturally possible to list a whole series of profound, theological reasons for the necessity of services,[5] although one sometimes gets the impression that a rather artificial answer is being sought to a question which was somewhat artificially asked. In view of the widespread problems, the observation of Uppsala, which may sound rather naive to some ears, that worship services need no justification is most comforting.[6] There can be no question whether or not there should be worship services; it can only be a question of "true or false worship."

At least it is decisive that, for the celebration of Holy Communion which constitutes the heart of the service, we have the express command, "Do this in memory of me," and that there "cannot be any other theological basis for the Church's worship which does not derive directly from the command, 'Do this in memory of me.' "[7]

This is the answer to the fundamental question "Why worship services at all?"[8] The only question is that of the form in which this gathering is to take place and that is the question which we shall be discussing below. To begin with, it should be noted as a positive factor that a general discussion of this matter has begun and that there is movement which indicates a certain liveliness. At least one cannot ignore the fact that worship has become the subject of controversies throughout the ecumenical movement. Not even the Orthodox church is exempt from this, of which it has been said that it owes its existence precisely to the fact that it is sustained by a form of worship which in no way is related to contemporary life. But there are some who, considering the changes in the Eastern European world in which the Orthodox Church lives, deny that it has a chance of survival precisely because of this form of worship.

However much the opinions on the question of worship may be diametrically opposed and in conflict with one another, nevertheless the Roman Catholic and Protestant churches agree about the heart of the matter. The heart of the matter is an openness to the world.[9]

The main theme is: surmounting the alienation from the world. The variations on it are: establishing relationships with technology, science, politics, social problems—the factors which determine the life of secularized man. This is the overriding starting point for all the endeavors directed to the goal of renewal. Although the point of departure for liturgical renewal used to be a "return to the sources," this starting point has been abandoned by the goal of being open to the world and has not been degraded to merely one point among many. The secular age requires something new, and the one-sided concern with what lies behind us has been abandoned in favor of a determined approach to today and tomorrow. Some would, however, maintain that "one should question the 'world-wide secularization and the decline of religion and religious institutions' which is continually assumed to be an unalterable fact throughout the discussion as a whole."[10]

After moving backwards for centuries, the pendulum has now swung with corresponding force in the other direction. While it is quite understandable that this results in one-sidedness, it is also obvious that it will be possible to cope with the shocks produced by secularism only by adapting to this swing. In other words, a responsible renewal of worship services will have to take account of the demands both of the secular age and of tradition. It is not possible naively to start from scratch; one has at least to take the experiences of our forefathers into account. The problem then becomes: In a "world without fathers" how is it possible to celebrate worship services which, in some way or other, are influenced by our fathers?[11] This problem can be solved only if tradition is not understood formalistically but in Jaurés sense: to maintain the tradition does not mean to preserve the ashes but to keep a flame burning. We shall come back to this again.

To start with, it should be remembered that the change which society is undergoing is not bypassing the church, which is part of society, and its worship without making any impact, and that the Roman Catholic and the Protestant Churches are prepared to accept the challenge. This can be said with a good conscience in this general way after the Second Vatican Council and the World Council of Churches' Uppsala Assembly of 1968, although the readiness to accept the challenge and the reactions to it are very different and have been evaluated differently.

II
The Second Vatican Council

Let us start with the Council. Its task was to draw up the basic principles for a thorough reform of the Latin rite. These have been summarized in the "Constitution on the Sacred Liturgy"and form the basis for a special liturgical commission (*"Consilium ad exsequendam Constitutionem de Sacra Liturgia*," now succeeded by the *"Sacra Congregatio pro Cultu Divino"*) which is responsible for working out the reform.

The constitution begins with the words, "This sacred Council has several aims in view: it desires to impart an ever-increasing vigor to the Christian life of the faithful; to adapt more suitably to the needs of our own times those institutions which are subject to change. . . . The Council therefore sees particularly cogent reasons for undertaking the reform and promotion of the liturgy."[12]

This renewal is far reaching [21]. Its goal is the conscious and active participation of all the faithful: "Mother Church earnestly desires that all the faithful should be led to that full, conscious and active participation in liturgical celebrations which is demanded by the very nature of liturgy. . . ." [14] The demand for "active participation" recurs in a variety of forms, in particular with reference to the celebration of the Eucharist [48]. It is really the key concept for renewal and can be identified with a fundamental principle of the Reformation.[13]

In order to make active participation possible the liturgical books are to be revised [25] and it was resolved that "the limits of" the employment of the vernacular "may be extended" [36], the "Prayer of the Faithful" (intercession) should be reintroduced [53] and an effort should be made to be comprehensible: "The rites should be distinguished by a noble simplicity; they should be short, clear and unencumbered by any useless repetitions; they should be within the people's powers of comprehension, and normally should not require much explanation" [34].

However obvious this all may seem—at least as a demand—to a Protestant and however revolutionary it may be for a Roman Catholic, it must still be soberly noted that the response of the participating congregation "can only be expressed in liturgical form. It is limited to the responses, prayers and acclamations set out in the liturgical formulations."[14]

From the very beginning, in order to prevent wild uncontrolled developments, individuals taking special measures, and arbitrary departures from liturgical formulations, the document also included the necessary restrictions: "Regulation of the sacred liturgy depends solely on the authority of the Church" [22, 1] in the form of the Pope, the bishop, and the bishops' organizations. "Therefore no other person, even if he be a priest, may add, remove, or change anything in the liturgy on his own authority" [22, 3]. And in the next paragraph it says, "Finally, there must be no innovations unless the good of the church genuinely and certainly requires them" [23]. And thus, since according to Catholic teaching the Holy Spirit is bound to the office (of the bishop), the demand for active participation is anything but a call for spontaneity from below; on the contrary, it is limited to what is laid down from above.

In spite of all the precautions which were included with wise foresight, it was unavoidable that, in the course of time once the machinery of reform had been set in motion, "arbitrariness" and an "abuse" of the new freedoms should occur. The German episcopate put on the brakes before or at the very moment of the departure of the train by means of a pastoral letter which it "sent home almost before the Constitution had been unanimously adopted with great joy on December 4, 1963: it contained serious criticism of all those acting on their own authority long before anyone could have read the text. . . ."[15]

Since the adoption of the Constitution the characteristics of the gradual implementation of the reform have been the alternation between the planning, systematization, and rules of the Commission and the Congregation on the one hand, and the wishes and additions of the bishops' conferences on the other. The instructions of the Commission, which, in its exemplary new editions of liturgical books, was thinking mainly of adaptation to local requirements, do not always correspond to the ideas of the territorial authorities or their needs. After a burst of enthusiasm at the beginning, the tensions which have arisen in the course of going through different parts of the work have resulted in the sober recognition that, first, the freedom is by no means as great as it appeared at first sight and that, second, there is a constant danger that the freedom granted will be misused. This is the reason why the accompaniment to the systematic work on a new liturgy is a continuous warning against arbitrariness. In order to prevent the whole hand reaching out with the finger that is pointing forwards and resulting so to say in deals made on the sly, the mighty Roman index finger at the same time has to be raised up in warning.

III
Uppsala 1968

On the Protestant side, where each individual has the "freedom of the Gospel" inscribed on his banner, there is all the more need for such a raised index finger (at least from the point of view of its owner). In fact many such fingers are raised but their effect is more limited than that which comes from Rome. At the Fourth Assembly of the World Council of Churches at Uppsala in 1968 the finger was fortunately never raised at all. Uppsala was the first assembly to concern itself with the question of worship. The report of Section V is of a very different nature from the Constitution of the Vatican Council and in this sense they cannot be compared. This report began by addressing itself to the questions based on the observation, "There is a crisis of worship and behind it a widespread crisis of faith."[16] It makes no attempt to produce a statement equally applicable everywhere but rather formulates some thoughts which "in the necessary reconsideration of worship . . . will offer a starting point" [4]. Secularization, with which the crisis of public worship is connected, "challenges us to find new ways by which worship in our churches can lead to Christian obedience both inside and outside the Christian community. Only such obedience will authenticate worship" [16].

The catalogue of questions is impressive: "We are bound to ask the churches whether there should not be changes in language, music, vestments, ceremonies, to make worship more intelligible; whether fresh categories of people (industrial workers, students, scientists, journalists, etc.) should not find a place in the churches' prayers; whether lay people should not be encouraged to take a greater share in public worship; whether our forms of worship should not avoid unnecessary repetition, and leave room for silence; whether biblical and liturgical texts should not be so chosen that people are helped to worship with understanding; whether meetings of Christians for prayer in the Eucharist (Holy Communion, the Lord's Supper) should be confined to church buildings or to traditional hours. In the same way in personal prayer should we not learn to 'pray our lives' in a realistic way?" [24]

IV
"Who Has the Answer?"

There is no doubt that these concrete questions strike the bull's
eye (or the purple), and methodologically it is certainly an advantage to begin with questions. But they are *questions* and questions
require answers. In this respect Uppsala was in the same position as
the musical "Hair" which was running at the same time (1967)
where someone says, "Who has the answer to my questions?"
    If things are not to follow the line of the well-known song by Bob
Dylan, "The Answer, My Friend, Is Blowin' in the Wind," that is, if
Section V at Uppsala was not just talking to the air, then there must
be someone who can give concrete answers to these concrete questions. Uppsala naturally addressed itself to "the churches" [24] and
in practice this means commissions. These then draw up their documents which contain analysis followed by questions. This question
game has now been going on for quite a long time. A typical example of this procedure is the report of Section IV of the Fourth World
Conference on Faith and Order at Montreal in 1963 which discussed
the subject "Worship and the Oneness of Christ's Church." The fact
that the question was asked there whether certain insights of contemporary theology might not be of relevance to forms of worship
demonstrates that merely asking questions may mean going round
in circles. If I really have a particular insight I must necessarily draw
the practical conclusions from it. An insight from which I can draw
no conclusions is not really an insight at all. If I have realized that
for certain reasons this or that is no longer appropriate to worship
but continue keenly to use it in the service as if nothing had happened, then in fact nothing has happened and I have really not
grasped the urgent necessity of the change.
    It is characteristic of our situation that we have an abundance of
insights (more than the formulators of the questions would have us
believe) but that we are too lazy to put them into effect. In this
way true insights become useless insights and it is unnerving to see
how slowly the gap in the church between theory and practice is
bridged.
    Even the consultation of the World Council of Churches on
"Worship in a Secular Age," which took place in 1969 in Geneva
and took up the Uppsala proposals, did not make any practical
progress. The papers[17] and discussions of that consultation served to

define the *status questionis* and to provide further evidence of the often bewildering variety of views on the question of worship. It was not possible to agree even on one interpretation of the term "secular," and there was as much controversy about the analysis of the situation and its evaluation as there was over the various alternative and proposed solutions. There was, however, an agreement that it is not possible to resolve the present crisis of public worship merely by adapting the traditional service and that, on the basis of the recognition that the key to the problem is to be found in an understanding of the Gospel, further studies are required. Granted, such studies are necessary. But while we are studying, consulting, drawing up lists of questions, reflecting, considering and procrastinating, time is passing and with it whole classes of confirmation candidates who pass through our services and finally out of them because they have received nothing to take with them.

Although almost everyone is convinced that it is necessary to change public worship, things in fact remain unchanged while committees pile right insights upon right insights in their documents and are supported in doing so by a flood of books and articles full of right insights. One can quote the authorities beginning with the New Testament and the Early Church, the Reformation and Luther, all the way down to learned experts from the fields of theology, psychology, sociology, and education; however clearly contemporary practice may demonstrate that certain things just cannot continue in this way and however audibly the chorus of voices from the parishes may express their grievances, nevertheless practically nothing happens. Because the place where something could happen, where something must happen, is the church in X in which Pastor Y is working and in which a congregation gathers every Sunday.

The worship service of this unknown, insignificant, average congregation is the subject of world conferences, books, and lectures; in order to explain its sad state whole armies of professors examine the course of the history of philosophy and culture and millions of grey brain cells are put to work; in order to end its troubles, appeals and proposals are issued and, despite the poor functioning of the church information channels, some of them even come into the hands of Pastor Y and his parish X. Many of these insights are also acceptable to Pastor Y, among other things because he had partially recognized them long before. He was just not in a position to formulate them in such a professional and systematic way. He is glad to see that apart from himself and his congregation authorities with a worldwide reputation are also of the opinion, for example, that three Scripture readings in one service are too many, and he is pleased to note that the university congregation in the town of Z left out one reading in an experimental Special-Evening-Jazz-and-Song-Pop service. Marvelous thing, that! But on the following Sunday he continues, only with a still more troubled conscience than before, to read obediently to his congregation, which cannot take in three Scripture readings, everything which is supposed to be read at this time. Because he has to take thousands of things into account—all sorts of regulations, higher authorities, colleagues, and traditions. By taking so much into consideration all those who are behind him, he does not consider those who are sitting in front of him, the congregation, secular man, his contemporaries, that is, those of whom he is supposed to take account first and foremost.

In a word, he lacks the courage. He lacks the courage to do the thing which he and others have recognized as the right thing to do. The question of really changing worship and of making concrete progress is to a large extent—however ridiculous it may sound—a matter of individual courage. Many things have been said and written and examined and proved; but, whatever the reasons may be, they have not yet been processed by the mill of church institutions and therefore still smack of illegality.

There are plenty of people who can present the most acute points in a conference room (far away from home) and on paper (paper is patient). But at the moment when they are standing in their robes at the altar they appear to have forgotten everything. But they have not forgotten it; they have suppressed it under the compelling force of church structures. It is not now so much a matter of making them aware of this suppression. Most pastors are only too well aware of this process of suppression and suffer very much from it. It is far more important to give the individual, who is standing on the touchline, the boundary line of events, the courage to act, indeed to compel him to do something.

As has already been said, enough has already been written and demonstrated; what we lack are courageous people who will risk the major step of taking small practical steps. However threateningly the index finger of those who warn us against "arbitrariness" may be raised against the horizon of revolutionizing worship, however threatening may be the roll of thunder from the authorities who have been caught out and were not consulted in advance, people must at last begin to act on their own.

However much the activity of the laity may be demanded today[18] and however right it is that a local pastor cannot proceed on his own, nevertheless one has soberly to admit that the attitude of the pastor is still the determining factor. (A clerical church will be abolished most quickly where the clergyman himself works against it.) And one must recognize something more: today it is no longer enough to allow experiments only at certain points. It is understandable that church authorities should endeavor to keep experiments under control. But it is simply not enough to grant liberties to a few special campus congregations which are denied to the normal parish. Today we need bishops and church authorities who will provide encouragement for experimentation and progress on the broadest basis, that is, at local level. But, because of the structure of church authorities and hierarchies as the guardians of order, they naturally always have one foot on the brakes, and what Kurt Tucholsky said about German authorities in general applies particularly to them: "The brakes are the most important part of the German car."

It would, thus, be unrealistic to hope for encouragement from above; we shall continue to hear a warning about arbitrary action from that direction more often than an encouragement to action. But even if one shares a horror for arbitrariness, one must admit that the sheer retention of positions which have been recognized to be wrong is no better and is at least as harmful as the arbitrariness of an isolated pastor who pieces his own service book together on his own. Moreover, one is making things too easy for oneself if one disclaims as arbitrary everything which has not yet been authorized by the governing bodies of the church.

It would be mere arbitrariness for a pastor, if, because of his justified aversion to the unevangelical black color of his gown, that old wineskin (Mk. 2:22), he suddenly appeared before his congregation in a homemade, pop-art-style colored gown and stole. But if this same pastor one fine Sunday stopped celebrating at the altar with his back to the congregation, this would have nothing to do with arbitrariness, even if he were the only pastor of his synod who was not facing the altar. Because what he would then be doing would not be a product of his own brain (like the imaginary robe); he can find justification for celebrating in this way in good theological arguments, in church history, in the express instructions of Luther and in widespread ecumenical practice.

It is still less permissible today than it was in Montreal, shyly to raise the question whether certain insights of contemporary theology might not be of relevance for new forms of worship. The cautious formulation of questions is irresponsible in the present situation of worship. The cautious formulation of questions is irresponsible in the present situation of worship, apart from the fact that this amounts to an insult to the work of contemporary theology, which is at last devoting itself increasingly to a correct, theological clarification of the problem of worship. It is criminal when faced with a man drowning before your eyes to deliberate whether certain insights of modern lifeguard associations might not perhaps be "relevant" to the man disappearing into the waters.

It is not our intention here to say anything against the necessary and essential work of specialized commissions. We hope simply to give the one who is on the crucial spot, the local pastor, working together with his congregation, the courage now at last to get done in a practical and concrete manner that which has already been proved to be a correct insight by numerous authorities and experiments, however much effort and courage this action may require. And we hope to give the church authorities the courage to take their foot off the brakes. "The church wins nothing but it loses a great deal if those who cherish tradition become the opponents of new experiments and keep their hands on the bell rope so that they may not be too late to start to ring the knell for those new attempts that have failed."[19]

V
Some Elementary and Practical Answers

No one can say with certainty today what form worship should take in the future. And nobody can demand this because we do not know the future and only vaguely sense the challenges which it will present to us. Therefore it is not a question of setting up models now which will be valid for the future but of finding forms which meet the requirements of the present. Once before, in the age of enlightenment, the church devoted itself to this task with great energy. "Certainly with the result that the forms created in this way were hopelessly outdated a few decades later."[20] It is still irrelevant to apply this judgment, however right it may be, to the experiments of today. Just as we cannot simply adopt the forms of past ages for today, so neither can we create forms for future ages. The most we can do is to prepare for them. Today's experiments will only serve as models for the future in the sense that generations to come also must find new forms for their time as we have for ours and our forefathers in the past for theirs. In others words, whatever forms we may find today can (and will) be out of date in a few decades. It is not a question of finding eternal values for the future but of providing an access to eternity for those who are alive now. Therefore, we have to demand that today's worship be adapted to the needs of today. There is no way of justifying this not being done. Because we know these needs and, as we have said, there are enough experts to provide us with the necessary insights. In the following we shall list some of these requirements which it is possible and necessary to meet.

Let us begin with something external, with the framework within which public worship takes place, with the building. Of course it would be quite effective at this point to make some profound statements about the place in general and the nature of the fellowship of the believers gathered there in particular. That has been done often enough by those better qualified to do so[21] and does not need to be repeated here or in later discussions. Instead, let us remain on the firm ground of practice.

The demand for comprehensible worship has been presented in arguments resulting from much theological effort. This demand rebounds from the walls of our enormous church buildings but is lost in the vast space between them for the sole reason that such large buildings are anything but conducive to fellowship. The Evangelical Church of Germany can never overdo its description of itself as "the church of the Word," but it does not do enough in order to make the words spoken in its services at least acoustically comprehensible. With the technical means of the twentieth century it is a minor detail to meet the most elementary requirement so that preaching can be relevant at least in this respect. But unfortunately, experience has shown that most people are blind to these practical points.

One should not underestimate the importance of these external factors which we theologians so easily dismiss as secondary. The predominant atmosphere in a building (arrangement of the seating, lighting, temperature, ventilation, decoration, etc.) and the question of acoustic understanding are of decisive importance, and it is to no avail to proclaim wonderful theological theories about the comprehensibleness of public worship if nothing is done so that it can at least be heard. Even the most perfect principles about the rhetorical aspects of the sermon remain rhetorical if the pulpit is in the wrong place (e.g., suspended too high above the congregation) or the preacher is forced by the size of the building to speak unnaturally slowly. It is useless to write notes about the pathos of the pulpit if one pays no attention to the pupits which, along with the large buildings, inevitably produce this pathos.

The best of sermons and the most devoted search for modern forms of worship can be torpedoed to death by the characteristics of the building, just as new attempts to celebrate Holy Communion can fail because of the wrong position of the altar. For centuries the altar has been standing in the wrong place in our churches—at the furthest end. In quite a few churches there is an empty space of 25 yards between the altar and the front pews of the church. The pastor stands with his back to the congregation and the congregation cannot see what he is doing at the altar nor in part hear what he is saying there. The effect of all this is a modern form of glossolalia such as Paul rejected, namely where someone praises God and speaks to Him but those standing round him cannot understand and therefore cannot say "Amen" to it.

We know how the communion table came to be moved from the center of the congregation to the furthest extremity and how the pastor came to be isolated from the congregation. We also know that Luther demanded that the celebrant stand behind the altar and sing, pray, and pronounce the words of institution, facing the congregation. And moreover we know that theologians are continually being called upon to listen to what Luther said on this point. We know, finally, that the Roman Catholic Church has been acting as Luther intended since the Council. But we do not know of anyone in the Lutheran church making a serious effort to free himself from a wrong development and going to stand behind the altar instead of in front of it. Where high altars make this impossible for technical reasons, one can follow the example of the Catholic priests who leave the high altar to be the high altar and set up a table at the front by the altar steps near to the congregation. This would be easily possible in most Protestant churches but although we know better and have the theological insight nevertheless we lack the courage to take this step.

At a time when the whole world is being stirred up, when the most revolutionary items appear on the agenda and when theologians themselves are busy writing books about a theology of revolution, theologians have not got the courage to take a few steps around their altars. At a time of major social changes and a reordering of the world, when next to nothing can remain in its traditional place and the whole world is involved in constant reconstruction, the church does not dare to move its altar a few yards nearer to the congregation! When one recognizes these circumstances one can understand why Manuel de Mello said of Section V at Uppsala, "Although we are living in an age of jet aeroplanes, in its worship life the World Council of Churches is still going by bicycle."[22]

This also applies, for example, to the Scripture readings in the service. Normally there are three readings: epistle, gospel and the sermon text. Only the latter is expounded. Luther himself demanded that all the texts read should be expounded, "and where this does not happen the reading is of no benefit to the congregation, as is the case so far in monasteries and seminaries where they have only been wafted to the walls" (*WA* 12, 35 f). There is widespread agreement that congregations are quite right to feel that two readings in addition to the sermon text are too much.[23] Moreover, in the churches where Luther's translation is normally used, Luther's version often contains language which cannot be understood (for which reason the revised edition is being revised again) and the listeners often cannot see the relationship between the various readings. But here, too, there is the same problem: the majority of pastors do not have the courage simply to leave out at least one reading and to use a modern translation, although this step would cause a general sigh of relief (apart from a few dyed-in-the-wool liturgy fans). Here too, it would be a good thing to listen to Luther who said, "One must not overwhelm the believers so that they do not become tired and bored" (*WA* 12, 36).

VI
Courage for Small Steps and Diversity

Since the service as a whole is made up of many (too many) separate parts, it is possible to take a large number of small steps without having to change everything radically at once. Even this demands a large amount of reflection, imagination, and, above all, time. No one who is involved in the preparation of worship, and above all the pastor, should hesitate to devote time to this point. Anyone today who "prepares" the service by slipping the markers quickly into the appropriate pages of the servicebook while the bell is ringing and then just reads them off is acting negligently and irresponsibly. The consequence of such laziness, which is often covered up by calling it the preservation of what has proved itself to be good, is often destruction. Everyone should take the trouble to formulate at least a new introductory prayer and prayer of intercession for each service, like the sermon, even if it takes many hours. In this case shortage of time is no excuse and anyone who uses it as an excuse should refrain from saying anything about new forms of worship.

The frequent use of this excuse, the actual shortage of time (which still applies even when the pastor prepares the services with a group), and the fact that one needs more time for this lead us to the sober admission that the method of small steps is the only possible form of action for the majority. Of course one can say of such small steps, which are really nothing world shattering, that they are only an attempt to mend the old wineskins when we should really be trying to find a completely new container for worship. That is true. The crisis cannot be overcome by means of repairs and minor modernizations. But to demand an immediate, radical, general transformation is totally unrealistic in the case of the majority of congregations.

Particularly if one is working towards a radical new order, small steps are necessary in order to prepare for this new order on a broad basis. When one considers for how many years and with what intensity the debate about new forms of worship has been conducted and how little has been put into practice in the majority of parishes, one has more reason to despair than to assume that radical solutions are likely to meet with success everywhere. Therefore, in the present situation it is necessary to encourage the individual pastor and his congrgation to take some small steps. This means, however, that the dogma of uniformity must be abandoned. Up to now there was a departure from this dogma when isolated congregations or groups received special permission to experiment. The experiments which are tolerated in this way normally take place somewhere else and at a diffrent time than the traditional gathering of the congregation. They are usually so-called special or extra services while the so-called main service has been kept as free from experiments as possible. But the distinction between main and extra services is theologically illegitimate. Worship which is not worship in the full sense is not worship at all. Peter Brunner, who considers that the main service should be the celebration of Holy Communion, writes, "In the Holy Communion the church of Jesus meets as a closed group. The doors to the world, which are wide open for the proclamation of the word, are now closed."[24] This omits the recognition that even the recital of the words of institution (in whatever form), which is constitutive for Holy Communion, is a proclamation of the word in the strict sense, and that the celebration of Holy Communion by the congregation gathered in the name of Jesus is itself an act of proclamation, a missionary act, "For as often as you eat this bread and drink the cup, you proclaim the Lord's death until he comes" (1 Cor. 11:26). Services in which "the church of Jesus meets as a closed group" do exist. But where "the doors to the world . . . are . . . closed" deliberately, one then cannot speak of worship.

The situation can no longer be perpetuated in which experimental services are merely tolerated, like stepchildren, on the periphery of the so-called occasional services. That time is now past. Within the context of small steps it would be enough to start with great success if they could now gradually find their way into traditional worship. But for this to happen it is necessary to tear down the idol of formal uniformity which enjoys the highest adoration in the church.

In recent years it has been said so often that the pluralistic society requires various forms of worship that this can already be called a platitude. There is now no one who objects today to the existence of early, midday and evening services for shift workers, academics, students, youth, beat, and, above all, Bach supporters, or that from time to time a "new form of worship" takes place in a motion theater or concert hall. Only the traditional Sunday morning service continues to be turned out unwaveringly and steadily throughout the country with scarcely any variation. Any variation would upset the basic principle of liturgical uniformity which even goes so far as to be used as a defense of the continued use of Greek. Instead of saying (rather than singing) "Lord, have mercy" in the vernacular of the various regions in the first part of the liturgy (if at all), the Greek form *Kyrie eleison* continues to be used with the argument that this demonstrates the unity of Christians throughout the world. One may doubt whether a supporter of this theory, when praying to

God in Greek, experiences an elated feeling of ecumenical fellowship. Even if that were the case, for the majority of those attending the service who have not studied Greek like their pastor, it is simply incomprehensible. Of course, it is an easy thing to teach the congregation the meaning of the Greek words, and the valuable time of many a confirmation lesson is spent on such teaching. But the question remains, "Why this complication?" Is it not possible to say it directly in the vernacular? Then one hears (see above) the allusion to worldwide unity, as if church Esperanto had anything to do with this. Thorough consideration should be given to Augustine's exhortation about the language used in worship (including hymns, prayers, and the sermon). "It is better for us to be criticized by the language experts than if the ordinary people not understand us."[25]

If the church is not prepared to dispense with its Greek linguistic remains and to do without uniformity on this purely formal point, one can easily imagine the difficulties involved in obtaining equal status for different forms of worship within the church and within one congregation. But the demand for this equal status and for variety must continue without relenting.

But demands alone, however well they may be argued, are not enough. The demands of the students for a reform of the universities remained ineffective as long as the students stuck to the academic rules of the game with petitions and proposals. These were "carefully considered" as "valuable suggestions" in order then to disappear into the waste paper baskets of the establishment. Only when it became clear to the students that in this way time was passing but nothing was happening did they adopt more drastic methods and force a hearing. Only when they became wild did the reorientation of the educational system really get under way. It is just the same in the church. Whoever wants to be heard in the church has to draw attention to himself in a noisy way. Sharp protests on paper frighten no one today; they are a normal part of the program just like the obligatory protest meeting outside the door of every conference room. Therefore there is only one option for someone who wants to achieve something—action.

Over the past decade the arguments, e.g., for and against new hymns, have gone to and fro.[26] Basically nothing new can be contributed to the debate. Anyone who is still not convinced that a large proportion of the hymnbook is hopelessly out of date and cannot be expected to be used (mainly because of the words[27]) will not allow himself to be convinced by a repetition of the arguments, especially since many prejudices hold sway here. So there is only one solution—to sit down and write some new hymns, set examples, offer some models. Sing the hymns and try them out. If they are no good they will disappear and if they are any good they will become established on their own merit, and their presence, their use in the congregation, will be better proof of their validity than theoretical negotiations and discussions. No one can deny the fact that the *Evangelisches Kirchengesangbuch*, the hymnal of the Protestant Church of Germany, for example, contains hymns neither for young people nor for children and that it not only has shortcomings with reference to many areas of contemporary Christian life but also gives most inadequate treatment even to the subject of mission, which is constitutive for the church.[28]

No one today would basically question the justification for new hymns but the church music experts are still reticent,[29] and they criticize the hymns based on jazz, blues, spirituals, folksongs, chansons and light entertainment for their lack of "high quality";[30] they observe a "tendency to the primitive" whereby primitive is not understood positively in the sense of closeness to the origin or genuineness but rather negatively. But complexity can no more be equated with high quality than can simplicity with lack of high quality, and it is probably easier to compose a motet than a church hymn. Making the words and music simple is what is most difficult. Purely as a consequence of their training, which is urgently in need of reform,[31] church musicians are scarcely prepared to tackle this difficult task— a problem which must not only be admitted objectively but also changed.

A respectable number of new hymns have become common property only because action was taken and new hymns were introduced without regard to the resistance of punctilious church musicians, and many a church musician has meanwhile quietly undergone a conversion. There simply comes a time when nothing more can be said or discussed and when action is called for. This point has been reached in the case of worship as a whole. Although many problems may still need to be clarified, and this clarification may be going on in the background, in the context of the event, on the level of the congregation which comes together Sunday by Sunday, action has got to begin even if the experts have not yet agreed on all the details. The subject of "livening up" worship can be talked to death.

The time for raising questions is past, long past, and the time has come for answers to be given, for action to be taken, and that in every congregation which comes together for worship.

VII
The Unrelinquishable Elements of Worship

In addition to the policy of small steps the tactics of radical solutions are also necessary. There are many Christians today—as Uppsala realistically recognized—for whom traditional worship no longer means anything. It has been of no interest to the world for a long time; services are regularly avoided by well over 90 per cent of our church members and the popular description of worship as an "institutionalized irrelevance"[32] is unfortunately true. There are many Christians for whom church services have become a ghostly museum, meaningless, and demanding more than one can bear. Among these are to be found particularly people who are making a special effort to take their faith seriously and to practice it in everyday life. It is impossible for them to take the usual worship seriously any longer precisely because it offers them no support in this endeavor. This is all the more reason why they should be taken seriously by the church because they are the spokesmen of the secular age. Romano Guardini was thinking of them when he (in connection with the problems and tasks of the Vatican Council) raised the question, "Is it perhaps the liturgical act, and with it everything which is called 'liturgy,' being so much rooted in history—antique or medieval—which should be given up completely for the sake of honesty? Should one perhaps work one's way through to a recognition that the man of the industrial age, of technology and of the psycho-sociological structures which it creates, is simply no longer capable of the liturgical act? And instead of talking about renewal should one not rather consider in what way the Holy Mysteries can be celebrated today so that modern man and his truth can relate to them?"[33]

In this case it is not so important in what form these ideas were expressed—it was typically in the form of a question—but by whom. For if even a man like Guardini, who once wrote the book "The Spirit of the Liturgy,"[34] can ask this question, then this is already an answer to it. Certainly E. Hertzsch believes that to say yes to this question "amounts to declaring the church bankrupt, or at least any church" which claims to accept the Augsburg Confession V and VII.[35] We shall see further on that this is not the case. But it would amount to declaring worship bankrupt, at least worship as it is traditionally celebrated today. For the time being this declaration of bankruptcy is being proclaimed only by the empty pews but in such an undeniable way that no theological tactics aimed at covering it up can in the long run escape the fact that traditional worship has failed. This is not a criticism of traditional worship itself but of those who continue to defend and maintain it in the present situation. For here repairs can do nothing anymore. The policy of small steps described above is meaningful only as an interim solution and can be justified only as preparing the way for new forms of worship without which church services will not be possible in the secular age.

The sort of worship which, in the sense of Guardini's question, "should give up completely for the sake of honesty . . . everything which is called 'liturgy' " is definitely possible for a church which is founded on Articles V and VII of the Augsburg Confession.

In Article VII the church is defined as "the assembly of all believers among whom the Gospel is preached in its purity and the holy sacraments are administered according to the Gospel." Although this Article refers not to church services but to the church, it surely expresses what is essential about worship as well since the service is the only place where the *notae ecclesiae*, preaching and sacrament, are visibly present. And although the term "worship service" is not used here at all, it is clear that that is what this refers to. Only when worship takes place can the marks of the church be recognized, only in the practice of public worship can one find the true touchstone for the true nature of the church, for "in such a gathering the epiphany of the church takes place."[36] "The question of public worship is therefore nothing less than the burning question of the truth of the Christian faith."[37] In all new experiments the sermon is therefore of decisive significance. It is not possible in this context to examine this problem but it must be emphasized that the renewal of worship stands or falls by the renewal of the sermon.

Thus according to the Augsburg Confession VII the constitutive elements of the church (read: worship) which are most important and vital are preaching and the sacraments, and this is followed by a satisfied *satis est* which indicates that everything else which may form part of the service is of secondary importance. So Article VII continues, "For it is sufficient for the true unity of the Christian church that the Gospel be preached in conformity with a pure understanding of it and that the sacraments be administered in accordance with the divine Word. It is not necessary for the true unity of the Christian church that ceremonies, instituted by men, should be observed uniformly in all places."

And there is the key word under which everything can be subsumed which might be counted among the relinquishable elements: ceremonies which are "instituted by men." This expression "instituted by men," *cerimoniae ab hominibus institutae,* proves to be an extremely helpful phrase. Preaching and the sacraments were instituted by God. Everything else is a human addition and therefore dependent on considerations of reason, usefulness (e.g., educational usefulness), taste, order, custom, cultural influences, etc. Basically the same distinction is to be found in Vatican Council's Constitution on the Liturgy: "The liturgy is made up of immutable elements divinely instituted, and of elements subject to change. These not only may but ought to be changed with the passage of time if they have suffered from the intrusion of anything out of harmony with the inner nature of the liturgy or have become unsuited to it" [21].

The confessional writings consider it to be a great danger if the same significance is attributed to rites, ceremonies, and church orders as to preaching and sacrament. This was precisely the situation the reformers were faced with, namely, the acceptance and following of certain orders instituted by men were considered to be "necessary for salvation."[38] The confessional writings protest against this error with all force and all sorts of strong expressions. "Thus it is the opinion of the Apostles that this freedom should remain in the church, and that no ceremonies, neither the law of Moses nor other laws, should be considered to be necessary worship. . . . But if one looks quickly through the Holy Scriptures and the Apostles one can simply draw a line through everything and pronounce clearly that in Christ we are free, liberated from all traditions, especially if one is supposed to obtain salvation and forgiveness of sins through them."[39]

Of course this is no longer the question which concerns us today. One is unlikely to find a theologian who will maintain that the observance of certain festivals and ceremonies is necessary for salvation. Nevertheless we cannot ignore the fact that today the times are in no way over in which latitudes are loaded with exaggerared significance and certain orders instituted by men are wrongly treated like dogmas. And here the problem is not the fact that variations are not recognized as such. In general, it is easier to obtain agreement on the basic questions than it is normally assumed. Thus, for example, on the question of the distinction between the sacred and the secular one can observe a consensus, which cuts right across the spectrum of theological opinion (see below), that this distinction has been abolished by Christ. But hardly has this observation been made when the inevitable big BUT comes in which opens both the back and front doors to practical sacralization. In the case of the service what happens is that everyone is more than ready to agree to the fundamental gospel principle that no fixed form of worship can be dogmatically established. But the necessary consequences of this principle are never spelled out (e.g., several forms of worship side by side with equal standing). And since *extra ecclesiam nulla salus est* and the present forms of worship make it impossible from the very beginning for large sections of the congregation (not to speak of the others) to have any access to salvation, any share in salvation is bound up practically again with the acceptance of these forms. And since only very few people are able and willing to make this sort of sacrifice, the orders instituted by men function as if they were necessary for salvation, although this is firmly denied by theory. And thus the prerequisite of circumcision, which Paul rejected, is in force today in another form, namely, as the acceptance of a particular style of music and of middle class gathering, of outdated conceptions of the universe and forms of language in the texts of the prayers and hymns, and so on.

The confessional writings are quite clear in their rejection of any burden of conscience which this can cause. The German text of Article XV of the Apology states, ". . . in the churches those ceremonies and orders should be used which can be used with a good conscience and without sin and which are helpful for maintaining order and peace." The preservation of "ceremonies" is here recommended on two conditions, first, that they do not represent a burden on the conscience (they may not be declared necessary for salvation) and, second, provided that they serve some educational or useful purpose. The most important aspect of the maintenance of "ceremonies" is to have a sense of proportion. In Article XXIV of the Apology it is first pointed out that a large proportion of the *traditiones* come from the Old Testament but that "the New Testament is concerned with other things, and that such outward ceremonies which may be necessary for the education of children should be kept in proportion."[41]

It is not only in the use of *traditiones* that the right proportion has to be found but also in their theological evaluation. The main attention of the church should be directed to the "main articles," and, if the church concerned itself with the really important things, then probably its "trifling and tomfoolery with albs, great tonsures, broad cinctures, bishops' and cardinals' hats and crosiers, and similar nonsense would soon be forgotten. If we would first carry out God's commands and precepts in the spiritual and temporal estates, we would find time enough to reform the regulations concerning fasts, vestments, tonsures and chasubles. But if we are willing to swallow camels and strain out gnats, if we let logs stand and dispute about specks, we might just as well be satisfied with such a council." (Smalcald Articles, Preface)

For those who are not able to keep these things in proportion— who consider ceremonies and human traditions as important for salvation as the sermon and sacraments—the confessional writings provide an answer which could hardly be more clear. In Article XXIV of the Apology (German version) it is said, "whenever our opponents set up their candles, altar cloths, images and other adornments as essential and therefore part of worship, they are the servants of the Antichrist. . . ." And with a similarly refreshing clarity Article XXVIII of the Apology (German version) states, "This is the clear and straightforward teaching about human regulations, namely that we should recognize that they are not necessary worship and yet that they should sometimes be followed in order to avoid trouble." Thus it is clearly stated here that human traditions are not "necessary worship" and that means, in other words, that they are relinquishable elements of the service. They can be used freely in order to avoid discord and for pedagogical reasons, although even here there is a warning against unlimited freedom, "To teach freedom and nothing else is also dubious and questionable since ordinary people need some outward discipline and guidance" (Article XVI of the Apology) . Therefore, as it goes on to say, one should "exercise Christian freedom in such a way as not to cause a scandal for the weak who are not versed in these things, and in such a way that the weak will not be frightened off the teaching of the Gospel by those who abuse freedom. And this is why our preachers teach that without special, cogent reasons nothing of the church's customs should be changed and that rather, for the sake of peace and unity, all such customs should be maintained as is possible without sin and burdening the conscience."

And above all of this there stands the word of the old canons to which the Torgau Articles refer, "That every custom, however old it may be and however long it may have lasted, must be subject to Scripture and the truth."[42]

Having referred so far to word and sacrament as unrelinquisable elements of worship, a further element of this sort which must be mentioned is prayer, which the reformers described as the highest form of worship and which occurs in Luther's famous definition in the Torgau Consecration Sermon of 1544 where he describes the worship service as the place where "our dear Lord himself speaks to us through his holy Word and we, for our part, speak to him through prayer and singing" (*WA* 49, 588). Indeed, worship does not only mean that the word is addressed to me but also that I respond to the word which I have heard. The basic form of man's response to God's Word is prayer, and singing can be subsumed under this heading. Thus the unrelinquishable elements of worship are word and sacrament and prayer. Therefore Luther wrote in "Concerning the Ordering of Divine Worship," ". . . that the Christian church should never meet together without the word of God being preached there and praying, however briefly."

The presence of these essential elements in a service, however, is not enough to guarantee that it will be acceptable and appropriate for our time. If I say, for example, that the essential elements of a car are at least three wheels, a propulsion mechanism, steering, and brakes, this applies equally to every vintage car. One cannot deny that it is still possible today to drive such a vintage car and reach one's destination, even though there are very few people who can allow themselves such an expensive and somewhat whimsical hobby. The average citizen of the twentieth century uses more modern, i.e., more practical, models which are better to drive. Thus the question of "How?" is in no sense secondary but is directly related to the matter itself. Questions of form are also questions of content. There will probably be Christians for a long time yet who can allow themselves the luxury of an exclusive, vintage church service, a museum piece which is artificially kept alive, But for the average consumer in a secular age it is not acceptable. In order to reach his destination he needs a modern model.

VIII
The Church Exists for Others

If, apart from the unrelinquishable elements mentioned, other elements of contemporary worship are to be given up, according to the confessional writings the following conditions apply. First, there must be special, "cogent reasons" which make it essential to change the church's practice and, second, the maintenance of these dubious practices must entail "burdening the conscience." The decision depends on one's particular concept of the church. Archbishop William Temple said, "The church exists for those who do not yet belong to it."[43] Dietrich Bonhoeffer wrote, "The church is church only when it exists for others."[44] And in the "German Mass" Luther defined worship as a "public incitement to faith and to Christianity" (*WA* 19, 75, 1 f) and said that it existed for those "who do not believe or are not Christians yet" (*ibid.*) .

In this connection it is interesting to see how Vilmos Vajta sums up Luther's attitude to ceremonies. "If the ceremonies restrict the conscience to outward behavior and direct attention away from one's neighbor towards God, they should be abandoned. Luther associates only one idea with church ceremonies: those who have not yet accepted the faith (like, for example, young people and the ordinary people) should be drawn by them nearer to the Word and sacrament where faith is born."[45] Luther's motive is still what counts today. Only today, and with precisely the same motive, the conclusions to be drawn are the exact opposite if ceremonies—particularly for young people—are no longer a helpful means of access to the Word but rather an unsurmountable obstacle. And whereas Luther in the German Mass, where he proposes three forms of worship, offers for those who "seriously wish to be Christians" (*WA* 19, 75, 5 f) a form without "much, mighty singing," but considers that more elaborate ceremonies are appropriate for the young and for simple people, then today the argument is exactly the opposite: the long-established congregation may still be able to cope with "much, mighty singing" but young people certainly cannot. For example, in the German Mass[46] Luther writes that he on no account wishes to give up the use of Latin in the service. The reason: "for I am very much concerned about the young people" (*WA* 19, 74, 5) . The same argument which Luther used to defend the continued use of Latin must be used today for the discarding of Latin, or of the ceremonies which have become an obstacle. The motive is the decisive factor! And the motive can be none other than love for one's neighbor, whether he be young, a nonbeliever, an outsider or the secular man of the industrial age. "Therefore a man's outward liturgical behavior, his decision for or against church ceremonies, depends always on the needs of his neighbor, and here the commandment of love applies."[47] If we take all of this seriously, it means that the church has no right to continue to insist on human traditions simply because the church itself is fond of them, when in reality they present an obstacle for its true task, that of existing for those who do not yet belong to it.

The basic prerequisite for this is that everything which happens in the service should be understandable for those participating, and here it should be noted that Paul, in 1 Cor. 14:23 f, takes not only the "uninstructed," *idiotai,* but even the "unbelievers," *apistoi,* as the criterion for comprehensibility. For Paul, "the person coming in from outside, the fringe member, or nonbeliever is the standard by which all preaching must be measured."[48] If the church were to adopt this apostolic criterion it would produce revolutionary changes in its present forms of worship. But up to now it has tried hard to avoid taking seriously this instruction from the apostle Paul. But the church will be able to measure up to the new situation of the secular age only if it follows this old apostolic precept. Moreover it becomes clear at this point that it is not simply a matter of replacing the old with something new, but that the tradition provides the basic guidelines and principles for forms of worship. It is only necessary to replace the "uninstructed" and "unbelievers" with the words "secular man" in order to see that one cannot be more up to date than Paul. But the church continues with its services undeterred as if Paul had never addressed himself to this question and in such a plain language.

It is obvious that, wherever work on new forms of worship is going on, energetic references are made to this passage in Corinthians. People, unless they are acting deaf for the sake of convenience, can argue against this Pauline criterion only by claiming that is all well and good but if one follows this principle consistently it breaks down over the celebration of Holy Communion. For what takes place in communion just cannot be made comprehensible; the deep mystery cannot be spread out on the flat drawing board of general comprehensibility. As if Paul did not know that best himself! As if the spokesmen for modern forms of worship were maintaining that they wish or were able to make the mystery plausible! But the manner in which this mystery is celebrated can and must take a transparent form. "But there are no hard and fast rules about the details of how we are to perform this remembrance. We have not even got a hard and fast formulation of the words of Christ in the institution."[49]

This very Holy Communion service must not be exempted like a final, impenetrable stronghold from the struggle for new worship forms. Even in the celebration of Holy Communion, where the congregation is normally a "closed group," the service has a missionary dimension. For when the church celebrates communion it proclaims the Lord's death until he comes (1 Cor. 11:26).

In present-day communion practice the vertical is in the forefront. Basically this is quite correct because fellowship between the communicants becomes possible only by virtue of their fellowship with the body and blood of the Crucified and Risen Lord. But a totally one-sided, dogmatically based overemphasis on the vertical has resulted in the complete neglect of the horizontal. This one-sidedness is a real perversion of the celebration of Communion.

The facts that a number of people are together in a building and take communion in successive groups, and that the organist, following the example of courtly ceremonial, plays some music while the others are eating and drinking, do not make clear to the "uninstructed" individual what the nature of this fellowship meal is. For him this sort of meal must look like a mystical snack where everyone eats alone, and is alone. It is of no use to point out the joyful nature of this meal when the whole setting is so weighed down with ceremony that no joy can possibly break through. It is of no use talking about enjoying fellowship together when the whole atmosphere makes it impossible for fellowship to come about. Although this solemn celebration is introduced with the exhortation "Lift up your hearts," it is so oppressive in the true sense of the word that one hardly dares to raise one's eyes on the way to the altar, to look at least once at the person standing and communicating beside one, let alone to greet him or even speak to him or have any contact with him. With the best will in the world the "uninstructed" cannot see what this individualistic narrow confinement has to do with fellowship. And yet eating a meal together is one of the few points at which secular man practices community. However incapable of community and lonely he may otherwise be, eating with others as an expression of fellowship is a natural reality of life for him as well. But precisely at this point, where the mystery of God's ways take physical shape, the church has swept the natural from the table, erected liturgical barriers, and obscured the horizontal dimension. "Therefore a sacrament of the Lord's Supper at which there is no real fellowship around the table is an abuse of worship in Paul's eyes."[50]

Nowhere is it more clear than in Holy Communion that the service must not only become more comprehensible and more missionary but also simply more human if it really wishes to be worship. Indeed Luther's Torgau definition of the service as the place where "our dear Lord himself speaks to us through his holy Word and we, for our part, speak to him through prayer and singing" is neither everything that Luther had to say about worship nor all that is to be said about it. Worship also has a dimension of Christian service which is expressed not in verbal formulas but in human actions. To be human and natural (in this case, e.g., to sit around the table and to replace liturgical formulations by conversation) is the prime command for any new form of worship.[51]

This has absolutely nothing to do with a theology which is only interested in the subject of *Mitmenschlichkeit* (human solidarity) and has thus become an anthropology; this is a matter of incarnation. Since the coming of Christ there is no place for a distinction between the sacred and the secular, there are no sacred persons, times, places, objects, and activities and no "cult." By now, this view of the question has become common ecumenical property and it would be carrying coals to Newcastle to start quoting prooftexts for this assertion.[52]

It is therefore unnecessary to conjure up the bogey of so-called modern theology when modern services put an end to the distinction between sacred and secular. Certainly it appears that in the background of many attempts at new forms of worship there is the emaciated theology of *Mitmenschlichkeit* or the God-is-dead nontheology which has done away with the transcendent personal openness of the whole man to the message of God's personal self-giving. This may be one of the reasons why theologically conservative circles are suspicious of new forms of worship and sense that something is being undermined.

In his analysis of the theological convictions which undergird the new services, Peter Brunner expresses the judgment that it is not only a question here of giving worship new external forms but that it is also a matter of "a change in the essence amounting even to a transformation of the essence."[53] Following this line further, he expresses fears about a "deformation" and "destruction" of Christian worship. These fears are unfortunately justified if the new attempts have the theological bases as Brunner has described them. But one must not tip out the baby with the bath water and should rather remember that avant-gardism in the field of new worship forms is by no means possible only hand in hand with the so-called "modern theology." It is therefore sad that the Lutheran churches are hesitant here, although their confessional writings should make them most open to new forms of worship, and the more open they are the more seriously they are taking their confessional writings. One cannot rid oneself of the suspicion that the hesitation of the Lutheran churches[54] on the matter of new forms of worship is not a consequence of their conservative "blue blood" but rather of reactionary "hardened arteries." If this is the case the only solution is a—perhaps painful— operation which would completely liberate the service from set phraseology, rigidity, unnaturalness, incomprehensibility, mercilessness, inhumanity, sacralization, lack of relevance to the world, etc.

IX
When the Pious Facade Comes Tumbling Down

To demonstrate, in conclusion, how necessary a radical reform of worship is, let us take the example of the church in East Germany. The situation of the church in the secular world is especially obvious in East Germany. After four centuries of common history, the development since 1945 has been different in the two halves of Germany. In the western part, under the label "Volkskirche" (established or national church) the church business has continued so far to run quite well. In the eastern part secularization in the form of Marxism has knocked at the door of the church and immediately brought down its pious facade. To see what this means in practice one can quote the example of an average parish of a large town. The tendency to decline in membership in such a parish is not an isolated case but probably typical for the church in the "secular city."

The parish which had about 18,000 members in 1945 had shunk to 7296 members in 1970. Of these, 4866 were women, 2430 men, and 3099 of them more than 60 years old. From the 7296 members, 1146 more should be deducted who without having bothered formally to leave the church are subject to church discipline for failure to pay their church taxes. So that in fact only 6150 remain, of whom about 300 take part in the life of the parish and about 150 come to worship services. There will be very few to take their place: there are 592 children under the age of 14. And since not all those who are baptized attend the Sunday School, and of those who come to Sunday School not all stay until confirmation, and since, moreover, not all of those who are confirmed remain faithful to the church, of these 592 children perhaps 150 will be left later on.

In a few decades these few young people will constitute the whole congregation. Even now, worship in its present form is unacceptable to these young people.[55] And this will not change in the future; on the contrary, the alienation will increase and, if no transitional measures can be found immediately, in the future there will be no one (apart from a few veterans) attending services. And yet it is precisely in the new situation of the future that the worship service as the gathering of the congregation will have a function and be of very special significance for true worship in the broad sense of Rom. 12, as an attitude of life, as the surrender of the whole man in concrete obedience in the everyday life of the world.

For worship in this sense does not exclude but rather includes worship in the sense of a meeting, because the church and the Christian life are not possible without some form of gathering.

NOTES

1. Cf. Trutz Rendtorff, *Die soziale Struktur der Gemeinde*, Hamburg, 1958.
2. It can be observed that in the New Testament "there are no religious, cultic concepts." Cf. Eduard Schweizer, *Gemeinde und Gemeindeordnung im Neuen Testament*, Zürich, 1962, p. 201.
3. This point of view is also presented by Peter Brunner in *Leiturgia*, Handbuch des evangelischen Gottesdienstes, vol. 1, Kassel, 1954, pp. 83-361.
4. "The predominance of this limited use of the term, by the way, arose only in the late eighteenth century," and it should be noted that "the use of the word 'worship service' is not really at home in Catholic circles whereas it is firmly rooted in Protestantism." Gerhard Ebeling, "Die Notwendigkeit des christlichen Gottesdienstes," in *Zeitschrift für Theologie und Kirche*, 67, 1970, vol. 2, pp. 233-234.
5. Gerhard Ebeling, "Die Notwendigkeit des christlichen Gottesdienstes," *ibid.*, pp. 231-249.
6. Bericht aus Uppsala 1968. Offizieller Bericht über die vierte Vollversammlung des Ökumenischen Rates der Kirchen, ed. by N. Goodall, the German

edition by W. Müller-Römheld, Geneva, 1968. English quotations here from *Uppsala Speaks*, Section Reports, p. 78.

7. We can find the same approach in Luther. Cf. Vilmos Vajta, *Die Theologie des Gottesdienstes bei Luther*, Berlin, 1958, p. 44.

8. But not for those who, like Helmut Gollwitzer in his commentary on the Arnoldshain Communion Theses (I, i), describe it as a "naive historical view that before his death at his last meal on Maundy Thursday our Lord instituted this meal in the way in which we now celebrate it." *Zur Lehre vom heiligen Abendmahl, Report on the discussions of Holy Communion in the Evangelical Church in Germany 1947-57 and Explanations of Their Outcome*, compiled by G. Niemeier in cooperation with H. Gollwitzer, W. Kreck, and H. Meyer, Munich, 1958, p. 24.

9. An indication of the new understanding of worship is the book "Fantasie für die Welt" (Imagination for the world), ed. by G. Schnath, Stuttgart, 1967.

10. H. Möllers, *Kirche und Religion im Widerspruch*, Witten, 1970, p. 10 f.

11. P. Selby, "Bringing Liturgy to Life," a paper presented in Strasbourg at the 1970 Ecumenical Seminar. This is now available in German in *Okumenische Perspektiven* 4, Frankfurt, under the title "Vergangenheit und Gegenwart im Gottesdienst."

12. *Vatikanum II*, Vollständige Ausgabe der Konzilsbeschlüsse, ed. by A. Beckel, H. Reiring, O.B. Roegele, Osnabrück, 1966 (Fromms Taschenbücher, vol. 44). English quotations from *Constitution on the Sacred Liturgy*, translated by Rev. Clifford Howell, S.J., Cirencester, 1963. References to the texts of the Vatican Council are indicated by the number of the paragraph in brackets.

13. Vilmos Vajta, "Die Folgen der Liturgiereform," in J. Chr. Hampe, *Die Autorität der Freiheit*, vol. 1, Munich, 1967, p. 609.

14. Edmund Schlink, *Nach dem Konzil*, Munich and Hamburg, 1966, p. 63.

15. J. Chr. Hampe, *Die Autorität der Freiheit*, vol. 1, Munich, 1967, p. 508.

16. *Uppsala Report*, loc. cit., p. 78 [3]. Hereafter the quotations from Section V are indicated by the number of the paragraph in brackets.

17. Karl-Friedrich Müller, ed., *Gottesdienst in einem säkularisierten Zeitalter*. A consultation of the Faith and Order Commission of the World Council of Churches, Kassel and Trier, 1971.

18. The view which has predominated so far, that the ordained pastor alone can do everything better than a layman, is just as false as the view which has recently become so popular, that everything in the church will automatically be better if it is entrusted to laymen. We have learned from the practical experience of working with laymen in the preparation of worship from the initial planning to the execution that laymen can be just as estranged from the world, anaemic, dogmatic, and incompetent as pastors. Therefore the decision about who should undertake responsibility for what part in the service should not be allowed to depend on whether one is a layman or an ordained theologian but rather on who has the necessary gift.

19. W. Jetter, in G. Wacker and P. G. Seiz, ed., *Gottesdienst im Gespräch*, Stuttgart, 1969, p. 13.

20. Peter Brunner, "Gottesdienst in neuer Gestalt," in W. Blankenburg, H. v. Schade, Kurt Schmidt-Clausen, *Kerygma und Melos*, Kassel, 1970, p. 104.

21. G. Langmaack, "Der gottesdienstliche Ort," in *Leiturgia*, vol. 1, loc. cit., pp. 360-436. Cf. in this volume also the contribution by O. Hartman.

22. *Monthly Letter About Evangelism*, no. 2/3, February/March, 1969, ed. by World Council of Churches, Division of World Mission and Evangelism, Geneva.
23. It is all the more strange that the Roman Catholic Church has gone over – albeit only for a trial period—to three readings since the Vatican Council.
24. Peter Brunner, in *Leiturgia*, vol. 1, *loc. cit.*, p. 220.
25. Quoted from J. Chr. Hampe, *Die Autorität der Freiheit*, vol. 1, *loc. cit.*, p. 509.
26. G. Hegele, *Warum neue religiöse Lieder?* Regensburg, 1964, R. Hagen, *Jazz in der Kirche?* Stuttgart, 1967. L. Zenetti, *Heisse Weisen*, Munich, 1966.
27. L. Schmidt, "Kirchensprache in der Gegenwart," in *Zeitschrift für Theologie und Kirche*, 63, vol. 1, May, 1966, pp. 88-133. Theo Lehmann, "*Swing und Zwang*," in *Calendarium spirituale '65*, Berlin, 1964, pp. 77-95.
28. In the main section containing 394 hymns only eighteen refer to mission. Cf. H. Bernewitz, "Der Sendungsauftrag der Kirche in den Gesangbüchern der Brüdergemeinde von 1927-1967 und im Evangelischen Kirchengesangbuch von 1950," Dissertation Halle, 1967.
29. Theo Lehmann, "Gottesdienst einmal anders," in *Deutsches Pfarrerblatt*, vol. 68, April, 1968, pp. 234-237.
30. W. Blankenburg, "Neue gottesdienstliche Musik," in W. Blankenburg, H. v. Schade, Kurt Schmidt-Clausen, *Kerygma und Melos*, *loc. cit.*, pp. 402-412.
31. D. Mendt, "Die Kirchenmusik in der missionarischen Gemeinde von heute und morgen," in *Die Zeichen der Zeit*, 24, Heft. 10, 1970, pp. 380-383.
32. Gerhard Ebeling, quoted by M. Lienhard, "Geburtswehen eines neuen relevanten Gottesdienstes," in *Lutherische Monatshefte*, no. 9, December, 1970, p. 614.
33. "Der Kultakt und die gegenwärtige Aufgabe der liturgischen Bildung, A Letter," in *Liturgie und Liturgische Bildung*, Würzburg, 1966, p. 17.
34. Romano Guardini, *Vom Geist der Liturgie*, Freiburg, 1953.
35. "Die Liturgie der Kirche in der Welt des Jahres 1985," in *ThLz* 94, 1969, no. 1, p. 15.
36. Peter Brunner, in *Leiturgia*, vol. 1, *loc. cit.*, p. 106.
37. Gerhard Ebeling, "Die Notwendigkeit des christlichen Gottesdienstes," in *ZThK*, 67, 1970, p. 233.
38. *WA* 19:73:30.
39. *Die Bekenntnisschriften der Evangelisch-Lutherischen Kirche.* 5th edition, Göttingen, 1963, pp. 303 f.
40. H. Thielicke, *Leiden an der Kirche*, Hamburg, 1965, pp. 136 ff.
41. *Op. cit.*, p. 365.
42. *Ibid.*, p. 107.
43. Quoted from H. P. Thompson, *Into all Lands*, London, 1951, p. 714.
44. Dietrich Bonhoeffer, *Widerstand und Ergebung*, Berlin, 1957, p. 211.
45. Vilmos Vajta, *Die Theologie des Gottesdienstes bei Luther*, Berlin, 1958, p. 325.
46. One cannot too warmly recommend an intensive study of Luther's German Mass because it contains a wealth of insights which could be extremely useful to us in the present discussion.
47. Vilmos Vajta, *loc. cit.*, p. 331.
48. Eduard Schweitzer, *Gemeinde und Gemeindeordnung im Neuen Testament*, Zürich, 1962, p. 206.
49. Peter Brunner, in *Leiturgia*, vol. 1, *loc. cit.*, p. 273.

50. Eduard Schweizer, *op. cit.*, p. 204.
51. Abbé Perrin accuses the liturgy of "dehumanization" (quoted from H.-R. Müller-Schwefe, "Liturgie heute," in *Deutsches Pfarrerblatt*, 64, no. 17, 1964, p. 454).
52. A carefully argued and remarkably well-balanced presentation with copious bibliographical references can be found in the paper "Neutestamentliche Marginalien zur Frage der 'Entsakralisierung'" by H. Schürmann, in *Jesu Abendmahlshandlung als Zeichen für die Welt*, Leipzig, 1970, pp. 103-160. Also in *Der Seelsorger*. Zweimonatsschrift für Praxis und Theorie des kirchlichen Dienstes, no. 38 (1968), vol. 1, pp. 38-48 and vol. 2, pp. 89-104. See also H. Mühlen, *Entsakralisierung, Ein epochales Schlagwort in seiner Bedeutung für die Zukunft der christlichen Kirchen*, Paderborn, 1971.
53. "Gottesdienst in neuer Gestalt," *loc. cit.*, p. 114.
54. An extremely praiseworthy and noteworthy exception is constituted by the document "Gottesdienst heute und morgen" from the Lutheran Liturgical Conference of 1969, which was commended to the member churches of the United Evangelical Lutheran Church of Germany as a working paper. It belongs to the documents which are full of right statements and far-reaching, practicable suggestions and that are only waiting to be put into effect at last.
55. Theo Lehmann, "Ich passe nicht in die Kirche," in *Deutsches Pfarrerblatt*, 68, no. 12, June, 1968, pp. 439-443.

GÉRARD SIEGWALT

Chapter 6

Authority in the Church:

Its Institution and Constitution

The extreme complexity of our subject is evident right from the start.[1] What do we mean by authority, for instance, and what do we mean by the church? Before one even begins to enlarge upon these terms one will doubtless recognize the authority of God or of Christ *over* the church in the sense of his lordship or kingship, but can one equally refer to an authority *within* the church? Does this mean the Pope and the whole hierarchy (the Roman Catholic solution)? Or does it, more generally, mean the church ministry in particular, together with those who exercise it, whether these be pastors, members of church synods, perhaps the bishop, theological faculties or still others? It could also be that certain of these only are meant, to the exclusion of others, or again all of them but in differing degrees and perspectives (this is the usual "Protestant" solution; there are numerous variations, depending on whether various viewpoints have been amalgamated or, on the other hand, shown to be incompatible). Does authority simply mean Holy Scripture (biblicism), or does it mean the confession of faith (confessionalism)? Does authority rest upon direct inspiration through the Holy Ghost (enthusiastic spiritualism) or upon the inner voice of the heart (mysticism)? If, then, the definition of authority *in* the church poses problems, should we replace it by that of an authority *of* the church? How, though, is it possible to define this church which has authority, and of what does this authority consist? So we are back to the original question.

In view of all these queries it is obvious that any consideration of the problem of authority in the church must be systematic and dogmatic. This is all the more essential because the dual crisis of authority and of the church, and thus also of authority in the church, invites the theologian to such considerations. It is impossible to tackle this crisis, so much in evidence today, at a lesser price. The theologian who knows himself to be in the service of the church of Jesus Christ cannot be content with a mere repetition of pronouncements concerning the church and authority which are based upon a norm other than that given to the church.

Every systematic consideration must be historically informed. History constitutes the memory of dogmatics, and thus also of ecclesiology. The problem of authority in the church has great need of historical clarification, for the solution of this problem is greatly hampered by the mists of history and can be tackled only from the basis of historical knowledge. In the absence of such knowledge, systematic reflection would become ahistorical, and could not therefore be considered legitimate; as the church is not ahistorical. Our first task is therefore that of presenting the way in which the problem manifests itself historically.

I
An Outline of Doctrine and History

The only way in which it is possible to present this outline is in the manner of a general summary. The aim is to reveal the range of systematic problems by studying history. In other words, the perspective will not be simply descriptive, but critical. This seems to presuppose the operation of a theological norm. If such a norm is indeed made apparent through our historical approach, and if in this approach history is dealt with in a systematic manner, the development of this point of view for its own sake will have to be reserved for our conclusion. Here our procedure could be termed critical in a sense which is above all phenomenological: to present history critically means in this sense to present a critique of history through itself. It will thus be shown that history demands a systematic review of given themes, for history is not its own norm. Our approach to history in this outline is intended to bring into focus the themes of the problems envisaged. The interest shown in history is an interest in the manner in which the themes of our subject are revealed there, i.e., in discovering the mutually critical forms and arrangements in which these themes appear. This phenomenological process, however, serves to promote systematic theological reflection.

THE ROMAN CATHOLIC DOCTRINE OF AUTHORITY

This chapter makes no claim to originality. It is simply a question of examining classical Catholic doctrine. For this purpose our expose is based above all upon the thorough research of M. Schmaus.[2]

Classical Catholicism understands authority in the church as a power. It distinguishes in this regard between ordinary power (of order), which is the power to sustain, deepen, and maintain in the spiritual life in man, and juridical power, which directs the church as a spiritual society or community. The power of order belongs in its fullest sense to the bishops, in union with the bishop of Rome; it is conferred on priests, and in a lesser and graded sense, on the different subordinates of the presbyterial order (principally the diaconate). Juridical power belongs essentialy to the bishops, under the primacy of the Pope. Power in Catholicism, therefore, has a hierarchical structure.

The two powers mark a division (the result of previous historical evolution and a simple question of expediency) of the one unique power given by Christ to the twelve apostles. It consists of the power of the keys (Mt. 18:18; Jn. 20:21 ff) exercised in the proclamation of the gospel by Word and sacrament (Mt. 28:16 ff; Mk. 16:15 ff; 1 Cor. 11:23 ff; Lk. 22:15 ff).

It might appear that the power given to the apostles, and through them to their successors, is nothing other than what is called the power of order, i.e., the power of the priestly ministry. In fact, this power is not given directly by Christ to the ministerial priests (the presbyters), over the heads, so to speak, of the apostolic successors, but only to the apostles and their successors. The latter are thus invested with a power of direction in the church. They have the fullness of the power of order, but they also hold the pastoral power as heads of the church. They may, when the carrying out of the task assigned to them by Christ demands it, confer the power of order on others, particularly the ministerial priests. But their power of direction or jurisdiction is not exhausted by that. Exercised for the whole church, it is on the one hand judicial or disciplinary and, on the other, legislative or doctrinal. The disciplinary task is given with the power of the keys, in the sense that loosing and binding are enforceable acts: "to loose and to bind" in relation to the Kingdom of God can mean to receive into the Christian community and to exclude from it, but also to impose obligations and to abolish them. The apostles and their successors are the earthly guardians of the kingdom and the guides who lead the way there. But their disciplinary task presupposes the doctrinal task; for if they are the representatives of Christ and his kingdom on earth, if they open and shut the door of the house of God, they must be the ones to decide what is right before God. The church being a spiritual reality, her legislative task consists in proclaiming normatively the gospel and, ultimately, in defining dogmas, i.e., affirmations of faith necessary for salvation. This proclamation necessarily implies consequences on the disciplinary level.

It should be made clear that the apostles and their successors employ this power not in their own name, but because of their institution in this function by Christ and for him. By the juridical power given to the bishops, Christ himself governs his church, just as by sacerdotal power or the power of orders he constitutes his church in each of its members. In other words, obedience toward the holders of juridical power in the church is obedience to Christ, and disobedience toward them is disobedience to Christ. But that does not mean that the apostles and their successors take the place of Christ. They do not bind men to themselves, but to the One whom they serve. That is to say, their power is not final, but instrumental. Christ works through them in a mediated, rather than immediate, manner. Ecclesiastical power may not be substituted for Christ by those who wield it, nor can it be mistaken for him by believers.

The power which Jesus conferred on the Apostles singled out Peter. This is first of all the result of Mt. 16:17-19: ". . . you are Peter, and upon this rock I shall build my church. . . ." The text is understood as instituting Peter, not only his confession of Christ but himself personally, as charged with a mission: to be the vicar, the representative of Christ on earth. Peter is the foundation of the church: it finds its unity and its continuity in him and in his successors. In him, Christ, the ultimate foundation of the church appears (1 Cor. 3:11; Eph. 2:20). Peter holds the power of the keys, in communion with the other apostles, but at the same time as the one instituted by Christ as the foundation of the church: he is the ambassador plenipotentiary of Christ (cf. also Lk. 22:24-32; Jn. 21:15-19).

The apostles in general, and Peter in particular, have successors. Apostolic succession[3] is implied in the very institution of the apostolic college, even if that does not signify the limitation of its successors to twelve. The institution, by the apostles, of collaborators is not only due to the expansion of the church in space, but it also carries the sense of assuring its extension in time. Apostolic succession is not constituted simply by Holy Scriptures, for "Christ has not set the principle of subject matter but the principle of persons as the foundation of the church."[4] Christ did not found the church on Scriptures, but on the ministry of the apostles. The latter, in the apostolic succession, certainly finds its norm in apostolic preaching, but cannot be reduced to it. In fidelity to the apostolic gospel there is a succession of the apostolic ministry. It must be understood that apostolic succession also includes the succession of Peter in his primacy.

Since the apostolic power, transmitted from the apostles to their successors, is conferred by Christ, the hierarchical structure of the church is of divine institution. It includes, according to the will of Christ, the difference between clergy and laity; the former are not the masters, but the servants of the latter, in the service of Christ. They exercise their power from the perspective of the coming kingdom of God and salvation for men. Their power—a spiritual power—is juridically defined. The church has a "Rechtsgestalt," a juridical structure given to it by Christ. There is no question of setting in opposition law and Holy Spirit, the church as institution and the church as event; for the ecclesiastical ministry defined by apostolic power is instituted by Christ for his church which, in turn, lives by the gift of the Holy Spirit. The church is indissolubly both christological and pneumatological. As Christ did not institute ministries only, but also ministers, and as he did not only confer apostolic power, but sent the apostles, the personal aspect is related to the institutional aspect: Christ places persons in the apostolic ministry. In other words, the ministry is both impersonal—or rather, transpersonal—and personal. Church law defines the juridical structure of the church *for* persons, the holders of the churchly ministry, and in view of service *to* persons, men called to the faith.

Because of this personal element in the church's juridical structure, the structure is not immutable. It participates in history, just as persons do. If what it receives from Christ is divine, thus making church law a *jus divinum*, there is still a human, historical element involved; consequently, church law is a *jus humanum* or *mere ecclesiasticum*. The latter varies in history according to the needs of the moment. Thus church law is made up both of immutable principles established by Christ and of specific historical examples of these principles. The making explicit of these principles will be proportionately more valuable and less contingent the closer one comes to the divine law itself. The church, in the exercise of its mission—which means, first of all, the ecclesiastical ministry—never exists in any other way but historically, in the finiteness of a given time. Moreover, it participates in sin, like the rest of humanity, even if it lives as a result of the victory of Christ over sin. Thus it cannot be regarded either as relatively infallible (in regard to history) or as faultless; nevertheless, in its totality it is indefectible. Its indefectibility in history rests on the promise of Christ and on the church's communion with him, in the Holy Spirit. In this way the church is assured of a charismatic truth which guarantees its infallibility, not relatively, on the contingent level of history, but absolutely, on the spiritual level. This infallibility is concentrated in the ministry of Peter and his successors when the ministry is exercised in conformity with the mandate of Christ, in his name and for the whole church. It is a doctrinal or legislative infallibility, i.e., in the proclamation of the gospel under the form of dogma, the *lex fidei*. At the same time, it is not an infallibility on the judicial or disciplinary level, since the latter is subordinate to doctrine: doctrine, so to speak, informs discipline. But even on this level, the church and, hence, the churchly ministry are assumed of the indefectible support of the Holy Spirit; he is promised to those who, in the freedom of their power of decision, serve the Christ who established them in their ministry.[5]

A CRITICAL APPROACH TO ROMAN CATHOLIC DOCTRINE

The doctrine of classical Catholicism which we have just examined must be looked at with a critical eye on history. Before even posing the question of knowing whether this doctrine, which claims to be founded on the Bible interpreted by tradition, is actually scriptural, we must ask how it has been lived in history; how is it lived in reality? We have already pointed out the historical aspect of the divine juridical structure of the church. The question appears legitimate from the perspective of Roman Catholic doctrine itself: has historical reality sometimes warped or altered or at least obscured the theological or ecclesiological truth?

We have already noted that classical Catholicism understands authority in the church as a power. But this definition is not self-justifying; it is the fruit of history and hence cannot be dogmatized. On the contrary, it must be regarded critically.[6]

It is very significant that the *Dictionary of Catholic Theology* does not include an article on "authority," but refers us to the article on "power." The complete title of this article is once again very instructive: "Power of the Pope in the Temporal Order." In fact, the article treats precisely what it says. Thus it constitutes undeniably a unilateral presentation of things, as we can see from the preceding discussion of Roman Catholic doctrine. First of all, the Pope is not the only one to have power in the church; papal primacy is written into episcopal collegiality; the Pope is the servant of the servants of Christ. Second, the Pope not only has a power in the temporal order: his juridical power is essentially a power in the church, and only accidentally a power in the world. Moreover, he has the ordinary power which belongs to every bishop and which is distinct from the juridical power, as we have said. The article in question is no less symptomatic: the definition of papal authority (and that of the bishops) as power is a consequence of the introduction, into theology and the church, of the ideology of temporal law and the state. It is because of the legalizing—in the sense of temporal law—and the sociologizing of theology and the church that not only did church-state conflicts become unavoidable (the church continually appearing and representing itself as a state within a state), but even more, the power of the Pope—and the bishops—was understood within the church itself as a juridical power bordering on and gradually approaching the temporal. The power of the Pope in the temporal order is a sign of the collusion between church and state; at the same time, it is the other side of the conception of authority in the church as a power, or rather, this power is the other side (or the consequence) of the determination of theology by temporal law and of the church by the State. It might be added that the definition of priestly authority in terms of power results from the same process.

This process combines two aspects: the legalization of ecclesiology in the sense of temporal law and the sociologization of the church. It begins, historically speaking, quite early. The tendency towards "statehood" and, hence, the recognized sociologization of the church begins with the edict of Milan (313), under Constantine. After the church became a state religion, a "power" (a term which is now appropriate, since it was extended from the state to the church) was officially recognized by the state as pertaining to the church; i.e., to the hierarchy and primarily to the Pope: spirtual power. In the church's exercise of the spiritual power given it by the state as its temporal subject, power conflicts manifested themselves little by little between them; these ultimately led to the church's affirmation of the supremacy of spiritual power (or the sword) over the temporal sword, of the *sacerdotium* over the *imperium*. This hierarchical theory reached its fullest expression in the Bull *Unam Sanctam* of Boniface VIII (1302). It affirmed that "the two swords belong to the power of the church, both the spiritual and the temporal. But the latter must be wielded for the church, the former by the church; the former by the priest, the latter by kings and knights, according to the consent and will of the priest."[8] The extension of the notion of power, whose natural domain is law and the state, to theology and to the church, explains this conclusion.,

The Middle Ages, followed by the sixteenth century, the French Revolution of 1789, and subsequent periods have gradually reduced, if not destroyed, the pretensions of the church, i.e., principally, of the papacy (and the entire hierarchy) to exercise a power in the temporal order (we are not speaking here of the civil principality of the Pope, the pontifical state). This loss of power has led the Roman Catholic Church to reflect anew on the nature of authority. But even if this authority is henceforth understood as spiritual authority, it will still continue to be designated as a power. In addition, *the problem of the relationship between spiritual authority and power* does not appear clear.[9] It is, in fact, a double problem: first of all it is the problem of the relation between spiritual authority and the juridical implications of that authority, a problem which arises when the spiritual authority is contested, either in a conflict between the holders of ecclesiastical authority in the exercise of their ministry, or in a challenge by those over whom they fulfill their function. In either case, since the authority is spiritual, i.e., in the service of the authority of Christ over the church, and since this authority is represented only in a mediated fashion, it cannot directly be decided, "To decide" is, in effect, a direct juridical act, one which is enforceable, while the exercise of spiritual authority is not direct, consisting rather of reference to Christ and of the proclamation of the gospel; for thus are hearts judged. Hence, the necessity of law arises as soon as there is a need to decide in cases of litigation. In traditional language one could say that church law must protect divine law. But the notion of divine law is an unfortunate one because of the inevitable human juridical understanding which it calls to mind. We, therefore, prefer to speak of spiritual authority on the one hand, and of church law on the other. The law must protect spiritual authority.

The spiritual authority established by Christ contains a juridical aspect from the very fact of its institution, certainly not in its content, which is spiritual and could not be dealt with in terms of law, but in its form. Church law is a necessary consequence of the institution of the ecclesiastical ministry by Christ. It does not establish this authority, but delimits it.

The second aspect of the problem of spiritual authority and power concerns the link between the church and the state. This problem has, in its turn, a double sense, since it relates both to the relation between spiritual authority and temporal power, and to that between the judicial implications of spiritual authority (hence, church law) and temporal law. As far as the first aspect is concerned, it can be defined only in the sense of a total freedom of the church in obedience to Christ on the one hand, and a critical submission to the state in conformity to the will of God on the other. The state, for its part, certainly cannot recognize what constitutes the church as spiritual reality; rather, there is a recognition of religious freedom, paralleled by a demand for loyalty from the church towards the state which recognizes this religious liberty. As for the second aspect, the strict separation of competencies, i.e., of powers, must be affirmed. In case of dispute, since church law protects a spiritual authority while temporal law delimits a coercive power, temporal law will be able executively to condemn what church law absolves, and church law will be able morally to indict what temporal law absolves.

The absence of clarification on this problem of the relationship between spiritual authority and power explains the ambiguity in classical Roman Catholic ecclesiology. This latter is quite clear: while accepting for better or worse the stripping of all temporal power imposed upon it by history, the Roman Catholic Church has certainly not renounced what we shall see to be natural and legitimate, the affirmation of the primacy of the Pope and, in a more general way, the spiritual authority of the ecclesiastical ministry *in the church*; what is neither natural nor legitimate is that the church should consider this authority as a juridical power. The latter signals a confusion of the spiritual and the juridical, which certainly refer to each other, but are not identical; the juridical is subordinate to the spiritual and the spiritual is delimited juridically.[10] The notions of power and the spiritual are not on the same level: if it is true, as we have said, that the spiritual implies a power, or authority a law, then the spiritual is not this power and authority is not this law. To

associate them to the point of identity is to confound the two levels
and to alter the nature both of spiritual authority and of juridical
power. Although they are not contradictory, the concepts of "power"
and of the "spiritual" are, nevertheless, not of the same nature, since
a power is always enforceable, whether in the church or in the state.[11]
This does not mean to say that the means employed by the church
and by the state are the same—they are most certainly different by
reason of the very different natures of the church, a spiritual reality,
and the state, a political reality; on the contrary, on the spiritual
level there is no coercion, except in the violation of conscience, no
matter what the means; rather, there is a free acceptance of authority
recognized as such, and understood as spiritual authority, i.e., as
pointing beyond itself to the author of spiritual or divine life. If
the authority of the ecclesiastical ministry is defined as a power, it is
then not simply spiritual, but, as a power, it is something else again:
at that moment the ecclesiastical ministry runs the risk of confronting man not with God, but with himself; of not proclaiming the
liberating Word of God, but of exerting pressure. This risk is
greater when it is not clear that the juridical aspect of the ecclesiastical ministry is simply the result of its spiritual aspect. Then the
different natures of church law and temporal law are blurred and
"spiritual power" is no longer clearly distinguishable from temporal
power. "Spiritual power" can, then, very easily become an actual
second temporal power, disguised as a spiritual one.

Moreover, it is necessary to say that the problem of the relationship between spirtual authority and church law appears in Catholicism itself, namely, in the distinction it establishes between the
"power" exercised over the heart—concerning the guidance of consciences or souls—and that directed towards external matters. This
distinction certainly manifests all the ambiguity of traditional Catholic ecclesiology: on the one hand the power is spiritual, in the case
of the care of souls; on the other hand, from the very fact that spiritual authority is defined as a power, it cannot be limited to the
conscience, for all power is immediate and enforceable. But is it
adequate to label as juridical this "power" exercised over the conscience, and is it adequate to qualify as spiritual this power as it is
exercised over external actions? In effect, if the juridical power of
the hierarchy is understood in the sense of the power of keys, as it
has been defined, it cannot be a juridical power; and if it is understood as different from the power of keys, it cannot bear on our

consciences if by that we mean, in a general sense, the complete man as a spiritual being. It must then be limited to external behavior. Hence the juridical power of the ecclesiastical ministry is legitimately exercised only in service to spiritual authority, over which it has no power.

In this way the question of the nature of the authority of the ecclesiastical ministry is clarified in principle.

The fact that Catholicism distinguishes between juridical power and ordinary power is well known. The latter, the *potestas ordinis,* is the power of the *ordo presbyterorum,*[12] i.e., of the priesthood or the sacerdotal ministry. The *ordo* is related to the eucharist; it is, according to the definition of the Council of Trent,[13] the "power to consecrate, to offer, and to distribute the body and the blood of Christ." But this power is seen in relation to the power of the keys, even if the connection between the power of eucharistic consecration and the *potestas clavis* is not specified. In addition, the definition cited adds "the power to remit and to retain sins." Thus, since for Catholicism the latter power is not only exercised in a general way in preaching the Word and administering the sacraments, but also in a specific way in the sacrament of penance, the power of order participates, on its level, i.e., the level of the sacerdotal ministry, in the *potestas jurisdictionis.* In other words, there is a juridical power implied in the ordinary power. But this power is limited to the level of conscience. As for the juridical power, it belongs to the Pope and the bishops. It is understood, as we have seen, as a governmental-disciplinary and doctrinal-legislative power. The latter is the power to watch over revelation, to transmit it and to explain it; the former is the power to guide the church as a society. The question is then the following: is this conception of the ecclesiastical ministry in conformity with the spiritual nature of authority?

It can immediately be seen that the two aspects of the juridical power of the ecclesiastical ministry are not on the same level. If the authority of the ecclesiastical ministry is spiritual, as we have said, and if it is possible to speak legitimately of ecclesiastical "power" only on a second level—that of the juridical implications of spiritual authority—then the relationship between the two aspects of "juridical power" must be just this: the power belonging to the ecclesiastical ministry, which is not a power but a mission-giving authority on behalf of Christ and his church, is "doctrinal power." This is true under the condition that we define doctrine, in distinction to the

oral proclamation of the Word such as it is performed by the ordinary ecclesiastical ministry, as a solemn proclamation, i.e., normative
of the church's gospel as such. Such a proclamation can be mediate
only, since it is necessarily the action of the church in obedience to
Christ, but not directly or immediately the action of Christ himself;
it is, in other words, *norma normata*, not *norma normans*. As far as
governmental-disciplinary power is concerned, its is a power and
should therefore be characterized as improper or foreign to the doctrinal authority of the ecclesiastical ministry: it is not, to use the
words of Luther, the *opus proprium* of the ecclesiastical ministry,
but its *opus alienum*. As implied by the *opus proprium*, governmental-disciplinary power is not improper in a pejorative sense, but
in the sense that it is not the primary proper mission of the ecclesias-
tcal ministry.

One might then say—thus raising anew the impact of temporal
law on traditional Roman Catholic ecclesiology—that classical Catholicism inverts the relationship between the doctrinal and governmental aspects of the ecclesiastical ministry; the doctrinal magisterium of the Pope and the bishops is subsumed, in effect, under
their governmental power: the *Corpus Juris Canonici* (C.I.C.) recognizes only the *potestas jurisdictionis* on the one hand, the *potestas
ordinis* on the other.[14] Doctrinal "power" (*potestas magisterii*) appears there as one particular aspect of the *potestas jurisdictionis*.
The latter is exercised in a governmental-disciplinary manner and
also, in a second way, doctrinally. Furthermore, even though this
second, doctrinal power is far from being considered secondary, it
constitutes the doctrinal and theological content of the *potestas
jurisdictionis*. Doctrinal magisterium refers to revelation, which
founded the church and which the church is obliged to spread. Because of the church's hierarchical structure it is the papacy and the
episcocapy to whom this task falls primarily. In addition, the juridical power given by Christ to Peter and the apostles, as well as to
their successors, is at the same time a *potestas magisterii*. The latter,
after a long evolution, has come to be defined not only in the sense
of the magisterial primacy of Peter (included in and given with his
juridical primacy), but also in the sense of the infallible magisterium
of the Roman Pontiff. The dogma of pontifical infallibility was
promulgated by the first Vatican Council in 1870.[15] It is important
to note that the Pope's infallibility where doctrinal material is concerned is derived from his juridical primacy.

There is, however, another way in which one can understand the relationship between governmental power and doctrinal power, in the sense of the above-mentioned evolution. We have already drawn attention to the collapse of the temporal pretensions of the church: it no longer really exercises power in the temporal order. Because of the interdependence between the definition of the authority of the ecclesiastical ministry as juridical power and temporal law, one could ask oneself whether the crisis of temporal power of the church is not simply the first stage of a more profound crisis, affecting the governmental-juridical power of the ecclesiastical ministry itself. This power is related to temporal law to such a degree, even in its very conception, that the questioning of what is temporal in the church cannot fail to affect it. In fact, the present contesting of the governmental "power" of the ecclesiastical ministry is a clear sign of this extension. The following question then has to be answered: if the church has progressively renounced the hierocratic theory as far as the state is concerned (in the sense we have suggested), should it not equally renounce it as far as the primacy of the juridical over the doctrinal is concerned? What would then remain of the recognized power of the Pope (and the bishops) is the magisterium.

It certainly seems that Vatican I prepared, in a way, a concentration of the juridical power of the Pope on the doctrinal aspect. The doctrinal aspect appears at the outset as the focus or center of papal power. Vatican I can be considered, first of all, as a sign of the renunciation of the hierocratic theory concerning the traditional relationship of the "spiritual" and the "temporal," since juridical power at the outset is limited to the church. Secondly, the Council represents the crystallization of the concept of authority as power, since it constitutes, properly speaking, a solemn dogmatization of this concept. Finally, it appears as the beginning of an understanding which centers juridical power in the doctrinal magisterium. Seen in this way, Vatican I prepared the way for a certain "detemporalization," i.e., a desociologization, but not yet a real dejuridization, of the Roman Catholic Church. This preparation may not have been apparent to the Council, but it is strikingly clear in retrospect.

This evolution was confirmed by Vatican II. Until then the church had very largely laid claim to the concept of the double office of the church (*munus duplex*), principally regarding the ecclesiastical ministry, its governmental-juridical office and its ordinary sacerdotal office. This conception was related to a similar understanding of the action of Christ, royal on the one hand, priestly on the other. Now, however, the church has adopted the conception of the triple office (*triplex munus*) : the royal office, the priestly office, and the prophetic office. This theory is built around the triple office of Christ. On the level of the hierarchy, the papacy and the episcopacy, the prophetic office designates the *potestas magisterii*. This magisterial power is henceforth placed on the same level as governmental power and priestly power. It appears above all in the texts of Vatican II in the enumeration of the three functions.

The substitution of the doctrine of the triple office for that of the double office had been developing in Catholic theology from the eighteenth century onward, undoubtedly under the influence of Calvin, who adopted it as his own, and from whom it was equally able to penetrate into the Lutheran orthodoxy of the seventeenth century.[16] Vatican II marks an evident approach towards Protestant theology in this respect. But Calvinist doctrine cannot be considered theologically sound, and hence it is difficult to see a satisfactory outcome in the replacement of the doctrine of the *munus duplex* by that of the *munus triplex* in contemporary Catholicism. The theory of the triple office undoubtedly has pedagogical value: the work of Christ is grouped under the rubrics of the three Old Testament ministries: priest, king, and prophet. The distinction is then extented to the mission of the church, and first of all specifically to the ministry in it; this extension is based on the indissoluble bond between chistology and ecclesiology, i.e., the fact that the church is a sign of Christ. Applied to the ecclesiastical ministry, the doctrine of the three offices leads to a distinction between the function of teaching (the prophetic function), the function of administering the sacraments (the priestly function) and the function of governing (the royal function). But what *theological* justification is there for this distinction? Why is the priestly function reduced to the administration of the sacraments? How does the prophetic function differ from the royal? Where is the unity in the three functions? Does it lie in the fact that they are fulfilled by the same Christ, and therefore by the same church and the same ecclesiastical ministry? In our discussion of the relationship between the govermnental and doctrinal offices of the ecclesiastical ministry, the question boils down to this: How does Christ exercise his royalty? To be precise, since it is not a matter of his cosmic royalty as creator, but his royalty as redeemer, we are talking about his royalty as Savior. That is what constitutes his authority. It is the authority of the Servant who gives himself as an offering to God for the salvation of men. The work of Jesus Christ is a priestly work: it ends in his death on the Cross. The preaching of Jesus, his miracles, give light and meaning to this priestly work; better yet, they are the radiance emitted by the priestly person of Christ, who is one with his work. Christ is king because he is high priest. His authority springs from his self-giving to God, and from his giving of himself for the salvation of men as Son of the Father, i.e., in doing the work of God. The authority or the royalty of the high priest is that of a person: because of this fact, it is a spiritual authority calling men to faith. This is true both for the earthly condition of Jesus Christ and for his resurrected condition, elevated to the right hand of the Father. The exercise of the royalty or authority of Christ is carried out in the same way in both cases: as priestly service. The royalty of Christ is a priestly royalty. This personal royalty is exercised through the Word (in the fullest sense, designating oral preaching of the gospel and administration of the sacraments) for the faith. That is to say, in our question concerning the double or triple character of the offices of Christ and thus the offices of the church and of its ecclesiastical ministry that the royalty of Christ does not constitute an office, properly speaking, but rather, it designates the quality or the authority of Christ as Son of the Father. Such an interpretation immediately undermines the theory of the *munus triplex*. Moreover, the royalty or the authority of Christ is his authority as Servant or high priest. This is the sole function of Christ: i.e., that of a priest. This argues against the theory of the *munus duplex*. The royalty of Christ is the royalty of the high priest: it is salvific. It is signified in the case of the historical Jesus by the unity of his preaching and his miracles, and it is exercised in the church through the unity of Word and sacrament. Christ exercises his priestly royalty in the preaching of the gospel and the administration of the sacraments, i.e., through the Word. There is only one office of Christ: that of priestly king; but this office is improperly designated either as prophetic office or as containing both the prophetic and priestly aspects. In the first case, we must ask if prophecy includes the administration of the sacraments; in the second, the question is in what way the oral proclamation of the gospel, designated as prophecy, is not a priestly activity, and how can the administration of the sacraments be dissociated from the spoken

Word? The churchly ministry, regardless of its diversifications (to which we must return), can fundamentally be one alone: the ministry of the Word and the sacraments or, according to the Catholic distinction, the ordinary, priestly, ministry, inasmuch as it implies the oral preaching of the Word. There is, if we can use the terms, one single *potestas* given by Christ to his apostles and their successors: the *potestas ordinis* which includes the *potestas magisterii* in the sense of the oral proclamation of the gospel.

In the light of these developments, the conclusion at first seems inevitable that the evolution we have described, moving in the direction of an ever-greater emphasis on the doctrinal aspect of the ecclesiastical ministry, must ultimately lead to the eviction of the juridical aspect and the limitation of the doctrinal element to the ordinary ministry, and thus to the prophetic aspect vis-à-vis the doctrinal. Such a conclusion would be erroneous in several respects. On the one hand, we have already recognized the place of the juridical in the church: church law is not only legitimate, but also necessary; however, it comes second to the real mission of the church and the ecclesiastical ministry. On the other hand, the oral proclamation of the gospel by the ordinary ministry does not exhaust the *"potestas magisterii."* The New Testament, and Paul in particular, gives to prophecy, by which is meant the actualization of the gospel *kerygma*, the double form of paraclesis (*paraklesis*) and teaching (*didaskalia*) ;[17] we might say that it is prophetic-paracletic and doctrinal. The gospel has a doctrinal element which cannot be overlooked. But it is important to see that this aspect may not be limited to the ordinary ministry, otherwise this ministry becomes the judge of the gospel, and hence of the Truth. The church, in its totality is certainly not the judge of the Truth, since it does not possess Truth, but is constituted by it and at its service. But the church delimits the spiritual authority of the churchly ministry. There is a response of the church *as church* to the gospel, and there is the response of each particular minister and each Christian within the church.[18] The response of the church as such takes the form of dogma and, in a general way, church doctrine. The only way to announce the gospel in an ecclesiastical manner, i.e., within the church's service to Christ, is under the control of church doctrine. Not that this doctrine would be anything other than *norma normata;* it is not the gospel itself. As the response of the church, it does not deprive the gospel of its freedom as it is proclaimed by the ordinary ecclesiastical ministry, but assures this freedom and gives it its value. So if doctrine in this sense is second in relation to the gospel, but is at the same time implied by it (just as church law is second in relation to the mission of the churchly ministry), then the elaboration of doctrine and the fixing of church law are of necessity the work of the ecclesiastical ministry. Since it occupies a second rank, this ministry ought to be distinguished from the ordinary ministry of the Word and the sacraments; at the same time, it should be coordinated with the latter as its necessary complement. Even though the designation of this form of ecclesiastical ministry as juridical ministry recalls our earlier objections, its legitimacy and its necessity may not be disputed in the sense defined. It is thus possible to speak both of legislative-doctrinal and of governmental-disciplinary aspects of the second ecclesiastical ministry.

But a problem remains: we have relegated what is termed the juridical ministry to the level of the second ecclesiastical ministry, while recognizing both doctrinal and governmental aspects in it. The relationship between this form of ecclesiastical ministry and the ordinary ministry was defined in terms of their coordination, and more precisely their complementarity. The doctrinal and governmental ministry was seen to be in the service of the ministry of the Word and sacrament (the latter being assured in the former). Consequently, the priority over the ordinary ministry attributed in Catholicism to the so-called juridical ministry in its double doctrinal and governmental aspect does not seem due only to the juridicalization, in the sense of temporal law, of ecclesiology, but seems also to cling to a reminiscence of the *royal* character of the ecclesiastical ministry. But it follows from what we said about the royalty of Christ that this royalty does not concern a particular aspect of the ecclesiastical ministry, even the juridical aspect, but concerns the ecclesiastical ministry as such. It concerns, first of all, the ordinary ecclesiastical ministry, particularly that of the Word and the sacraments, and secondly, the general, doctrinal and governmental ecclesiastical ministry. The royal character of the ecclesiastical ministry expresses, on both levels, that it is invested with the authority of Christ, i.e., that on both levels it is instituted by him and carries his authority wherever it is exercised in submission to him.

The critical approach to Roman Catholic doctrine, starting from history, has thus led to a result which in a Protestant, and particularly in a Lutheran, theological perspective might be surprising. For whatever reserves and even rejections have been tendered vis-à-vis classical Catholic doctrine, and whatever developments of Catholicism in connection with Vatican II have been seen to surmount certain earlier, contestable emphases, we cannot isolate the Catholicism of Vatican II from classical Catholicism; rather, we find in both, i.e., in historical Catholicism as it emerged at Vatican II, certain themes which should not be lost. The "ecumenical opening" of conciliary Catholicism ought not to be interpreted unilaterally as a rejection of classical Catholicism, or as a "protestantization" of Catholicism. If this "opening" is undeniable, if the influence not only of Protestant, but also of Orthodox theology on contemporary Catholicism is clear, and if, moreover, classical Catholicism has divested itself, either in part or more deeply, of certain vulnerable historical aspects, it still remains no less faithful to the affirmation which constitutes it, properly speaking, as Catholicism: the hierarchical structure of the church which is maintained to have been instituted by Christ.

If we have largely taken exception to the historical comprehension of this structure, we, nevertheless, recognize, even before informing ourselves further, the ecclesiological justification behind the affirmation of the ministerial structure of the church. This recognition does not exclude the characterization of this structure as hierarchical, on the condition that we define this hierarchy in terms not of power, but of service, as reciprocal order and subordination, within the ecclesiastical ministry, of both the first specific ministry, that of the Word and Sacraments, and the second, general ministry of doctrine and government, within the one service of Christ. The result leads to the conclusion that the hierarchical ministerial structure of the church is not a factor in the ecclesial division between the Roman Catholic Church and any Protestant church subscribing to the result enunciated. In making this conclusion, we must take into account the fact that it implies the recognition of the ecclesiality of the Roman Catholic Church to the extent (i.e., in the hypothesis) that in it it recognizes itself as essentially guaranteed in its dogmatic self-comprehension. But is this result acceptable to a Protestant, and particularly to a Lutheran, theological perspective? Is it possible to recognize the statute for this second, doctrinal and governmental ministry in the episcopacy, for the entire church? And it is possible to recognize, within the episcopacy, a papal primacy? Would not such a recognition be a self-denial, i.e., a negation of the very principle of the Reformation?

II
Systematic-Theological Reflection

In the course of the preceding study we have spelled out a provisional result which constitutes the question for this second part. This result is contained in the affirmation of a hierarchical ministerial structure for the church, hierarchy being understood in the sense of service, i.e. (as we shall see), of responsibility. We have distinguished two poles in the ecclesiastical ministry: the first, or ordinary ministry (in the sense of *ordo*), is that of preaching the Word and administering the sacraments. We might call this the ministry of edification. The second, doctrinal and governmental ministry, we shall term a ministry of unity. The question then arises: what is the scriptural base for this distinction?

But we cannot attack this question at once, for the problem of the ecclesiastical ministry is not itself the first problem. That does not mean that it is secondary. Just as the ministry of unity is second in relation to the ministry of the Word and sacraments without being subordinated to it, but is precisely and adequately coordinated in it, in a similar way the problem of the ecclesiastical ministry (referring to the structure or the constitution of the church) is second in relation to the problem of what calls into both the church in its entirety and the ecclesiastical ministry in particular. In effect, the ecclesiastical ministry responds to the question of how the church becomes the church. But this question raises another: through what agency does the church become the church? It could also be asked: who is the author of the church, i.e., in the etymological sense of the word, from which is derived the word "authority": who makes it exist and grow (*augere*)?[19] The problem is that of authority, thus giving us the two terms of our subject: authority in the church and its constitution. The. word "constitution" is taken, first of all, in the active sense, i.e., that of the Latin words which end in *-tio*: it refers to the manner in which this authority is constituted. The result of this operation might also be called "constitution," but the latter must finally be seen as the result of a dynamic process and must always be grasped as such, and never separately from this process; if not, the result (the constitution) becomes frozen and petrified, and a gap is introduced between constitution as dynamic process on the one hand, and constitution as institution on the other. The latter then tends to dominate the process and to force its submission, i.e., to move from its legitimate second place to the first. In this way the dynamic process of the constitution of authority is slowed down and sometimes stopped. But the organization of the church is only legitimate as an expression of the organ which it serves. When it ceases to be a servant and becomes the master, it interposes itself between the organ and its rightful function. It is then no longer theonomous but tends to make the theonomous organ heteronomous in submitting it to a law other than its own. In other words, even if the two aspects of authority and constitution are indissoluble, the second can be treated only in relation to and as dependent on the first.

The subject of this section thus concerns two questions: As a result of what, and how, does the church come into existence? Each part must be treated according to its specificity, and the close relationship between the two must be demonstrated.

AS A RESULT OF WHAT DOES THE CHURCH COME INTO EXISTENCE?

This first question poses the *problem of authority*. It is Christ who calls the church into being, and it is the gospel which causes its growth. This distinction between Christ and the gospel corresponds to that between the source and the content of the gospel (Christ) on the one hand, and the form in which Christ attests and offers himself (the gospel understood as Word and sacrament) on the other.

This distinction appears as early as Eph. 2:20: "You are built upon the foundation laid by the apostles and prophets, and Christ Jesus himself is the foundation-stone." Since we have Christ only in this gospel form (even if in giving himself in it completely, he simultaneously transcends it), we can simply say that it is through the gospel that the church becomes the church. In other words, there is no church other than the apostolic church. This word is understood in the dogmatic sense which it also has in the Nicene Creed (*Credo unam sanctam catholicam et apostolicam ecclesiam*) where it means: founded on the apostolic gospel. The "missionary" sense of the word—the church is apostolic inasmuch as it is sent—is dependent upon the first sense indicated: the church cannot be missionary except as a church founded on the apostolic gospel. The question of authority, therefore, concerns the apostolicity of the Church.

This is why the authority in question is not that of the church itself, for the church does not exist by itself. Even if one can speak in a derivative sense of the authority *of* the church, as we shall see, the problem of authority is first and fundamentally that of authority *over* the church.

1. The authority of Christ over the church: Its nature.

It follows that he who has authority over the church, i.e., he who causes the church to be and to grow, is God or Christ. If there is an authority *of* the church and also an authority *in* the church, it comes from this source and, if it is legitimate, only from it. But we cannot be satisfied with this purely formal affirmation that Christ has authority over the church. The decisive question here concerns the nature of that authority, since it determines the nature both of the authority of the church and of authority in the church. Thus, in what does the authority of Christ consist?

We will limit ourselves to a few central affirmations.[20]

a) The authority (*exousia*) of Jesus manifests and imposes itself as much in his preaching and teaching (Mk. 1:22) as in the miracles he performs (Mk. 1:27) and the forgiveness of sins he offers as sovereign (Mk. 2:10). Jesus' authority, however, is not coercive; if it is imposed, it is as personal authority which should be freely recognized in faith. (Mk. 8:27 ff; 11:27 ff) .

b) The authority of Jesus is qualified by its content. The content is that of a mission. Jesus is the One sent by God (Heb. 3:1; Jn. 3:17, 34; 17:3); as such, he received an authorization (*Bevollmächtigung*) from the God who sent him.[21]

c) The mission of Jesus is that of a savior: he is sent for the salvation of the world. The authority of Jesus is the authority of the Savior; he is Lord because he is Redeemer. Jesus is the gift of God to men. As such, he is not authoritarian but appeals to the freedom of man. The authority of Jesus is therefore an authority *a contrario*, an authority which is the absence of authority, in the sense of power or might; his authority is that of humility or suffering, the authority of the Crucified (Phil. 2:5 ff) . It is, as we have seen, the priestly authority of the Servant of Yahweh.

d) This is true both of the earthly and of the heavenly condition of Jesus. Raised to the right hand of the Father who, unlike the earthly Jesus, has the power of his authority (Mt. 28:18; Phil. 2:9 ff), Christ exercises it sacerdotally (Heb. 7:24 f). Just as the almighty power of God is recognized from the experience of the authority of his redemptive love, so the cosmic kingship of Jesus also appears through the recognition of his saving kingship (Jn. 1:1 ff; Col. 1:16 ff; Heb. 1:1 ff).

e) The saving character of Jesus is manifested in its fruits, which verify what was said about the nature of Jesus' authority. These fruits are: 1. Faith, i.e., the recognition of the authority of Jesus, as opposed to nonfaith. In this double contrary effect (faith on the one hand, nonfaith on the other) the personal character of Jesus' authority is made manifest: it is the authority of a person which calls forth a personal response. In the free response to Jesus, man finds his true freedom (Jn. 8:36; Rom. 8:21). 2. The church. The authority of Jesus is not only recognized in faith; it also gathers believers around him. The gathering authority of Jesus breaks forth with the gift of the Holy Spirit at Pentecost.

We are thus led to speak of the church. Our subject is clear: authority *in* the church. But there is no direct relationship between the authority of Christ over the church and authority in the church, since the latter depends both on Christ and on the church, as we shall see. Before speaking of authority in the church, it is therefore necessary to speak of the reality of the church as it is constituted by the authority of Christ and as it is thus itself invested with authority. The authority of Christ over the church engenders the authority *of* the church. It is in the church as characterized and endowed with authority that authority is exercised in the sense in which we will refer to it in Section 3.

2. *The authority of the church, bearer of the authority of Christ in the world.*

Once again, we will content ourselves with a few essential affirmations.[22]

a) The church does not have independent authority. Its authority can be derived only from that of Christ: it exists in the absence of authority proper. The authority of the church consists entirely in submission to the authority of Christ: it is in this submission that the authority of Christ becomes transparent through the church and that the church becomes the bearer of the authority of Christ.

b) The church participates in the being and the mission of Christ; hence it participates in the royal priesthood of Christ. This is derived especially from 1 Pt. 2:4-10. The royal priesthood of the church is defined as consisting in its self-offering to God, which can be done only by following Christ, and in its proclamation of the great deeds of Christ, which accompanies and gives meaning to its self-offering.

c) Hence the church becomes the sacramental sign of Christ on earth and of the saving plan of God. This also means that it becomes a sign of contradiction, as it follows Christ and abides in him (1 Pt. 2:4 ff). The struggle of the church, understood as true church, is always simultaneously the struggle of Christ through the struggle of the church itself.

d) Apropos of this struggle it can be said that: The struggle of the church as bearer of the authority of Christ is the normal condition of the church (Mt. 10:24 f; Mk. 8:34). Jesus, in his mission and in the face of struggle, has only one weapon: obedience to God. The weapon by which Christ challenged and challenges the attack leveled against him is also the only (legitimate) weapon of the church.

e) The church is a community in which individuals are referred directly to Christ and at the same time, by him, to each other. This means that the authority of the church is a community authority. Community authority must be defined as dialogical, i.e., becoming concrete in the dialogue between different individuals in the midst of the church community or between different church communities.[23]

3. Authority in the Church.

The problem of the authority *of* the church, about which we have just spoken, does not respond to the question of knowing as a result of *what* the church becomes the church, but to that of the identity of this church which comes into being through the authority of Christ over it. The church itself shares in the authority of Christ by submitting itself to him. Thus the development of the theme of the authority of the church involves a reflection not directly relevant to the subject. But this reflection was necessary in view of the discussion of authority in the church, since this second authority is an authority in the church which already exists. In this sense the church is preexistant to that which creates authority in it. But at the same time the church exists only by virtue of the authority in it: the latter is, in this sense, preexistant to the church. The authority *of* the church and authority *in* the church are thus indissolubly linked. They are simultaneous.

Like the authority *of* the church, authority *in* the church is second to the authority of Christ over it. But if the first form of authority characterizes the church in its being, the second characterizes it according to that which gives it being. Both of these are responses to the authority of Christ, but the second is the way in which the authority of Christ over the church sustains the church. We have already seen that Christ exercises his authority over the church by the Word (in the sense of both oral preaching of the gospel and administration of the sacraments). Authority in the church pertains to the space made by and in the church for the Word. It is, under this heading, an ecclesial act. But this act is sustained by Christ: the church is led by the authority of Christ. His authority sustains not only the church by making it the carrier of his authority, but also authority within the church.

The recognition by the church of the authority of Christ over it constitutes authority within the church. In other words, there is an authority in the church which is derived from the authority of Christ over it. The authority in the church is given by the church's response to Christ's authority over it. Hence, authority in the church (as recognition of the authority of Christ over it) must be seen as making Christ's authority concrete. The one does not exist without the other. Christ and the apostolic gospel, as authority over the Church, even if they transcend history, do not exist other than in, with, and under history. We have neither Christ nor the gospel outside of the response given to them. Even the scriptural witness and, hence, the apostolic gospel are a response to the Word which is Christ.[24] But the response which constitutes the apostolic gospel is given prior to that of which we are speaking and which is second to it. We have Christ or the apostolic gospel only in the historical response given by the church and based on the foundation of Scripture. What is this response understood as being more than the response of faith, i.e., that of the individual and of the church but also as that same faith as it takes ecclesial form and bearing? The response is, on the one hand, preaching, i.e., the constant transmission and actualization of the gospel in the oral proclamation and the administration of the sacraments; on the other hand, it is the confession of faith as the response of the church to preaching. The difference between the response of preaching and the response of the confession of faith is the fact that the first establishes the second.

The response of preaching, i.e., of the transmission and actualization of the apostolic gospel by the Word and sacraments, is authority, first of all, in the church, because this is the way the church comes into being. It comes into being through Christ as he gives himself and actualizes himself in the Word and sacraments; i.e., as he gives himself and actualizes himself in the response which, on the part of the church, constitutes the preaching of the gospel, and as he sustains that response. But since preaching demands a response, it can never render itself absolute. The response is certainly *necessary*, in the sense that Christ or the apostolic gospel uses it to lead the church by his proper authority; but this response necessarily remains referred dialectically to Christ and to the apostolic gospel as constituting authority over the church. Even though we have Christ and the apostolic gospel only in, with, and under history, they manifest themselves there precisely as a norm, and therefore remain sovereign over all response given to them. It is because of this dialectical relationship between Christ and the apostolic gospel as authority *over* the church, and preaching, in its character of response, as authority *in* the church, that a constant control is necessary by the church itself of the faithfulness of the response which it gives in preaching. The confession of faith constitutes this control. In effect, as ecclesial response to Christ and the preaching of the gospel, it is secondary to the gospel. In the same way as the church responds to the apostolic gospel in preaching, it controls its preaching, i.e., its understanding of the gospel as it is expressed in preaching by the norm of the gospel. Although second to preaching, the confession of faith as verification of the truth of the preaching of the gospel is also normative for preaching, since it accentuates the normative character of the apostolic gospel vis-à-vis preaching. There is, therefore, a dialectical relationship between preaching and the confession of faith. But the confession of faith is only secondarily normative; it is *norma normata*. One could certainly also say that preaching is secondary, and that it should not be substituted for Christ and the apostolic gospel themselves. This ensues that neither of these responses can be taken as absolute. It is the "relative" character which is expressed in the necessary reference of one to the other, without the reference of preaching to the confession of faith depriving the former of its necessary freedom. But, as we have already said, there is a price to pay for that freedom.

In any case, Christ and the apostolic gospel remain for themselves always free and beyond this double dialectical response which refers preaching and the confession of faith to one another. Christ and the

apostolic Gospel are the only *norma normans,* and because of that
we cannot dispose of them. That is why the authority of Christ and
the apostolic gospel over the church is also the freedom of that same
Christ towards the response made to him, whether that be in
preaching or in the confession of faith.[25] It would, however, be false
to conclude from this that only the freedom of Christ can and must
be affirmed, to the exclusion of the response of the church to Christ;
for this freedom of Christ, like his authority which is one with it,
exists only *in,* with, and under history, although it is certainly not to
be confused with history. If then the freedom of Christ does not
undermine the authority of the response of the church given in
preaching and the confession of faith, but on the contrary establishes
that authority, it seems, nevertheless, that authority in the church
can never be given once and for all; it is always in a state of becoming. A church which believed itself to have regulated the question
of authority in it would already be unfaithful to Christ. Conversely,
a church which refused to consider the question of authority in it
would also be unfaithful to the gospel, since it would in that very
act deny the historicity (the historical character) of the church and
the gospel. The church, being neither simply historical nor simply
eschatological, but both, will never lose its pilgrim character.[26] The
necessarily dialectical relationship between the normative gospel
with its ensuing historical response, and the necessarily dialectical
relationship between the response of preaching and the response of
the confession of faith, must both be seen as something *living.* This
is true for the first relation because the norm, Christ and the apostolic gospel, is itself living, and thus sustains, judges, and purifies the
response of the church. It is also true of the second relationship, a
fact which appears in the function of theology or the doctrinal ministry, which refers the two forms of response to each other as well as
to Christ and to the scriptural gospel.

But it is not enough to characterize this double relationship as
living; it must be indicated that it concerns a personal relationship.
In the case of the relationship between Christ and the apostolic
gospel on the one hand, the response of the church on the other, it
seems clear that the content of the apostolic gospel—Christ—is personal, and that the response it sustains is a response of persons, of
men who through their relationship with Christ become free and
responsible persons. The relationship with Christ and the double
response to which it leads is, therefore, not simply the relationship

between Christ and preaching or the confession of faith, but—in every case—between Christ and the preacher, between Christ and the one who confesses his faith in Christ. Just as we have no access to Christ except in the apostolic gospel, neither does the relationship of Christ with the preacher and the confessing church appear except in preaching and in the confession of faith. But these responses are nothing without the personal reality which carries them, just as the apostolic gospel is nothing without the reality of the apostles. The relationship of Christ to the gospel goes through the apostles, just as the relationship of Christ to preaching and to the confession of faith by the whole church, passes through the successors of the apostles.

As far as the relationship between the two forms of response to Christ and to the apostolic gospel is concerned, it is the relationship between the ministry of preaching in the church, on the one hand, and the confessing church, on the other. Here, too, we are dealing with a personal relationship, in the sense that the ministry of preaching is a personal ministry just as the church is a personal reality. But even if this is true, the affirmation should not be understood in a subjectistic sense, as if there were only the relationship of Christ with the preacher on the one side, and His relationship with each member of the church on the other. The ministry is, at the same time, greater than the minister, and the church is also greater than its members. The preacher does not preach himself but Christ and the apostolic gospel; the church does not confess the individual and subjective faith of each member, but its communal and objective faith created by Christ himself. Preaching is, of course, the work of the minister or the preacher, and he fulfills a ministry which is in no way independent of his person; however, it transcends him simultaneously: his ministry is thus both personal and transpersonal. In like manner, the confession of faith is certainly the affair of the church. The church, though, is not simply an aggregate of individuals, each of which, in the church's confession of faith, declares his individual belief; neither is it simply the present community of believers. It is the church of yesterday, today, and tomorrow. The confession of faith is thus the fact both of the members of the church *and* of the reality of the church which transcends its members as it transcends time.

Consequently, authority in the church, which stems from the recognition of the authority of Christ by the church, cannot be more than signified. It is always second, relative, always subject to revision. It cannot, by its very nature, be codified, even if preaching and the confession of faith can and must necessarily take form. As we have already pointed out, the church is not founded simply on a principle, but on a person. It is not founded simply on Scripture in its necessary transmission and actualization, but on the apostolic and ecclesiastical ministry. The living relationship, both personal and transpersonal, between Christ and the double response which he sustains, on the one hand, and the two wielders of this double response, on the other, appears precisely in the very reality of the personal, ecclesiastical ministry, understood as a ministry of edification and as a ministry of unity. It is that ministry which signifies authority, without itself being authority. Thus the preaching of the gospel, in Word and sacrament, and the confession of faith necessarily imply the personal, ecclesiastical ministry without which they become anonymous and, hence, impersonal. Instead of being edifying, they would then be destructive of personality.

Our question "as a result of what does the church become the church?" thus leads directly to the other question: "How does the church become the church?" The problem of authority in the church is by nature linked with that of the constitution of this authority.[27]

HOW DOES THE CHURCH BECOME THE CHURCH?

This question, which poses the *problem of the constitution of authority* in the church, is the question of the ecclesiastical ministry. We have seen, in effect, that the authority of Christ over the church is manifested historically as authority *in* the church, and that authority *in* the church means the preaching of the gospel by Word and sacrament and the confessing of the faith, in constant openness to Christ who is the authority *over* the church. But then the question presents itself; first, how is preaching effected, and second, how is the confession of faith effected? The first question draws attention to the difference between the general mission of the church, or its royal priesthood, on the one hand, and specific ministry in the Church on the other: this ministry is understood here in terms of what we have called the ministry of edification, or of the Word and sacraments. Preaching is effected through this ministry. The second question refers to the confession of faith as it expresses the *consensus ecclesiae* or what we might also call the doctrine of the church;[28] it raises the problem of knowing how this consensus is realized and how it is lived. It is realized and lived through the ecclesiastical ministry understood as a ministry of unity.

We are thus led to speak of the ecclesiastical ministry according to its two poles of edification and unity. The first question which comes to mind here is that of the biblical foundation for this distinction. But this question leads to a second, for is it possible simply to copy primitive Christianity? The second question therefore concerns the organization of the Church.

1. The New Testament Doctrine of the Ministry in the Church.

Recourse to the New Testament is not just a matter of form. It is an essential step, since Scripture is the fundamental historical norm for the church. All doctrine of the ecclesiastical ministry must take Scripture as its pattern, i.e., it must, in the ultimate analysis, proceed from Scripture and be covered by it. The New Testament must be searched for a theological model for the ecclesiastical ministry.

a) The historical problem of the New Testament doctrine of the ecclesiastical ministry.

The search for a New Testament model of the ecclesiastical ministry runs into an apparently insurmountable difficulty: there exist in the New Testament at least two traditions concerning ministries. Let us put to one side the Johannine ecclesiology where, except for the function of the apostles, there are no indications concerning one or several particular ministries, and where all the emphasis is on the church as a fraternal community living from the Word by the witness of the Holy Spirit. There then remain the Pauline (gentile-Christian) and Judeo-Christian (or Palestinian) ecclesiology.[29]

Pauline ecclesiology is charismatic. The accent is placed on the fact that the church, the body of Christ, is made up of members each of whom has a gift of grace (charisma) to be used for the common good of the church (Rom. 12:3-8; 1 Cor. 12:4 ff). Among these gifts, there are some which give rise to true functions in the church, i.e., to a functional hierarchy which is not a hierarchy of value. Although there is no fixed and exclusive catalogue of these functions, it is still possible to distinguish two essential lines, of which the first is basic: the services of proclaiming the Word (apostle, prophet, teacher; 1 Cor. 12:28) and the services of mutual help and unity, or of direction (1 Th. 5:12; Rom. 12:8; 1 Cor. 12:28). These two groups of services are closely tied together, as we shall soon see. In fact, this bond has already appeared in the fact that the functions of the Word and the functions of unity and mutual help derive from the unique apostolic function, which is both foundation (*Kirchengründung*) and direction (*Kirchenleitung*). These ministries, however, are exercised *in* the church community in which each member has a gift for the use of the whole body (1 Cor. 12:7). Moreover, these ministries are controlled by the community (1 Cor. 14:29).

Judeo-Christian or Palestinian ecclesiology is found in the Book of Acts and the pastoral epistles (and also in the synoptic gospels), i.e., principally Judeo-Christian and late gentile-Christian communities. It is an ecclesiology in which the instituted ministries are far more strongly accentuated: first of all, that of Peter (Mt. 16:18 f; Acts) who appears as the head of the early church; then that of the presbyters or elders who direct the local communities and who are collaborators and successors of the apostles (Acts 15:2, 4, 6, 22, 23; 16:4; 21:18; 1 Tim. 5:17 ff; Tit. 1:5—Acts 14:23; 20:17 ff—Jas. 5:14; 1 Pt. 5:1 ff.). These leaders are instituted by the laying on of hands and they in turn repeat this act in order to call to the ministry and consecrate to the service of God in the church those who have received the necessary charisma (1 Tim. 4:14; 2 Tim. 1:6). Called presbyters in Judeo-Christian communities, they are termed *episcopoi* (bishops) in Greek communities. Their ministry is to watch over the church; the identification is made in Acts 20:17, 28. But while the presbyters constitute a college, the *presbyterium* and are always designated in the plural, the monarchical episcopacy was sketched very early in the singular and termed *episcope* (cf. 1 Tim. 3:2; Tit. 1:7). If the presbyterial and the episcopal functions were indistinguishable at the outset, the difference indicated between the presbyterial college and the monarchical episcopacy is one which concerns the extent of competence: the *episcope* is metropolitan, charged with watching (*episcope*) over a given area; this function dates from the era of Ignatius of Antioch. There is therefore no difference between presbyters and a bishop as far as the content of their ministry is concerned. It is a *pastoral* function in both cases (Acts 20:28; 1 Pt. 5:1-4; 2:25; cf. also Phil. 1:1; Eph. 4:11—pastors!). Their ministry is one of unity or of direction (pastoral.) Generally the deacons are associated with them (Acts 6:1 ff; 19:22—in Acts, certain deacons seem to have been presbyters by reason of the function exercised; cf. Stephen, Timothy; 1 Tim. 3:8 ff; cf. also Phil. 1:1).

These two conceptions do not simply follow one another chronologically, even though there is an evolution in Pauline communities from the first to the second way of thinking; this evolution can be traced by comparing the great Pauline epistles and the pastoral epistles. But the two conceptions coexisted for a long time, having been born independently of each other. This diversity makes any ecclesiological fundamentalism impossible, in the sense of a pure and simple repristination of the ministries of first century Christian communities—for which of the two traditions should we take? But while such ecclesiological fundamentalism is impossible, neither can we accept a relativism which says: because the early church cannot be copied, all these questions are theologically irrelevant and simply concern matters of expediency. Such a view is inadequate because the church is the church of Christ and her ministries should signify Christ and be derived from him. The diversity of ecclesiologies should be seen in relation to the unity of the church, and vice versa. It is not a matter of harmonizing, but of ordering diversity in unity, and unity in diversity. For the great New Testament proclamations on ministries are not simply of a historical order, but are at the same time, beyond all historical influences, of a theological order, i.e., of an ecclesiological order in a fundamental and permanent sense.[30] They can thus provide us with a theological model for ministries in the Church.

b) Functions or ministries according to the New Testament.

The two concepts of ministry, gentile-Christian (Pauline) and Judeo-Christian (Palestinian), should both be studied from the viewpoint of their common foundation in the ministry of the apostles. Christ gave his fundamental form to the church through the apostles, through their apostolic ministry, and he continually forms and reforms his church in a fundamental way through the ministry of those whom he calls in the Holy Spirit, through his church, to be the followers of the apostles. This "apostolic succession" is related to different aspects of the apostolic ministry. The apostles were preachers of the gospel, by which the church was founded, and they were also the leaders of the church, watching over its needs and its unity. Pauline ecclesiology, which belongs to the time of the founding of the church in a Greek and gentile milieu, insists on the first aspect. The ecclesiology of the period during which the church was organized (in an originally Judeo-Christian milieu, where the gospel had rapidly created communities, and later in a gentile-Christian milieu, as we see in the pastoral epistles) accentuates the second aspect. The two ecclesiologies and their respective accents appear fundamentally complementary from the perspective of the relationship of Christ with his church. Christ is, in effect, both the cornerstone and the keystone of the church. He is the One on whom the church rests and in whom its unity is assured in love. The building up, or edification, of the church is situated between two poles: the foundation, which is the preaching of Christ's gospel, and the unity. These two poles are visible within the apostolic ministry, as seen in the two complementary ecclesiologies. Those ministries in the church which continue the different aspects of the apostolic ministry should also be "transparent" to these two poles, and thus to Christ, who is indissolubly the foundation and the One who perfects the building in unity. We are here at the source of a theological model for the ministries.

The distinction between the two poles or functional (ministerial) lines is a distinction in the unity of Christ, not in the unity of ministries. The latter will fulfill one function or the other, or a particular aspect within each function. Even though there is an overlapping of functions from the fact that Christ, the founder and builder, is also the unifier, there are nevertheless and at the same time two poles which define two groups of ministries or functions. There are ministries of the Word and ministries of unity or communion. We will see where the two overlap, and we shall also see that the ministries of communion do not exist without the ministries of the Word.

We should make it clear that when we speak of functional ministries we mean much more than duties. The latter case is a matter of a social statute which does not concern us here. Although ministries can become duties, they are neither necessarily nor always so. It is always essential that the function be fulfilled but it must not necessarily always constitute a duty.

i) *The Functions of the Word*: These are the functions or ministries by which the preaching of the apostolic gospel is continually founded and actualized; specifically, these are the functions of prophet and teacher.[31] Let us say that the first prophets and teachers were the apostles themselves, who, in addition to the proclamation of the fundamental gospel of Christ, always went on to realize to this foundation and actualization. According to 1 Cor. 12:28, these are, in effect, two principal functions which emanate from the apostolic ministry. Prophecy, in the Pauline sense of the term, serves the building up of the church (1 Cor. 14:3, 5 . . .; Rom. 8:6 ff). Although the prophetic function can overlap the teaching function, in the sense that the prophetic word can be a word of instruction (1 Cor. 14:31), its specificity is not in teaching. According to the etymological sense of the word, it is both consolation and exhortation (1 Cor. 14:3); on the other hand, this paraclesis is not reserved exclusively for the prophet since, in Rom. 12:6-8, he who consoles and exhorts is distinguished from him who prophesies. It might be said that prophecy is an actualization of the apostolic gospel and that its function is to enlighten, by means of the gospel, the individual or ecclesial existence of Christians, i.e., to illumine their way. It must be added that prophecy is a community gift (1 Cor. 14), but that this does not rule out the existence of specific ministerial or functional prophets (1 Cor. 12:28).

If the character of the prophetic function is one of actualizing the apostolic gospel, then the character of the teaching function is that of establishing the Gospel in all its fullness. The teacher is the man of Scripture (of the Old Testament in New Testament times) and of its interpretation, who establishes the apostolic gospel in Scripture and transmits it (2 Th. 2:15; 1 Cor. 11:23; 15:3). He is the one who draws from the gospel moral or paranetic instruction (e.g., 1 Cor. 4:17), and even wisdom in the sense of instruction in the full scope of the design of God's salvation (1 Cor. 2:6 ff; 3:1 f; 12:8). Teaching can be close to prophecy (Acts 13:1) or close to the ministry of communion, i.e., the pastorate or presbyteriat (Eph. 4:11; 1 Tim. 5:17 . . .). It is nevertheless specific as a teaching function, even if every member of the faithful may have some instruction to give to the church (1 Cor. 14:26).

These two functions of the Word are not only a historical reality but are also theologically and ecclesiologically meaningful. The apostolic gospel must continually be realized and grounded. This is why the prophetic or teaching functions are *necessary* to the church and to its edification.

ii) *The Functions of Communion:* This is the name given to the functions of unity and mutual aid already testified by Paul alongside the functions of the Word. These functions take a primary status in Palestinian ecclesiology: the presidents—those who lead, etc.—correspond in effect in their function to the presbyter-bishops (and also pastors) which we have mentioned. They are typical of Palestinian and late or post-Pauline ecclesiology (Eph. 4:11; the pastoral epistles). The function of the presidency is pastoral or unifying. It appears closely linked with the more specific function of diaconal or

mutual aid. Presidency and diaconate are thus profoundly linked.[32]
This relationship is what impels us to call these functions (presidency
or leadership, diaconate or mutual aid) functions of *communion,*
i.e., of ecclesial communion. They are in the service of communion,
or of the unity of the church in love, which is the same thing. This is
true in any given ecclesial community or any complex of such communities. Such functions have the purpose of building up the church
on the basis of the foundation laid down and continually realized
and grounded by the ministries of the Word, in view of its ecclesial
unity and the reality of its fraternal community.

The characteristics of the functions of communion are various. In
their leadership aspect they overlap, as we have said, the prophetic
and teaching functions (1 Tim. 4:11 ff; 5:17; 2 Tim. 4:2; Tit.
2:15 . . .). They have the particular task of watching over and safe-
keeping orthodox doctrine in order to maintain unity (1 Tim. 1:3 ff;
4:6 f; 6:20; 2 Tim. 1:14; 2:14 ff; Tit. 1:9 ff; 3:10), as well as instituting ministries to fulfill, in their turn, the functions of communion
(1 Tim. 5:22; 2 Tim. 2:2; Tit. 1:5). This could be called a function
of leadership, but it is really the guidance of the Word, according to
the image of Christ who leads his church by the Word. It is also a
spiritual function: leadership within the church is a ministry of
Christ. But we prefer the expression "function of unity" to "function of leadership," since the leadership is in the service of the unity
of the ecclesial community or communities, i.e., the service of the
church. And the relationship of this function with the diaconal
or mutual aid function shows that the function of presidency or
leadership cannot be in the service of unity except in love.

It is difficult to characterize the functions of unity or communion
in as clear a way as that in which we indicated those of the Word. In
the latter case, it was a matter of actualizing and grounding the
apostolic gospel, i.e., of proclaiming Christ through the Word. As to
the functions of communion, if we associate indissolubly the functions of leadership and mutual aid. They are not in the same way
functions of the Word. Mutual aid, or the diaconate, certainly proceeds from the Word, is in fact its fruit, just as it is in the service of
the Word and as such a sign of its meaning which refers us back
to it. But it is not a function of the Word. What is it, then, that
brings about the unity of the functions of communion, both leadership and diaconate? In other words, how is the church built up in
view of its ecclesial unity and its communal fraternal reality?

Let us begin with the fact that the deacons serve at table (Acts 6:1 ff) and that these meals for the poor followed the example of Jesus eating with the poor, the publicans, and the wretched of the earth. Let us also consider that these meals were an extension of the brotherly agapes in the framework of which the Eucharist or the Lord's Supper was celebrated (1 Cor. 11:17 ff; Acts 2:42).[33] It can then be said that, centrally, the ecclesial communion is realized in the Eucharist. This is where Christ, present in his body, forms his people into an ecclesial body (cf. 1 Cor. 10:17: "Because there is one bread, we who are many are one body, for we all partake of the one bread") in brotherly communion (Acts 2:42, where the brotherly communion and the breaking of bread are cited side by side). The bodily presence of Christ in the Eucharist is effected by the Holy Spirit and the ministry he sustains in conformity with the institution of Christ: "Do this in remembrance of me." (1 Cor. 11:24, 25). This is the ministry of presidency and unity. The diaconal ministry is like the extension of Christ's gift of himself, such as it is received in the Eucharist, directed both towards the brothers and towards the poor and the publicans. This is why the ministry of presidency and the diaconal ministry are called ministries of communion in every sense of the word. And it can be seen how the Pauline and Palestinian traditions come together here, even if for the Palestinian tradition the relationship of the ministries of unity and Eucharist is only retrospectively evident (except for Acts 2:42 and 6:1 ff). Beginning with the second century, like Ignatius of Antioch it centers the pastoral or communion functions (in the hierarchical sense of bishop-presbyter-deacon which does not interest us here) around the Eucharist (Philad. 4:1).

The Eucharist, which is the source of the ministries of communion, is nothing without the Word. For this reason the functions of communion do not exist without the functions of the Word. The two groups of functions are fundamentally coordinated and complementary. The second group must integrate the thrust of the first into the church, and the first must prepare the Word which, ever new, keeps the church constantly in movement. The second group of functions is as necessary as the first, because Christ is not only the foundation but also the One who calls to unity. His call to unity is a call to openness towards those who do not yet sit at the Lord's table, and for whom the crumbs of love that He gives are intended.

Is one group of functions subordinate to the other? No. The two are both necessary in their complementarity and in their coordination with each other. It is Christ, giving himself in Word and sacrament, who is their common unity.

The result of the New Testament doctrine of the ecclesiastical ministry seems at first glance irrelevant to our subject for three reasons: First, the ministry of the Word and sacraments does not necessarily appear as one ministry. Not only are these two forms of the ministry of the Word—the prophetic ministry and the teaching ministry—but even these ministries of the Word are not necessarily ministry of the sacraments at the same time, and particularly the sacrament of the Eucharist. Even if the ministry centered on the Eucharist cannot be separated from the Word and is always associated with its ministry, but not necessarily in the form of a personal union, the ministries of the Word, while necessarily coordinated with the Eucharist as the ecclesial locus *par excellence*, have, however, a certain independence, although certainly not an autonomy, since their independence is within the church. Thus the ministry of the Word and sacraments appears to be constituted, or at least, can be constituted from different ministries. The diversity of the aspects of this ministry—which must be designated in the singular, since there is but the one function of building up the church despite its different forms—cannot adequately be evaluated except by differentiating this ministry into a diversity of ministries.

Second, the ministry of unity or communion in the New Testament is different from that which we have hitherto mentioned. It is evidently not a second ministry, but a first ministry. It constitutes the ministry of the Word and sacraments; it designates an axis for them. Thus these two groups of ministries—that of the Word and that of unity—really refer to the same ministry of Word and sacrament, according to its two fundamentally complementary lines. This shows that the ministry of unity is not additional to the ministry of edification, but is already with and in the latter. Then the question arises: in what way is it a second ministry, such as we mentioned in the first part? Why envisage a second ministry of unity?

Third, we spoke of the confession of faith which expressed the *consensus ecclesiae* and we said that the second ministry of unity is its organ, permitting it to be realized and lived. But if that is true, on what New Testament data is this affirmation based?

2. The Organization of the Church.

a) The problem. The New Testament doctrine of the ministry in the church answers the question: how does the church form itself or become itself? We can now say that it becomes or takes form fundamentally in the gathering of the community. For the preaching of the Word, under whatever form, and Eucharistic celebration are cultural acts. So the response given seems to be limited to the local community. There the church comes into existence, i.e., takes form, forms itself in the gathering of worship. It takes form through the action of Christ as he gives himself in the Holy Spirit by the Word and sacraments. Christ is the author of the church in its gathering together. It is certainly possible to point out that the church, in its local reality, is not the church only in this form of cultic gathering. The church is not only a worshiping assembly; it is also a supracultual reality. Like faith, the church is a total reality or it is nothing. But—and this is the important thing—although the local church is not just a cultic assembly, it takes form as a church only in that fashion, for worship is the source of the church.

It must then be noted that the church is not simply a local community. Certainly, it does not exist without the local community. Moreover, this one is entirely church, but is not the entire church. This demonstrates both the truth and the error of congregationalism. The truth is that the local community is entirely church; its error is not in overlooking the fact that the local community is not the entire church—congregationalism recognizes a multiplicity of local congregations—but in not considering the problem posed by the contention that the local church, although it is entirely church, is not the entire church. This problem is that of the correlation between different local communities. In other words, how do different local communities become or form together the church, or one single church? This question can be limited to the sphere of a single church just as easily as it can be expanded to the sphere of universal Christianity, thus envisaging the problem in terms of the relationship or the correlation among different churches, i.e., among different complexes of local communities grouped together into distinct churches.[34] The problem thus posed, whether limited to the relationship between different communities within the same church or extended to the relationship between different churches is, properly speaking, the *ecumenical problem* of ecclesiology. The word "ecumenical" brings together, in the usage it has assumed, the two notions of universality and unity.[35] The term can be understood in a limiting sense (in which it is rarely used, but that does not prevent us from using it in this sense) and applied to a particular church, i.e., to a particular complex of different local communities united in one church. This might be described as an ecumenical ecclesial microcosm: a *micro*cosm because universality is reduced to one given church; but nevertheless a micro*cosm*, because of the fact that that church is envisaged from the angle of its unity. The term "ecumenical" can also be understood in the more current sense, the extensive one, and can be applied to the relationship between two or more, or even all of the individual churches. In either case it is a question of the ecumenical problem of ecclesiology.

b) The hierarchically structured ministry: We have already noted the insufficiency of Protestantism's response to this problem. Certainly, the necessity of a common doctrine, or of what we have also termed a common confession of faith, is clear—it is necessary only to recall article VII of the Augsburg Confession on doctrinal consensus. But apart from a certain amount of unity already implied in the realization of such a common confession, the question of its manifestation remains. This is really the question of the ecclesial significance of doctrinal unity: what result does doctrinal unity have on the church level, i.e., for relations either among different local communities within one church or among different churches having the same doctrinal base?

Protestantism in general finds itself either empty-handed before the problem or approaches it in a manner above all pragmatic, assuming that it does not simply copy certain aspects of the Catholic "organizationalism," while inevitably dissociating them from the total ecclesial reality claimed by that organization. The manner in which Protestantism generally approaches the question lacks theological seriousness. The problem is treated not as a question of ecclesiology but as one of ecclesiastical practice. Although practice plays an undeniably important role, and although ecclesiology here as always consists indissolubly both of "theory" and of "practice," nevertheless all that pertains to the church concerns ecclesiology. It is in this respect that Catholicism in general and the second Vatican Council in particular constitute an extraordinary interpellation for any kind of Protestantism whatever. As far as Lutheranism is concerned, Catholicism poses the question of the ecclesial consequences to be drawn from doctrinal agreements, the *consensus doctrinae (ecclesiae)*. Catholicism also insists on doctrinal consensus, but it does not assert that this consensus is sufficient for the church to become one, unlike article VII of the Augsburg Confession. It contends, on the contrary, that this unity must still take form ecclesially. As for Calvinism, Catholicism does not stop at a pragmatic definition of a unifying ecclesial structure by a superficial resource to the New Testament,[36] but has a theology of the structure of unity. In the first part, we attempted to show in what way we feel this theology can and should be accepted. We might recall here that the structure of unity on the general church level is the affair of the ministry, since everything in the church is personalized. The structure grows out the "second" ministry which is a ministry both of doctrine and of government. Hence, unity is realized and manifested through the men charged with the ministry of unity.[37]

This statement demands to be deepened and also verified by the following remarks:

First, the aforementioned structure of unity appears even at the New Testament stage. It appears first of all in what was later called *visitation*.[38] In early Christianity, this is the work both of the leaders of the Jerusalem community (Acts 8:14; 9:32, etc.) and of Paul, who constantly revisits the Christian communities founded by him. Moreover, he maintains a relationship with the Jerusalem community both by going there himself (Gal. 1:18; Acts 9:26 ff . . .) and by organizing the collection for its aid (1 Cor. 16:1; 2 Cor. 9). Visitation, first by the apostles, then by their successors, realized and manifested the communion among different local communities. In addition, the structure of unity as it appears at the level of early Christianity is the *synod* or the *council*. Acts 15 (cf. also Gal. 2:1-10) speaks of a meeting at Jerusalem uniting Peter and James and the apostles in general, as well as the presbyters of the community of the city, with Paul and Barnabas. At Antioch a serious disagreement had arisen between Peter and Paul in the understanding of the Gospel. A consensus is brought about here by a common confrontation with the preaching of the two apostles. This synodical or conciliar confrontation places the preaching of each one in the light of a single norm, purifying and making preaching transparent to that norm. The encounter thus led to a recognition of the preaching of both as an authentic proclamation of the gospel. This reciprocal recognition is signified by the hand of friendship given to the different partners. It testifies as to the collegiality of the ministry in the church (Gal. 2:9).[39] Moreover, it might be noted that we have the explicit sign of such a reciprocal recognition of different ways of preaching the same gospel in the early church's settlement of the New Testament canon. It constitutes for the church, in its various expressions, the only apostolic witness, the unique gospel. Visitation and synod are the two complementary ways by which the relationship is lived out among the different local communities and, later on, among the different churches. This relationship is rooted in and proceeds from the same faith. It is, at the same time, in the service of that faith. The common confession of faith is expressed in a living way through effective communion among local communities and different churches, such as it is made concrete in this double manner. We might say, following up what we already mentioned apropos the dialogical authority of the church, that the structure of unity is the *dialogue* of faith for this is, in effect, what constitutes the content of the visitation and the synod. The church cannot exist except through permanent dialogue if it really wants to experience unity. But that implies the necessity of a ministry of unity. The double structure we have noted is simply a framework which does not exist for itself; it is the form created not in view of the ministry of unity, but—if we refer to the New Testament—by the exercise of that ministry. The structure does not exist prior to the ministry, but the ministry creates the structure. It has no meaning except as a function of the ministry of unity in its reality. This ministry, like every ministry, appears as both personal and transpersonal. It is personal in the sense that it is lived by persons (ministers) for persons (members of different local communities or churches); it is transpersonal because this ministry transcends the persons who exercise it and the persons for whom it is exercised. The ministers of unity are in the service of Christ, who is himself the true minister of unity, and the different Christians are a part of the Church of Christ.

Second, it might be asked why the dialogical reality of the church calls for a ministry of unity and cannot be lived without it. Should the indicated New Testament data not be considered simply as contingent? We have already pointed to the fact that because of the plurality of New Testament ecclesiologies, no ecclesiological fundamentalism is possible. Does not the New Testament material dealing with visitation and the council appear to have been unduly emphasized in relation to its significance? We may respond by saying that the authority of Christ over the church is constituted in the church by the ministry. We saw that Christ not only sustains individual faith, but gathers together a church. That is to say,[40] Christ himself acts in the sense both of founding and of edifying his Church on the one hand, and of unifying it (koinonia), on the other. The double form of the ministry-edification on the one side, unity on the other (on the supralocal ecclesial level), is the expression of this double complementary action of Christ. It is also clear that the two poles of the ministry in the church meet, as we have seen, at every stage and in every sector of the first century church. It follows that this ministry, according to its two axes, is a part of the very being, *esse*, of the church. If that does not yet tell us anything about the variable forms that such a ministry can assume in history, it is nonetheless possible to state that God himself, or Christ as he sustains the church, sustains in it also the ministry according to this double line. The ministry of unity is *the* ministry in the church in the totality of all its aspects, i.e., in its collegial reality, inasmuch as that reality is lived as ministry of unity. In this regard, it is doctrinal and governmental, in the same sense that seemed to be inadmissible in Roman Catholic ecclesiology, on the general church level (whether for a given church or for the universal Church). Inasmuch as doctrine, understood as the church's response to the gospel of Christ, is second to preaching, and inasmuch as government, understood as the service of church unity, is second to the building up of the church, the ministry of unity is a "second" ministry. But just as that is not meant to imply "secondary," so neither does the fact that it is second signify that it is not instituted by Christ. We saw that the contrary is true: the bipolar nature of the ministry is of divine institution. It even appeared to us that, on the local level, the two poles coexist and overlap one another. On the wider ecclesial plane, the ministry of unity is second in the sense that it is nothing without the ordinary first ministry, and that in truth it is in the service of the latter just as the latter, the ministry of edification, is open to the ministry of unity. The two poles are complementary, but in the sense of a necessary coordination which the ministry of unity must realize. Moreover, it must be made clear in view of what we said in the first part about the juridical aspect of the ministry of unity, that the latter is, in turn, second to the service of unity which is its proper content. We distinguish therefore in the ministry of unity, second to the ordinary ministry, an element which is first and a juridical element which is second. The latter is not established by divine law, as we said in the first part; but by church law.

Third, we saw that if the ministry in the church is, according to its twin poles, part of the very being, *esse*, of the church, the forms that it takes are not always the same in history. This is already true on the level of first century Christianity, as is clear from the different New Testament ecclesiologies. We are compelled to conclude that the *organization* of the ministry in the church arises not out of the *esse*, but the *bene esse*, the good order of the church,[41] and this means that no claim to an absolute systematization can be sought in this domain, providing that it is clear that we are speaking of the good order *of the church*, and that this order and the forms taken by the particular ministry should be transparent to their real being. This is why, on the one hand, article VII of the Augsburg Confession can say that church organization does not arise from the confession of faith, and why, on the other hand, the Confession of La Rochelle can say that church organization is not a matter of no importance. The statement that the organization of the ministry in the church, under its double form of edification and of unity, cannot be systematized in a necessary and rigid theological sense shows the nonabsolute and, in its hierarchical-clerical form, disputable character of the traditional conception of the three-level ministry: bishop-presbyter-deacon, to be a conception that goes back to Ignatius of Antioch. Certainly, having been traced at the end of the first century and possessing in addition to its great antiquity an extraordinary ecumenical weight, the three-level scheme of ministry should seriously be taken into consideration when the hierarchy is conceived as one of service rather than one of tutelage, exercised collegially, thus renouncing every kind of juridical and "clerical, sacramental systematization," such as has long characterized Catholicism.[42] Such a scheme is certainly possible, simply because it is transparent both to the pole of edification and to the pole of unity within the church's ministry. But if the diaconal aspect is a constitutive factor of the ministry of unity, as the New Testament data shows, then it might be asked whether or not the (relative) independence which characterizes it in Ignatius is imposed. It seems to us that it must be integrated into the ministry of unity, thus affirming its diversified and necessarily collegial character.

The distinction between the *esse* and the *bene esse* of the church, as far as ministry is concerned, implies another distinction: that between the unity of the church and the union of local communities or different churches. If we accept the ambivalence of the church, a reality that is both divine and human or, what is really the same thing, both eschatological and historical, then the One Church is the church which we believe *within* the church in which we live.[43] No real church is that One Church, but to the extent that it is the church it participates in the One Church. However, the participation of a real or historical church in the One True Church is the order of faith; the real church is not itself, inasmuch as it is real, of the order of faith, but of the order of fact, of what is given; what is of the order of faith is its participation in the True Church. This participation must be historically realized, for the real church is a church only through this participation. This takes place (as we saw) by the transmission and actualization of the apostolic gospel in Word and sacrament, under the control of the church's confession of faith (understood in the sense of doctrine).

The organ of this transmission and actualization and the organ of this control, an organ instituted by Christ himself who establishes it in and through the community, is the particular ministry in the church according to its double pole of building up and of unity, or rather union, communion. But it appears here—the close connection established between the ministries of edification and unity on the local level allows us this assertion—that the ordinary ministry is in fact itself a ministry of unity, and that what we called the "second" ministry, that of unity, is, on a wider church level, both ministry of unity and ministry of union, or better yet, of communion. The ordinary ministry is a ministry of unity in the sense that by it, i.e., by preaching the Word and administering the sacraments, Christ attests and signifies and realizes the unity of the church in faith, i.e., the unity confessed and lived thanks to the apostolic gospel.

The "second" ministry of unity is a ministry of unity in the same sense, because it is in the service of Christ in the unity of his body and it can only be rooted in the preaching of the Word and the administration of the sacraments. It is at the same time a ministry of union, or communion, in the sense that it watches in love over the union of different members of the church and, consequently, over the different ecclesial communities or churches.[44] Unity is of the order of faith; union or communion of the order of love. Unity is the vertical dimension of the church; union or communion the horizontal dimension. The real church is situated at the intersection of this vertical and this horizontal. The ministry in the church, as ministry of unity, whether it concerns the ordinary ministry or "second" ministry, is a ministry of truth, and, as ministry of union or of communion, it is a ministry of charity.

It is then easy to understand how, being situated in both the vertical and horizontal dimensions, the ministry in the church arises indissolubly out of the *esse*, "being," and the *bene-esse*, "good order," of the church. Insofar as the church is historical, human, it is a union, a communion of Christians, and by extension, of ecclesial communities. Such a union, when it is composed of a certain number of ecclesial communities or even of several churches, can only be formed around a confession of faith which expresses the vertical dimension of the church—here we have the doctrinal aspect of the "second" ministry of unity—*and*, it must be added, around a church *constitution* (*Kirchenverfassung*) which expresses the horizontal dimension of the church—here we have the governmental aspect of this "second" ministry. "Constitution" is understood here not in the active sense, but in the sense of a given constitution (*Verfassung*). The constitution is connected with the way in which the ministry of unity and communion is conceived and lived; at the same time, it deals with the discipline of the church.

Fourth, the ministry in the church is a responsible ministry, and therefore, even hierarchical. It is Christ who, in the different forms of ministry, locates the men whom he calls, and who then have to give an accounting of the way they fulfill their ministry. The collegiality or conciliarity of particular ministers in the church does not mean anonymity and irresponsibility. The transpersonal character of the ministry, under whatever form it is understood, presupposes the tension between the holder of the ministry—a person—and the ministry itself in the mission which it constitutes: it therefore signifies the responsibility of the minister. The ministry which we said has no power does have a responsibility towards Christ who instituted the ministry in its two poles, and who institutes men, through the church, in certain given aspects of the ministry. On the one hand, it is the church which is responsible for the way in which it "organizes" the ministry in it; on the other hand, each holder of a ministry is responsible for the way in which he fulfills his given responsibility. The communal reality of the church and the fact that the church is the place of individual freedom do not exclude, but rather include, the responsibility of the ministry, since individual freedom is lived only in responsibility, and the church is only a community through the responsibility of its members. Collectivity is anonymous; it is not a community. Responsibility is thus constitutive of the church in its different aspects, since the church exists in and through Christ. Responsibility cannot, however, be understood in an individualist sense, which would be the very negation both of the church and of Christ, its head; it is a responsibility vis-à-vis Christ and *in* the church, a responsibility, therefore, in truth and love.

If the concept of the ministry is linked with that of responsibility, then the hierarchical constitution of the ministry in the church is self-evident. The ministry is diversified; on the one hand, it has two poles; on the other, each of these poles is composed of several possible ministries. While the different responsibilities, which according to the different ministries make explicit the ministry in the church, are complementary, neither their nature nor their field of action is identical: hence the ordinary ministry is, by its nature, different from the ministry of unity and communion, even though the nature of one participates in that of the other. Moreover, the ordinary ministry, the ministry of edification or building up, is exercised in the local community but is the ministry of unity in the larger church. Here is where the legitimacy of the concept of hierarchy appears. There is hierarchy because there is responsibility. The hierarchy is certainly not ascendant, as in Catholicism, but, understood as a "reciprocal order and subordination within the ecclesiastical ministry of the 'first' ministry which pertains in particular to the Word and the sacraments, and of the 'second,' which is a general ministry of doctrine and government, in the unique service of Christ" in the church, it must be defined as dialectical.[45] But if hierarchy, because of its dialectical character, cannot develop into monarchy or oligarchy either in the local community or the larger church, since each of its elements must be referred to every other lest it assume undue importance, and since responsibility at every "level" must always be lived within the collegiality of the church, then this necessary and essential insertion of responsibility in the whole of the church is not sufficient in and of itself to define responsibility which also implies personal decision. The minister who is situated in the collegial reality of ministers, and in the communal reality of the church, cannot, "after having listened to the church," be dispensed for his responsibility in the exercise of his ministry.

The same is true, moreover, for the individual member of the church. That is the reason why the church is both human and, as such, the place of the possible action of God. Personal decision is both the risk and the chance which God runs with man and the church.

Because of this notion of responsibility, with its implications for the hierarchy, the words of Jesus which give a particular place to Peter do not have to be interpreted in a sense which can be justified neither by the texts themselves nor by the general New Testament pronouncements on ministry. The problem of Papacy arises both from *esse* and the *bene-esse* of the church. If, in effect, the conciliarity of the church is to be responsible, it must necessarily lead to the recognition of a presidential ministry within the council. Collegiality and presidency[46] refer to each other: there is no responsible collegiality without a personalized ministry of unity, and hence a ministry of presidency in its midst, as there is no responsible presidency except within the collegiality of the church's ministry. The problem of Papacy cannot legitimately be a problem of ecclesial dissension and a cause of schism if the presidential ministry is conceived and lived in this way.

But the problem of the Papacy is no more important than other aspects of the ecclesiastical ministry. They are equally vital.

NOTES

1. An immense literature exists on the problem of authority and especially on authority in the church. Although we are not able to discuss it specifically within the limits of this study, we will indicate below (cf. II/A) in what sense we speak of authority in the church as well as the meaning of the word "authority." Here are several titles: (1) Writings centered on the relationship between authority and freedom for historical interest: A. Sabatier, *Religion de l'esprit et religion de l'autorité*, Paris, 3rd ed., 1904; More recently, E. G. Rüsch, *Kirchliche Autorität und Freiheit des Gewissens*, Göttingen, 1967; H. Küng, *Kirche in Freiheit*, Einsiedeln, 2nd ed., 1965. (2) On the relationship between authority (power) and love: J. L. McKenzie, *Authority in the Church*, New York, 1966; J. Drane, *Authority and Institution*, Milwaukee, 1969. (3) On the relation between authority and submission, A. Dumas, *L'ordre dans l'Eglise: autorité et soumission*. In *Foi et Vie*, 1955, pp. 489-514; similarly, *"La soumission mutuelle dans les épitres."* In *Verbum Caro/Communion*, 1970, No. 4, pp. 4-19. (4) On the crisis of authority, W. Anz, G. Friedrich, H. Fries, K. Rahner, *Autorität in der Krise*, Regensburg/Göttingen, 1970; N. Lash et al, *Nennt euch nicht Meister. Die Autorität in einer sich wandelnden Kirche*, Styria, 1968. (5) Writings identifying authority with the churchly ministry: *Evangelische Autorität – Katholische Freiheit*, Rottenburg/Bad Boll, 1959; cf. also the bibliographical references given below, particularly under II.

2. *Katholische Dogmatik*, München, last ed. 1960 ff. Cf. in parts III/1, para. 167c, 172, 176a, and IV/1, para. 278 ff. Studies on this subject are innumerable. One might cite in part. Ch. Journet, *L'Eglise du Verbe incarné*. I. La hierarchie apostolique. Paris, 2nd ed., 1955; Dom A. Grea, *L'Eglise et sa divine constitution*, Paris, 1965; cf. also the following articles in RGG³: Jurisdiktion, Kirchengewalt, Kirchenrecht, Lehramt, Lehrgewalt, Ordination.

3. Cf. also Y. Congar, "Composantes et idée de la succession apostolique," in *Oecumenica* 1966, Minneapolis, 1966, pp. 61-80.

4. Schmaus, *op. cit.*, III/1, p. 189. "Christus hat nicht ein Sachprinzip, sondern ein Personalprinzip zur Grundlage der Kirche gemacht." On this subject cf. also Y. Congar, "Apostolicité de ministère et apostolicité de doctrine. Réaction protestante et tradition catholique." In R. Baumer – H. Dolch (ed.), *Volk Gottes* (Festschrift für J. Hofer), Freiburg/Wien/Basel, 1967, pp. 84-111.

5. On infallibility, cf. F. Hofmann, "Reichweite und Grenzen der kirchlichen Lehrzucht," in *Evangelische Autorität – Katholische Freiheit*, pp. 42-53.

6. A critique of the Roman Catholic doctrine of the principally priestly ministry, a critique carried out on the basis of the preoccupation—characterized as existential—of Luther, is found in the Catholic theologian D. Oliver, *Les deux visages du prêtre*, Paris, 1971. We ourselves will not go beyond the perspective indicated by the title of this chapter.

7. Paris, 1930 ff.

8. Denzinger, *Enchiridion Symbolorum*, p. 469 (our translation).

9. This problem is singled out by K. G. Steck, "Wie weit reicht kirchliches Recht?" In *Evangelische Autoität – Katholische Freiheit*, pp. 62 ff., in part, p. 68. But while Steck certainly differentiates law and authority, he does not see that a law is implied in authority. For Steck, law is not second, but secondary. Cf. similarly, "Recht und Grenzen kirchlicher Vollmacht," in *Theologische Existenz heute*, 1956.

10. We can but mention here the recent Protestant works, on the theology of church law, of J. Heckel, H. Dombois, S. Grundmann, J. Ellul, and others.

11. What we said above comes into play in cases of litigation between church power and political power.

12. Cf. the decree on the ministry and the life of priests—*Presbyterorum ordinis* – of Vatican II.

13. Denzinger, *op. cit.*, p. 957. Cf. also p. 938.

14. Cf. also the Roman Cathechism, in Mirbt-Aland, *Quellen zur Geschichte des Papstums and des römischen Katholizismus*, Tübingen, 1967, p. 683, no. 1057.

15. Denzinger, *op. cit.*, pp. 1821 ff, esp. pp. 1832 ff.

16. For a presentation of the doctrine of the *triplex munus* moving from Christ to the churchly ministry, cf. Per Erik Persson, *Repraesentatio Christi. Der Amtsbegriff in der neueren römisch-katholischen Theologie*, Göttingen, 1966. There is also a sketch of the evolution of Catholicism, from the doctrine of the *munus duplex* to that of the *munus triplex* (pp. 167 ff). But Persson does not pose the question of the theological legitimacy of either conception. Cf. also Dom A. Grea, *op. cit.*, esp. chapter IX. For a more critical approach, cf. Schmaus, *op. cit.*, III/1, pp. 714 ff, and above all W. Pannenberg, *Grundzüge der Christologie*, Gütersloh, 2nd ed., 1966. On the other hand, R. Prenter takes up the doctrine of the *munus duplex* in an original way; cf. *Connaître Christ*, Neuchatel, 1966, pp. 162 ff, and *"Das kirchliche Amt als königliche Vertretung Christi und als priesterliche Ver-*

tretung der Gemeinde," in *Oecumenica* 1967, ed. V. Vajta, Minneapolis, 1967, pp. 253 ff.

17. Cf. on this subject our book, *La loi, chemin du salut,* Neuchatel-Paris, 1972, 1st part II B/1.

18. Cf. on this subject our article "Unité de l"Eglise et confession de foi," in *Oecumenica* 1969, ed. V. Vajta, Minneapolis, 1969, pp. 271 ff.

19. On the meaning of the word authority, cf. the article "Vollmacht," in *Biblisch-theologisches Wörterbuch,* ed. E. Osterloh – H. Engelland, Göttingen, 2nd ed., 1959; the article "autorité," in *Dictionnaire Encyclopedique de la Bible,* by A. Westphal; etc.

20. For a development of these affirmations, cf. the original French of the present study: *L'autorité dans l'Eglise. Son institution et sa constitution.* In: Revue de droit canonique Strasbourg, 1972, nos. 3 and 4.

21. On this subject, cf. *Theological Dictionary of The New Testament* (Kittel), the article *apostellein* and the article *pempein.* It is possible to apply the rabbinical notion of shaliach to Jesus. The schaliach is a "Bevollmächtigter," one "authorized," one charged with power, a plenipotentiary.

22. Cf. *supra,* n. 20.

23. Apropos of this, cf. in the volume *The Gospel and Unity,* Minneapolis, 1971 (ed. V. Vajta) , the contribution of V. Vajta, "Theology in Dialogue," pp. 25-66. Cf. also *Oecumenica 1969,* where most of the articles deal with the theme of dialogue.

24. Cf. our article "Unité de l'Eglise et confession de foi," in *op. cit.,* p. 278.

25. On this subject, cf. K. Barth, *Church Dogmatics,* 1/2, paragraphs 20 and 21.

26. "Die Kirche kann nicht in Ruhe bleiben; der Kampf um das Wort gehört zu ihrem Wesen." R. Stupperich, in K. Herbert, *Um evangelische Einheit,* Herborn, 1967, p. 35.

27. On the relationship between authority in the church and church constitution, cf. R. Mumm, *"Rechtsgestalt und Vollmacht,"* in *Kerygma und Dogma,* 1968, no. 3, pp. 229-248.

28. In this context we do not distinguish between confession of faith and church doctrine, although strictly speaking church doctrine is nothing more than the doctrinal content of the confession of faith, which has other dimensions than simply doctrinal.

29. Out of the immense literature on the problem of ministry and ministries, we can only indicate several titles. E. Schweizer, *Gemeinde und Gemeindeordnung im Neuen Testament,* Zurich, 1959; M. A. Chevallier, *Esprit de Dieu, paroles d'hommes,* Neuchatel/Paris, 1966 (I owe a great deal to this book) ; H. Frh. von Campenhausen; *Kirchliches Amt und geistliche Vollmacht in den drei ersten Jahrhunderten,* Tübingen, 1953; G. Dix, *Le ministère dans l'Eglise ancienne,* Neuchatel, 1955; E. Molland, "Das kirchliche Amt im Neuen Testament und in der alten Kirche," in *Oecumenica* 1968, ed. V. Vajta, Minneapolis, pp. 15-38; L. Goppelt, "Church Government and the Office of the Bishop in the First Three Centuries," in I. Asheim – V. R. Gold, eds., *Episcopacy in the Lutheran Church? Studies in the Development and Definition of the Office of Church Leadership,* Philadelphia, 1970, pp. 1 ff; Göttingen, 1968, pp. 9 ff; similarly, "Das kirchliche Amt nach den lutherischen Bekenntnisschriften und nach dem Neuen Testament," in *Lutherische Rundschau,* no. 4, 1964, pp. 517-536; "Eucharist and Ministry," vol. IV of *Lutherans and Catholics in Dialogue,* 1970; O. Semmelroth, *Das geistliche Amt,* Frankfurt, 2nd ed., 1965; H. Küng, *The Church,* New York, 1967, esp. E/II.

30. On the relationship between a more charismatic ecclesiology and a more "institutional" ecclesiology, cf. J. L. Leuba, *L'institution et l'événement,* Neuchatel, 1950; K. Rahner, *Das Dynamische in der Kirche,* Freiburg, 1958; G. Hasenhüttl, *Charisma. Ordnungsprinzip der Kirche,* Freiburg/Wien/ Basel, 1969; cf. also M. Honecker, *Kirche als Gestalt und Ereignis. Die sichtbare Gestalt der Kirche als dogmatisches Problem,* München, 1963.

31. Cf. H. Greeven, "Propheten, Lehrer, Vorsteher bei Paulus. Zur Frage der Ämter im Urchristentum," in *ZNW,* no. 44, 1952, pp. 1 ff.

32. On the relation between these two aspects, cf. L. Goppelt, "Kirchenleitung und Bischofsamt," in *op. cit.,* pp. 14 ff. On the diaconal aspect of the ministry of unity, cf. J. Colson, *La fonction diaconale aux origines de l'Eglise,* Paris, 1960; P. Winninger – Y. Congar (ed.) *Le diacre dans l''Eglise et le monde d'aujourd'hui,* Paris, 1966. On the episcopal aspect of the ministry of unity, Fr. J. Leenhardt, "Les fonctions constitutives de l'Eglise et de l'épiscopè selon le Nouveau Testament," in *RHPR,* 1967, no. 2, pp. 111-149; J. Colson, *L'évêque dans les communautés primitives. Tradition paulinienne et tradition johannique des origines à St. Irenée,* Paris, 1951; K. E. Kirk, *The Apostolic Ministry. Essays on the History and the Doctrine of Episcopacy,* London, 3rd ed., 1962; P. Brunner, "Vom Amt des Bischofs" in *Pro ecclesia* I, pp. 235-292; W. Stählin, E. Fincke, L. Klein, K. Rahner, *Das Amt der Einheit. Grundlegendes zur Theologie des Bischofsamtes,* Stuttgart, 1964; Y. Congar – B. D. Dupuy, ed., *L'épiscopat et l'Eglise universelle,* Paris, 1962.

33. On this subject, cf. J. Jeremias, *Die Abendmahlsworte Jesu,* Göttingen, 4th ed., 1967.

34. On the relationship between *ecclesia particularis and ecclesia universalis,* as well as that between both of these and the *ecclesia spiritualis,* cf. S. Grundmann, *Der lutherische Weltbund,* Köln/Graz, 1957, pp. 86 ff; cf. also D. Pirson, *Universalität und Partikularität der Kirche,* München, 1965; H. Sasse, "Uber das Verhältnis von Gesamtkirche und Einzelgemeinde im Neuen Testament," in *In statu confessionis,* pp. 131 ff.

35. Visser 't Hooft defines ecumenism thus: "It could express the nature of the modern movement for cooperation and unity which seeks to manifest the fundamental unity and universality of the Church of Christ." In R. Rouse – S. C. Neill, *A History of the Ecumenical Movement* 1517-1948, Philadelphia, 1967, p. 740.

36. It is well known that Calvin simply took up pragmatically the New Testament data as far as ministries were concerned, without any understanding of the highly complex historical reality of the first century church, and without thinking through the problem of the ministry theologically. Cf. A. Ganoczy, *Calvin, théologien de l'Eglise et du ministère,* Leyden, 1964.

37. On the problem of the ministry of unity in Lutheranism, cf. I. Asheim – R. Gold, *op. cit.,* esp. the article by B. Lohse, pp. 51 ff. Cf. also S. Grundmann, *op. cit.,* pp. 91 ff; G. Tröger, *Das Bischofsamt in der evangelisch-lutherischen Kirche,* München, 1966.

38. On this subject, cf. H. Diem, "Kirchenvisitation als Kirchenleitung," in *Sine vi, sed verbo,* München, 1965, pp. 161 ff. On this whole section, cf. also H. Küng, *Strukturen der Kirche,* Freiburg, 1962; J. Bosc, *L'unité dans le Seigneur,* Paris, 1964.

39. Cf. on this subject our article, "Unité de l'Eglise et confession de foi," in *op. cit.,* p. 283 f. Apropos of the idea of conciliarity, cf. *Councils and the Ecumenical Movement* (World Council of Churches Studies, 5), World

Council of Churches, Geneva, 1968; J. Pelikan, *Luthers Stellung zu den Kirchenkonzilien*, ed. K. E. Skydsgaard, Göttingen, 1962; N. Seils, "Das ökumenische Konzil in der lutherischen Theologie," in H. J. Margull, ed., *Die ökumenischen Konzile der Christenheit*, Stuttgart, 1961; J. L. Leuba, "Das ökumenische Konzil in der reformierten Theologie," in Margull, *op. cit.*; L. Vischer, "Joint working group between the Roman Catholic Church and the World Council of Churches," report presented to the Central Committee of the W.C.C. at Canterbury, in August, 1969.

40. Cf. on this subject our article, "Structures d'unité possibles dans la diversité et la mouvance actuelles de nos Eglises," in *op. cit.*

41. Here we are again following closely our article cited in the previous note.

42. Cf. Y. Congar, "Ministères et structuration de l'Eglise," in *La Maison-Dieu* (review of pastoral liturgics), no. 102, 1970, pp. 7-20; cf. p. 9. There is no need to point out that clericalism is an inherent temptation in the exercise of any ministry in the church, whatever the denomination is. On the ministry in the early church, see the work by that title of Dom G. Dix, Neuchatel/ Paris, 1955. A theological reflection on this question is found in M. Thurian, *Sacerdoce et ministère*, Taize, 1970.

43. For the following, cf. our article, "Structures d'unité pour nos Eglises," in *Positions Luthériennes*, no. 2, 1971, p. 109 f. On the relationship between the eschatological character and the historical character of the church, cf. P. Brunner, "Die Einheit der Kirche und die Verwirklichung der Kirchengemeinschaft," in *Pro Ecclesia* I, pp. 225 ff.

44. A parallel to this distinction between unity and union is found in the division made by J. Heckel between the spiritual and the institutional church, or between divine law and human church law. The latter, which must be referred to the former, has to be reasonable, i.e., has to be able to respond by itself to human reason enlightened by faith. On J. Heckel, cf. S. Grundmann, *op. cit.*, pp. 54 ff. It might also be said that the union arises from the form of the church (*Kirchengestalt*) ; cf. H. G. Göckeritz, "Verkündigung und Kirchengestalt," in *Fragen zur Kirchenreform*, Göttingen, 1964, pp. 60-79. Cf. also W. von Rhoden, *Unio et confessio*, Witten, 1957; K. Herbert, ed., *Um evangelische Einheit*, Herborn, 1967; P. Brunner, "Die christliche Kirche und die Verwirklichung der Kirchengemeinschaft," in *op. cit.*, and above all "Koinonia. Grundlagen und Grundformen der Kirchengemeinschaft," in *Pro ecclesia* II, Berlin/Hamburg, 1966, pp. 305-322.

45. Cf. above. On the notion of hierarchy, cf. H. Dombois, *Hierarchie. Grund und Grenze einer umstrittenen Struktur*, Freiburg, 1971.

46. On this topic, cf. Y. Congar (ed.) , *La collegialité épiscopale. Histoire et théologie*, Paris, 1965; K. Rahner – J. Ratzinger, *Episkopat und Primat*, Freiburg/Wien/Basel, 1961. Cf. also N. Afanassieff, N. Koulomzim, J. Meyendorff, A. Schmemann, *Der Primat des Petrus in der orthodoxen Kirche*, Zurich, 1971.

Chapter 7

The Life-Style of the Christian Congregation

The word "style" originally referred to the stylus used for writing, then to the use of this stylus, and finally to the writer's personal way of presenting things. Thus it entered into the vocabulary of aestheticism. There it means the

"collective characteristics of the writing or diction or artistic expression or way of presenting things or decorative methods proper to a person or school or period or subject, and the manner of exhibiting these characteristics."[1]

"Style," therefore, is a form of expression, a language, which presupposes, however, in the individual artist a personal conviction, and, as language of a period or culture, a certain community of values.

From there, it is not far to an ethical use of the word. But used in colloquial language, it often loses the special connotations which the word "style" nearly always has in its artistic meaning. It then simply refers to conduct, divorced from motivation or reasons, and without presupposing that it should have its roots in a community of values.

If one wants to extend the meaning of the word in this direction, one usually adds the word "life"—"life-style." That happened when the General Assembly of the World Council of Churches in Uppsala in 1968 discussed questions of individual ethics. The report of Section VI talks about "new life-styles."[2] Motivation is not forgotten: there are different Christian life-styles, but all are motivated by one and the same hope. True Christian life must express joy and gratitude for the possibilities of being God's fellow workers.[3] But the emphasis of the report is on the discussion of different ways of conduct and behavior. The younger generation is to share in the processes of decision making.[4] We are to use time and money in such a way as to guarantee true care for our neighbors.[5] The relationship of men and women is to be characterized by true partnership.[6] It must be said that these discussions have drawn current problems into the ecumenical debate which for too long had been regarded as peripheral to the life of the church. The dangers of the concept of "style" become apparent in a certain centrifugal tendency within the document, and what is said about motivation cannot fail to give the impression that, in any case, everything depends on what we, as Christians, plan and achieve. There is no hint that this "effective" style could be used as a flight from life; no inkling that it might help to repay a debt; not a word about the necessity of being still and waiting for the hour of the Lord. The closing words, on the contrary, say: "He who makes all things new is drawing us on."[7]

In spite of these dangers, this chapter aims to discuss the life-style of the Christian congregation. Which congregation? In this article, it is the congregation as described in Augustana VII and VIII. How old-fashioned and harmless this congregation gathered around the preaching and the sacraments seems to be, compared with the congregation of the dynamic style of Uppsala, 1968.[8] Here we find faith, holiness and sin—that is all that is said about the membership. Two considerations are important for our subject here:

First, preaching and the sacraments are seen to be independent of the style of any particular church in any particular time. A style is bound to a time and place, while word and sacrament are free to use different styles in different circumstances. Changes in society mean new tasks for the congregation of the Word, but do not threaten its identity.

Second, where there is a Christian congregation, there is the whole church. It is the "assembly of all believers." That is catholicity. Style separates. One can see straight away, for instance, in an ecumenical procession, who belongs to the one or to the other confession. It is obvious from the style. But the gospel knows no such limits.

Nevertheless, style and the gospel do not belong to different worlds. It would be schizophrenia if they tried to live without any relationship to each other, and it would be a mortal danger to the congregation. Articles VI and VII of the Augsburg Confession ask serious questions about the style of life; and the principles of the

Reformation underlying the concept of congregation show the way to a continuous renewal of the life-style of the Christian congregation.

I

The fact that the Christian congregation has a life-style is of relative significance. It is relative because every style is historical, whereas the congregation proclaims "an eternal gospel" (Rev. 14:6). The concept of congregation guarantees its freedom over against different styles. But if this is so, then there is a place in the congregation where the structures of society lose their power. Style is no meteorite which dropped straight from the sky but a phenomenon of society, a result of its economic structures and a means of exercising its power. "Do not be conformed to this world" (Rom. 12:2)! This is no moral exhortation to stick to what is old and well-tested, but rather a proclamation of freedom. Every new style is spread through propaganda which promises freedom, but is just as authoritarian as the traditional way. Within the congregation, it is possible to stand back far enough to examine critically what otherwise may be taken for granted, and this is very important, because all that is taken for granted can exert an especially powerful authority.

This criticism of contemporary style is not raised from the vantage point of another style, for instance, an older one. It is customary to consider traditional forms of life to be "holier" than modern ones; Gregorian music "holier" than jazz. It is "more pious" to dress in an old-fashioned way than to follow modern fashion, and it is considered more trustworthy in the congregation to bring up children according to the old, strict norms than to learn from modern child psychology. It is particularly difficult to counteract the power of old life-styles if these come from groups which once were the means of a renewal in the congregation. In many countries, for example, the Puritan ideal of life is seen as the style of the Holy Spirit, not to mention the recommendations of the biblical writers to their contemporaries. The claim to absolute authority made for these recommendations has been disastrous in the fight for rights and justice in society. The apostolic exhortations to the *douloi* of a slave society are still sometimes being applied to modern labor relations to suggest that strikes and other forms of passive resistance are non-Christian. "Workers, be submissive to your employers with all respect."[9] Among the considerations of style which are not necessary for the unity of the church, the Augsburg Confession mentions only "ceremonies." It should be remembered that New Testament traits of Christian life-style should not be excluded when discussing contemporary, ethical life-styles for the congregation.

Confronted by the gospel, any life-style is relative. There only appears to be a contrast between "old-fashioned" and "modern"; soon a new style grows old, and revolution turns into an established society. To claim absolute authority for any life-style, be it old or new, means to paralyze life; it produces arteriosclerosis.

Not only the fact that any style is historical but also the experience that attitudes are deceptive should stop the congregation from claiming absolute authority for its life-style. The Christian congregation should have learned to mistrust the "semblance of a godly nature" (2 Tim. 3:5)—but it has not. "The same people who confess their faith in the Fall, and in the sinful nature of man, cannot, for their life, stand the books which testify to this," says François Mauriac.[10] Protestant authors have said the same thing.

When a certain life-style becomes "constitutive" for the Christian congregation, as it frequently does, this brings with it at least three dangers. First, questioning people who see through the "semblance of a godly life" will ask what they are to believe. When, during his prayers with Dr. Drew, Babbitt peeped through his fingers (for he was piously holding his hands in front of his face) and saw that, without interrupting the flow of his words, Dr. Drew took out his watch and consulted it, Babbitt hurried away as fast as possible. This was one of a chain of events which led Babbitt away from these bourgeois style-patterns into a new congregation which at least acknowledged ritualistic influences.[11]

The second danger is despair which seizes those who see through their own style-pattern. In a letter to a friend, N. F. S. Grundtvig tells how, during his enthusiastic period, "I took off everything that seemed un-Christian to me, except arrogance." He continues:

"Doubtlessly, in this way I would have become one of the most arrogant enthusiasts who ever walked this earth, unless the good God had had mercy, and had torn away . . . the veil. Suddenly it was like scales falling from my eyes; my arrogance and hardheartedness became evident to me. . . . Now I was near to despair."

This crisis brought him near to madness. During a journey, he told his companions that the previous night: "I had felt the devil winding himself round my body like a snake."[12] What saved Grundtvig was the particular character of the evangelical congregations:

what it is, and what it can give its members remains there, when all life-styles break down.

The third danger is Pharisaism. I would like to recall what Gruntvig said in the above-cited letter about this threatening future, in which he sees himself as an arrogant enthusiast. A church which in its style is "constitutive" presupposes that, for its members, their life-style also is constitutive for their Christianity. That means that they believe in their style and conceal its hollowness from themselves. This is Pharisaism: not that the style is more Christian than the witness of one's own heart, but that one has to lie, both to oneself and to the world. It is what I have called in a novel *The Holy Masquerade.* The reason why this phenomenon can frequently be observed in pastors, although they of all people live near the de-masking Word, is that the "masquerade" is a congregational phe-nomenon: it is expected of the *representative of the congregation* not only to have a life-style and live it, but also to *be,* down to the very depth of his personality, as Christian as his style. This expecta-tion, however, is a death trap. Nothing hampers the true develop-ment of a "man of God" as disastrously as the belief that he has fulfilled such expectations (2 Tim. 3:17).

Such Pharisaism often creates "establishments of obduracy"—col-lectives—in which all help and support each other's faith in their chosen style. This produces a security so hardened that where there should be mercy and understanding, the outside world can find nothing. This in turn awakens the hatred of the world—and the despair of those who seek for mercy. It is not as if such congregations don't preach mercy. But their conduct contradicts their preaching, and nobody knows whether or not to take their words seriously.

The life-style of a congregation always includes the possibility of isolation. That is evident already in the relationships with those who are socially or spiritually different. Lars Ahlin tells in his novel *Natt i marknadstältet* of a man named Pig-Lasse.[14] This man called himself "Noah's Ark" because, to his amazement, he lived on this side of the Flood and hadn't drowned, and because he believed he had the whole of creation within his body. He lived by scavenging on a rubbish heap for things he could either sell or feed to his pig. When he went to a church one day, people fled as soon as he ap-proached them—he stank. A voice inside him finally ordered him to leave. Who spoke? "The man who went to make room. You have been baptised in my name. You have been written into the book of life, and there your name lives." Pig-Lasse added: "And so I who am Noah's Ark here on earth, hurried out of the church."

The congregation did not just fail to exercise mercy towards him who was different; such behavior raises the question of the church's catholicity. There is no room for man in the church. For no one. Man is too big for the church.

I do not need to explain this story. Recognizing the relativity of its style is the only means for the congregation to do justice to the catholicity of baptism. Document VI from Uppsala rightly condemns all racism or national discrimination. But it does not say anything about the prejudices against those who think differently, about the physically handicapped, the old, or the alcoholics.[15]

Many still believe that a believing Christian cannot be an alcoholic because the abuse of alcohol is a sin. I do not agree, because alcoholism is an illness. But what if alcoholism really were a sin? The Smalkald Articles say that "manifest and impenitent sinners" must not be admitted to "the sacrament and other fellowship of the church until they mend their ways and avoid sin."[16]

At this point, there is a tension between the Smalkald articles and Augustana which states that "even open sinners remain among the godly" and are members of the congregation.[17] But above all it says that it is not the life-style which constitutes the Christian congregation. That means that even a sinful style of life cannot break up this community. One might find a parallel here in a theological exegesis of law and gospel. But I ask whether it was not the old style-patterns of the early church and the first Christian centuries, and the demands of sixteenth century society, respectively, which were the real background for the particular church discipline as it was practiced. We might have here an example of the aftereffects of old style-patterns, and of government influences. "Spiritual punishments" were, in practice, often a help to the police, although the preacher was not to "mingle" spiritual and worldly punishments.[18]

We find a tendency here to try to fit the Christian congregation into the style-patterns of society. Particularly unfortunate in this context is the use of the word "public" in Augustana, which means that the outside appearance of life becomes all-important. Anybody who has tried to get an ex-convict a place among "honest" people knows the power of public opinion, even within the Christian congregation—a power stronger than the gospel. Certainly, "public sinners, too, can receive forgiveness." "Too"! But they will still bear the stamp of second-class citizens. The tax collectors and whores in the Gospels are people we read about. They comfort us when we think of our "respectable" sins. We never identify them with the antisocial people of our own time, especially as we remember that Jesus and his disciples were their friends. As I have written elsewhere:

"Such groups (as the organized congregation) often make bourgeois respectability and an outward appearance of Christianity a condition of membership. Those who do not conform often have difficulties in being taken into the community, and in being allowed to share its warmth, because members hesitate to accept what is strange and unknown. Instead, they disappear to the outside, into other groups where perhaps their antisocial behavior is the norm, and the presupposition of their membership."[19]

Finally, to recognize the relativity of life-style must mean openness to criticism. The masquerade which I mentioned is performed in front of the world.[20] It is in front of the godless world. As if the morals of the members of the congregation were a guarantee for the Gospel! Remarkable in this context is a story by Boccacio in the *Decameron*: A Jew who had previously refused to be baptized was ready, after a visit to depraved Rome, to become a Christian. He explained it to a Christian friend, who had expected a different outcome to the visit, in the following way: since the Pope and his people, in spite of their best efforts, had not managed to destroy the Christian religion, it must evidently be upheld by other powers. "I think I must really recognize that it is the Holy Spirit who supports and upholds it."[21] There is more of the gospel in this anecdote than in many a sermon attempting to show how Christians should convince the world by their behavior. This kind of sermonizing often strengthens the fear of exposés, and thereby awakens the suspicion of the world.

The masquerade is performed specially for the benefit of the pious world which exists inside the congregation, and is therefore all the more powerful. In this context, the Pauline words about the duty to "welcome the weak in faith" (Rom. 14:1) are often quoted and explained. That is a strange confusion. According to Hugo Odeberg, Paul is not thinking here of "the people who condemn, may they be ever so grand and meticulous Christians in their own eyes, but rather of those who are really weak, and can be tempted to fall away from Christ by my actions." Professor Odeberg adds: "On the contrary, a Christian must always be ready to have the 'just' lined up against him."[22] That is relativizing of life-styles.

II

The Reformation commented on abstract principles of form in the polemic against the enthusiasts "who imagine that without means, without the hearing of the divine Word and without the use of the sacraments, God draws man to himself, illuminates, justifies, and saves him," for at the center of faith, there is something earthly. This attitude affirms the necessity of a style, in conscious opposition to those who only admit of a purely spiritual center, and consequently reject all regular forms of worship.

Only when we deny the biblical doctrines of creation and incarnation can we consequently reject any necessity to have a style. If, with Platonism, we believe that all evil comes from matter, we are able to free ourselves from concrete expressions—words and pictures—in order to be able to reach God beyond the material world. According to biblical faith, however, God has pronounced the things of this world to be good. The divine, eternal, and invisible Word through which the world was created (Jn. 1:3) has even himself become part of its creation; that means he has submitted himself to the relativity of a style, just as the young Messiah did when he was "obedient to" his parents (Lk. 2:51). The paradox of faith is that the eternal has become temporal.

This means that we cannot understand God at all unless we see him in the relative (Jn. 1:18). To understand, to create, or even to want to be the absolute is a characteristic of satanic nature (Gen. 3:5), whether it reveals itself in a style, or in freedom from style. God has revealed himself in his intervention, in a new creation, but not in his absolute nature. It happened here, in the flesh, in a relative situation, subject to styles.

It happened in the realm of the human, in a way which revealed the meaning of an original but hidden picture of creation, and extended it; the picture of the grain of wheat. What is human is shown here to be an affirmation of, not an objection to, the Divine. The call to man to be "co-creator" with God (Gen. 2:15, 19) was fulfilled on earth again, not in rivalry with God (as happens when man claims the absolute), but in the honoring of the Father (John 8:49).

Many attempts at claiming absolute validity for a style or life-style are characterized by a desire to be free from the body and from

God's creation. The same is true in art. A modern example is Kandinsky's suprematism: technology and religion are still tied to desire and to matter, art alone rises above all this to cosmic harmony and freedom.[24] The same happens in religion, and not only, as just mentioned, in the sphere of worship, but also in the ethical consequences of religion, leading to a contempt of marriage, of food (Col. 2:16) and of the other material gifts of creation (1 Tim. 4:3).

Curiously, the move from claiming absolute validity for a life-style to affirming a total lack of style is quite short. The one is a denial of God's creation, the other a rejection of God's call, in creation, to become his "co-creators." As in Gnosticism, contempt of the body can express itself in licentiousness as well as in exaggerated asceticism.[25] In morals, just as in worship, it is impossible to do away with style: we are always set in a pattern because we find ourselves within creation which is the opposite of chaos. Even the devil has to ape God in this—there are patterns of destruction, just as there are patterns of construction (Lk. 1:17 ff). These antistyles not only destroy the spiritual life, culture, or what could be termed the "higher life," but especially body, nature, and soil. It is characteristic of the true life-style of the Christian congregation that, in its faith in creation, incarnation, and calling, it confesses and defends man's physical existence.

It is easy to find examples of this denial of a life-style in the congregation. When the gospel tells us that God is interested in the body, and, in the Word made flesh, that he is fighting against sickness, and death, then the congregation thinks of spiritual sickness, spiritual death, and spiritual healing. When He brings reconciliation and breaks "the curse on the earth and on bread," the congregation manages to spiritualize this to the point where those who receive the bread of reconciliation do not even notice that they are eating "daily bread." And in the marriage service, as prescribed in the 1942 service book of the Swedish church, the word "flesh" has been omitted, and the pastor says: "They shall be one."[27]

In consequence, the dangers of sexual sins have been exaggerated (seen as admission of sexuality, not as damage to it), and sins committed in the name of mammon, that is to say, sins against bread and the body, have been underestimated through the centuries. The figure of the young Messiah has been frequently depicted, both in preaching[28] and in art,[29] as one of a pale, intelligent, obedient pupil, quite in keeping with an educational system in which intellectual achievements are highly valued, whereas the creative ability of the hands is relegated to the status of "technical subjects" without any credit. This corresponds to a hierarchy of professions in which work with abstract subjects like philosophy, mathematics, or economics is highly esteemed, while manual work counts little. It must be added that the ideal of the "good" child, whose joy of living and whose impulses are kept in check, if not repressed, has been astonishingly widely accepted in church, school, and society, and similar demands have even been applied to adults.

The church still proclaims the dignity of the body at the beginning and at the end of life, in baptism and the burial service. It is also a community of those who respect the unborn life which cannot yet, by intelligence or reason, give proof of its humanity.[30]

Carl Malmsten, who renewed the style of wooden furniture and pioneered educational ideas which took account of the whole psychophysical personality, suspected a link between such an educational theory and the gospel of Creation and Incarnation:

"He was a simple man of the people, from childhood well-versed in things of this earth, accustomed to building with his hands, radiating a healing and sustaining power. Among all other renewers of religion, he is distinguished by this beneficent power of his hands. Without it, he would not have been the Son of Man who cares for his brothers, the sons of men. It is symbolic that the powers of this world nailed these serving hands to the cross."[31]

Here we find an understanding of the call to become co-creators allied to respect for the body. It has been shown that such an association can produce an astonishing renewal of the whole personality, even of the intellect of the young.[32]

It is impossible, however, to talk about man's physical existence without mentioning his animal nature. This animal nature has often been considered, both by the pious[33] and those who believe in progress,[34] as a heritage with problems. Chesterton was right when he called man the only savage beast.[35] It is regrettable that the romanticism which marked the years between World War I and World War II and which saw the "golden age" in our animal past[36] has so rarely been recognized by Christians as a renewal of part of the biblical faith in creation. Now such a renewal is sometimes found in the discovery of the cosmos as the true body of man.[37] We are experiencing the consequences of the fact that, for centuries in the Western world man's call to become co-creator has been set against his organic unity with the rest of creation—often in practical application of the biblical command to man to subdue the earth (Gen. 1:28). The command to "till" and to "keep" the garden (Gen. 2:15) has not been proclaimed so much. An early and good example of such a proclamation was Joseph Sittler's introduction to the question of unity, given at the ecumenical Assembly in New Delhi in 1961. He starts from the theme of the conference, "Jesus Christ—the Light of the World."

"When millions of the world's people, inside the church and outside of it, know that damnation now threatens nature as absolutely as it has always threatened men and societies in history, it is not likely that witness to a light that does not enfold and illumine the world-as-nature will be even comprehensible."[38]

He then develops such a statement on the basis of the cosmic vision of Colossians which does not only include history but "all," be it thrones or dominions or principalities or authorities. Not only man, but the whole of creation has been reconciled to Christ. He who is baptized in Christ witnesses to this cosmic redemption, and it is his task to serve creation in this light.[39]

Wherever man subdues the earth, Christ is the key to his dominion. He has shown us what rightly deserves to be called power and lordship.

"The royal power which he has over the whole of creation, and which he passes on to man—is it really a power which he exercises over nature in the same way as other lords and masters use their power? Or is he there, too, among us like a servant? And what are we to be?"[40]

Therefore, if the Christian congregation accepts the need for a life-style, and believes that God has created the cosmos, and has reconciled it in Christ, then this belief must influence the kind of life-style they will have: it will have to be characterized by respect for the human body, and for the whole of creation. The respect which, in the liturgy, is paid to the blessed gifts is really due to the whole of God's blessed cosmos.

It is the task of ecologists, naturalists, and politicians to prevent the fatal development outlined by Sittler. But it is the task of the Christian congregation to be the home of convictions which will result in the necessary regulations, and it is the task of its preaching to defend creation against men's reckless profit seeking.

If the Christian congregation accepts that its life-style derives from the eternal word having become temporal, it also has to recognize history and society. Recognition of history is the antithesis to any one epoch's claim to absolute validity. History means change. Christ was born "in the time of Herod," but this does not make that time particularly holy; it means a sanctification of all times with their changing forms of society and styles of life. Not as if it didn't matter what form of society and life were predominant. Through Christ, the changes have received a goal; it is no longer an eternal repetition, or a series of human whims, but a drama. Therefore no period as such is better than any other; each period of time must be subordinate to the goal, and must be judged by its relationship to this goal. "Great times" of history—or church history—are thus often robbed of their glamour, whereas apparently insignificant epochs appear in their true light.

Like so many religions, Christianity speaks about a golden age; but it is not historical, it lies before history— and after. In this light, the fault of the past is not to be old enough and of the present not to be new enough. When Harvey Cox says, quoting T. Wieser, that "the *Kyrios*, the risen Christ, always goes *before* the church into the world"[41] this fits well into his evolutionist scheme, in which every great event of the past was just one step nearer the secular city[42] which represents the "new era." His zeal in de-sacralizing the past goads him into an overinterpretation of Mk. 16:7, forgetting what Galilee meant for the disciples. He overestimates the importance of the "facts" of time over against the "acts" of the congregation, as if the most remarkable thing in the Acts of the Apostles were the openings for mission, and not the gospel and its proclamation into these openings. Quite logically, Cox says: "Canon and tradition function not as sources of revelation but as precedents by which present events can be checked out as the possible loci of God's action."[43] If the past wants to mean more, the best answer is Cox's classical one: Iconoclasm.[44] But what is iconoclasm if not a sacralization of one's own time and one's own theology? The Prostestant reformation saw this; note here the mild irony of the Swedish Church order of 1571: "Likewise, although it is an old custom and common to all Christians, do we use salt, light, robes, sponsors, etc. in Baptism."[45] In the name of Christian freedom and against the claims of both Catholic traditionalism and Calvinist iconoclasm, it is said: "We do not let ourselves be caught under the yoke of their bondage, may it be evil or sweet to them."[46]

If one wants to follow Cox's prescription and look up occasions in the past through which present events can be understood, it would be fitting to read Is. 40 where the prophet invokes God's sovereignty against the Babylonian astrologers: "Who created these? He who brings out their host by number" (Is. 40:26). Astrology was the futurology of those times. Naturally, there is a great difference between the two ways of investigating the future; they share, however, a tendency to foster fatalism. An obvious way of sacralization in our time is to feel oneself to be just a figure in the machine of the future, impotent as Israel was in Babylon, or wanton like the businessmen in Jas. 4:13-15, threatened or pampered by "fate." The prophets believe that the future lies in God, and can be changed by the forgiveness of sins: Is. 1:18-20 speaks of sins like scarlet and crimson and of God's power to make them "white as snow." This is the gospel of Christ who goes before his people. This forgiveness is not predictable, it is beyond reason because it is of God.

This is the gospel of the holiness of all ages: they are God's, Christ has suffered through them, he opens their seals (Rev. 5). This happened for the sake of man whom he loves. The past is not just a pattern to which man must adhere; it belongs to men who, through the power of Christ's resurrection, live among us as full members of the Christian congregation.

Artistically, inconoclasm was a catastrophe, but not because it prevented idolatry of the past. Rather, it stops the development of the present which thus loses what should be developed. "Some say, 'the dead authors are far from us, because we know so much more than they did.' Yet, it is them whom we know."[47] These words come from T. S. Eliot, the traditionalist, who was one of the fathers of lyrical modernism. Church buildings imitating for instance the Gothic style exemplify the same poverty of spirit as these modern churches which have no element of the past in them at all. Both witness to a state of mind which does not dare to let the past live. Therefore, the present cannot live in them. Both are, frankly, very dull.

It must be admitted, however, that many of the old stone churches resist change, and that the liturgical conservatism of Lutheranism has often prevented renewals for our time. This in turn has produced attempts at solving liturgical problems which try to avoid any link with the past and, therefore, seem remarkably harmless, uninteresting and without a future. Unfortunately, many of our church architects repeat the concern of their predecessors, to build churches to last for centuries, and not decades, and thus stifle the initiative of the new generation. This is to claim absolute validity for the present-day style. But there are newly built churches in which the past is really present, and which still clearly speak modern language. Some of them are made from very perishable materials, suffer frequent changes of liturgical layout, and are even transportable. They witness to a time of change and to their own transitoriness.[48]

Style in art is part of the style of life, and what I have said about one part holds equally true for the whole: it is the confrontation with the past which makes development possible, and we must be ready to be questioned by the future in order to let it develop. Between the past and the future we are to live honestly and humbly in the time which, of all the ages, is ours. It would be easier if we were to come to know the past not only as a series of styles, patterns, principles, and commandments, but in the way the Augsburg Confession teaches about the congregation's relationship to the saints: "saints should be kept in remembrance so that our faith may be strengthened. . . . Moreover, their good works are to be an example for us."[49] Thus we have to live in a personal relationship with the past in order to be able to deal personally with the future.

This last point is of great importance for the relationship between young and old churches. What a generosity there was on the part of the Jewish apostles to free the Gentile-Christian congregations from the Jewish style of life (Acts 15:1 ff). What an anxiety there is on the part of Western missions to tie the young churches to Western lifestyle. "Hinduism has to die into Christianity, so that the best of what their philosophers, saints, and ascetics have been longing and praying for may live," said J. N. Farquahrar.[50] And this is not only true for India. There are areas of concern in the Indian tradition which highlight parts of the gospel vital to the West, like the unity of, and communication between, all living things.[51] The same is true for other, non-Christian traditions. Dialogue with them is not missionary method, it is a life-style.

The openness of different Christian life-styles to each other presupposes a degree of political flexibility which is not possible under all forms of government. Augustana XVI says that "all government in the world and all established rule and laws were instituted and ordained by God." In reality, this doctrine is amazingly open to different political traditions. The doctrine of the regiments to which it belongs was originally directed against the tyranny characterized precisely by a mingling of wordly and spiritual powers.[52] But it is, nevertheless, the background to Lutheran conservatism in political issues. Protestant ethics either have been relatively indifferent to existing social structures, or have accepted them with a relative lack of criticism.[53] Gustaf Wingren reminds us that orders which are good in themselves can be abused;[54] the gospel possesses a "critical function" which makes the Christian free from "rules and conventions."[55] Why has there been so little evidence of this critical power? In innumerable sermons it has been applied "downwards" but rarely "upwards," thus often giving rise to the suspicion that faith is a tool in the hands of the ruling classes, to keep the people in check.

In my opnion, the conference at Zagorsk in 1968 showed this at an important point, by asking whether or not the traditional understanding of providence contained an element of fatalism irreconcilable with our experience. It is the task of theology "to find a new connection between man's sense of responsibility for the way he manages the world, and the assurance of faith, that God is Lord."[56] What has limited the Lutheran doctrine of vocation is the belief that God"s institution of worldly authority gives absolute validity to the status quo, so that whoever attacks it is in fact questioning God's providence. This is to reason as if the capacity to produce, by the appropriate means, a better order of society was not also God's gift and our responsibility. As the conference in Beirut said in 1968, it is God's will that the world be developed.[57] It is necessary to give to the doctrine of vocation a dynamic dimension, in order to free it from its imprisonment within static ideas about society.

The Geneva conference in 1966 was, therefore, right to say that Christian commitment in political life means a questioning of all unjust systems and demands opposition to all forms of oppression.[58] But is the Christian congregation allowed to say this? Should it get involved in worldly affairs?

The Reformation did not forbid preaching about "how everybody in his position should live and act in a Christianlike manner."[59] Later on, it has often been forgotten that the realm of the Word is not only relevant to matters of inner life. The boundary between the two realms is not identical with the boundary between body and soul, nor with the boundary between congregation and society (as if the Christian congregation were not part of society). The boundary does not run between law and gospel either. It runs rather between

the word of God, and the words, actions, and possibilities of
others.

This means that the status quo of the world is not sacrosanct. As
God's creation, the world is subject to changes which emanate from
the Word. God has said "yes" to society in becoming a member of it
in Christ, while at the same time most severely criticizing world
history and those in power, as we see in Christ's preaching. I only
need to recall that he, too, was one of the prophets, and that his
preaching has to be seen in this context. It is not true to say that the
preaching of Amos or Isaiah against those in power was intended to
lead to social and political changes, whereas Christ's preaching was
only to lead to the conversion of the individual soul.

Furthermore, we cannot develop new forms of worship without
either accepting or criticizing the structures of society. This is already clear in the Epistle of James, where both a rich man and a
poor man are assigned certain places in the assembly (Jas. 2:1 ff).
When Section V at Uppsala says that our communion with Christ
means that we are also to share our bread with our hungry brethren,
this is not only an exhortation to draw such implications from our
worship, but also to encourage us to construct our worship in a certain way. The same paragraph condemns any form of racial or class
discrimination in worship.[60] To accept or reject this statement is a
political act.

The same can be said about *diakonia*, service, which seems to be
such a politically innocuous form of congregational life. Small groups
who, within unjust structures of society, represent forms of life foreign to their structure, are the vanguard of a new order and not,
as the Marxists say, temporary relief agencies which only delay the
revolution. Their voice, or even the voice of an individual, may, in
a prophetic sense, be the voice of the whole church.[61] Especially
important seems to be the spontaneous exercise of genuine Christian
solidarity in times of political change.

"In Eastern Europe, the effective social witness does not lie in legislation
or political pressure, or idealistic resolutions but in the independent
relationships, in the feeling of mutual solidarity and responsibility. . . .
And this feeling of independence and solidarity goes beyond any narrow
definition of Christian community. . . ."[62]

If the Christian congregation, in its basic functions, can both ap-
prove of and criticize society, this does not mean indifference to the
individual. As I have already hinted, there is a sharp difference here

between the work of renewal of the Christian congregation and of Marxist organizations, because the Christian congregation must never forget, or even sacrifice, the individual in order to bring about new structures of society. The church may be an assembly, but an assembly of believers.[63] And faith is a personal matter.

In the present situation, the Christian congregation has an alternative to the way society is developing in both East and West. The consumer society is interested in the individual, but only as a target for advertisements. Innumerable demands are made of him without ever really expecting a personal answer—for his money, his vote, his declarations are hardly part of his personality. Has he any real existence at all?[64] He no longer decides for himself, he is led by others, he is directed by others,[65] a mere group phenomenon. We remember Gadara, where Christ's word is addressed to this legion, and asks for the name of him who is possessed by so many voices.[66]

The Christian congregation should show a different kind of interest in the individual. It should not search him out for its own sake, but for his sake, so that we come to existence. His "yes" or his "no" to God is spoken in his own voice—and so is his protest. Even when the congregation cares for his body, he is not just an object, and he is not expected to give his money or his assent, but to give himself.

The Christian congregation is perhaps most effective in the present-day situation through individual pastoral care—not only by saying what it is called upon to say, but also by listening to the depth of a person. This is "client-centered therapy," even if we do not follow all the recommendations of Carl Rogers.[67]

To sum it up, the Christian congregation must beware of claiming absolute validity for a style of life. No style can be constitutive for the congregation. It always has to be open to dissenters and to any form of criticism. On the other hand, it has to recognize and defend the physical character of man and nature, and that in itself is already a style of life. Both in art and in life, the Christian congregation will use styles of different epochs and different cultures. It says "yes" to society, not least by its criticism of all unjust structures and by its defense of the individual. This is not possible without getting involved in styles and patterns, even sometimes getting stuck with them. How can the Christian congregation be suspicious of all styles, and yet accept them? How can it live in them, and yet remain free of them?

The answer is that a congregation's center is neither pattern nor discipline nor principle but something alive, something like a heart. It has a life which breaks through styles and creates new styles, in order to discard them again. Style is language, but this language has a definite content.

III

To say that "forgiveness of sins, life, and salvation" is the theme for the life-style of the congregation means, in the first place, that subject matter is to be central. Otherwise the congregation has nothing to say to the world. A life-style determined by the law is not specifically unique to the church. For "the natural law which coincides with the law of Moses, and the ten commandments" is "inborn and written in all men's hearts."[68] The pressure of law, both inside and outside the congregation, is so great that the gospel of a different kind of justification has to be proclaimed loudly and clearly if it is to be interpreted by all who hear it as yet another law. It, the gospel, is so "unbelievable" that one can scarcely believe that it means what it says.

The style of the Christian congregation is part of this clear proclamation. The style of church buildings alone can either strengthen the proclamation of the gospel, or give it the lie. We soon notice whether a building has been constructed for saints or for sinners, whether it rebuffs or welcomes, whether it frightens or calms. In the same way, the worshiping congregation, through its attitude, can either chase away a sinner, or accept him in the name of God's mercy. What form of mercy could have reached Pig-Lasse during his last visit to church?[69]

Like no other modern theologian, Einar Billing has managed to build the gospel of universal grace into the structure of the congregation. "The people's church is forgiveness of sins"—he saw a straight line "from the innermost religious center to the congregation, from the thought of forgiveness, from the universal, prevenient grace, to the Church in her wide, inclusive organization—*the people's church*" (*folkkyrka*).[70]

It follows that the Christian congregation is not founded on the faith of its members, but considers, in radical openness, all those within earshot as belonging to the church. There are different degrees of assuming and exercising responsibility in the congregation, but it is not a special sector of humanity: its home is with God—as the children of Korah sing about Zion: "The Lord records as he registers the peoples, 'This one was born there' " (Ps. 87:6).

We must not separate baptism from the church, lest it become like a door standing in an open field. It is a door into the inner room of the church, and there are forecourts outside. Word, baptism, Eucharist are one and the same movement of the grace of God. Luther says of baptism in his Larger Cathechism, "that faith must have something to believe in, something to hold on to, and on which to stand and ground itself." Baptism is a confirmation of what the Word has said already. This confirmation does not limit the gospel to something private, but works at the roots of society itself: it is part of teaching all *peoples*, and it extends its work of grace to the whole of life in the human community. Grace does not lead away from humanity, but into the heart of the world where Christ gathers all together. If this is true, it links the Christian congregation with people and soil, with erring souls and obedient stars.

In this context, the state-linked national church has great advantages. It shows clearly that it is not only the individual and his soul that are encompassed in the gospel, but the whole of man and the whole of society. The whole of national life is judged and blessed. Under these circumstances, those who are estranged from the church will become conscious of the fact that there is someone in the congregation to whom they are not strangers. But this pact with the state also usually involves a certain degree of establishment, whereas the gospel itself can never be "established." When it seems to get established, we must recall that such a gospel is unknown in the New Testament. Those who need the gospel most are afraid of such a respectable congregation.

At times when such people have been edged out of the official churches of one or of the other kind, there sometimes arise, inside or outside these churches, some disestablished and informal groups in which discussion and Eucharist are open to all who happen to come. These groups often provide the initiative for a renewal of style both in the church and in the whole of society.[71] Often it is groups like these that best translate the gospel for their times.

I have warned against claiming absolute validity for a moral style by referring to its practical consequences. Would the alternative be a different kind of justification, proceeding from a cosmic amnesty which, through Christ, is open to all? We could also suggest that, what we said at the beginning about style being the "personal conviction" of an artist, could be applied here. This new kind of justification is not identical with any style-pattern, but radiates from a personality which, from time to time, expresses itself in different forms, customs, and patterns. These traces of Christ always lead into certain directions. I would like to follow up a few of them and discuss their significance for the present situation.

The first result of Christ's presence is forgiveness, and that means *unconditional community*. The radicalism of this kind of justification has provoked astonishment and criticism from the very beginning. When Christ was called a "friend of tax collectors and sinners" (Mt. 11:19), this did not sound as pious as it did later on, but was taken very seriously. The same cannot be said for the Christian congregation.

In the established congregation, the link between forgiveness of sins and respectability was established by assuming that "real" sins were not involved. A Swedish author recently told a short story about a "real" sinner. During the Creed, he had reflected that "the sinners with a small 's' " go to church, while the others have to seek their comfort elsewhere.[72] That is "gospel in the conditional tense,"[73] forgiveness with conditions. What is at stake here is not only a consequence of the gospel, but the possibility of its being understood at all. As long as there exists for Christians a minimum of moral prerequirements to be fulfilled, the stumbling block of the gospel is hidden, and Christ is screened in by better-versed people.

It is quite clear that other conditions—like race, wealth, cultural level—are just as deadly for a weak faith. I have already mentioned that the Assembly at Uppsala in 1968 declared that we, as Christians, must refuse to participate in any form of racial or class discrimination in the congregation.[74] The good Samaritan clearly is still afraid of the Jews' interdiction to share house or food with him. He gets himself "represented" by his money.[75] Doesn't this fit with the doctrine of vocation? If the great-grandson of "Ol Captain" in Purlie[76] wishes to become a member of a black congregation—isn't he deviating from his vocation as white man? Paul answers this question in Eph. 2:14, when he says that the "dividing wall" between Jews and Gentiles has been broken down in Christ. Similarly, Jas. 2:1ff breaks down the invisible wall between rich and poor in the congregation. For faith in Christ cannot tolerate it.

There are other walls in the congregation, for instance, between priests and laymen. But the ordained ministry exists because of the faith which breaks down the walls of style and of law. Augustana V expresses this most clearly: "To obtain such faith God instituted the office of the ministry, that is, provided the gospel and the sacraments." The experience of liturgical experiments in Sweden has shown that where there is nobody who is specially commissioned to preach the gospel, the gospel remains silent. The changes of style in modern liturgical life often fetch the preacher down from his traditionally high place into the midst of the congregation. That means that he is one of the congregation. But that is not the whole truth, for he is also the one among the laymen whose responsibility it is to see that the gospel be not ignored. The sole authority in the congregation which must not be contradicted is the authority of absolution. Therefore, what counts is not the authority of a person or a doctrine, but the authority of a definite promise.[77] But as soon as the authority of absolution is claimed for persons, church orders, or doctrinal systems, the wall of quality reappears, cutting across the absolute authority of the gospel in order to protect human authority.

Only when the absolute authority of the gospel is proclaimed and practiced against other authorities will men dare to let the gospel's light shine into the depths of the soul, where anonymous guilt is hidden like a ghost. The law "in power" drives the individual to strengthen his guards at this door, while the gospel "in power" asks "Why are you afraid?" till the guards are withdrawn, and the "dark countercenter of evil in our nature" lies open to the light of forgiveness.[78] Individual pastoral care has a special task here.[79]

Finally, I want to recall that "faith" itself can become a wall in the way of faith; this happens when it is intellectualized to the point where a certain degree of belief in the truth of doctrinal statements takes the place of New Testament faith. Jesus repeatedly speaks about faith where obviously no such qualifications for belief exist, e.g., Mt. 8:5, 15:28. The situation of faith is the encounter between deep distress and Jesus. There are no other conditions.[80]

The second effect of the presence of Christ and of his justification is that we experience the cross and identify ourselves with him. The broken-down walls in the congregation are prophetic signs of what is to happen in the world. The forgiveness of sins which knows only one class and one grace exercises a revolutionary pressure on the

structures of the world. Instead of these structures questioning forgiveness (as they have done so often in church), God's great amnesty
always questions the structures of this world with their punishments,
sanctions, and wars.

These consequences are mainly derived from the fact that in the
gospel God has identified himself with the lowest of man. The man
who is right at the bottom has, thus, been shown to be the principal
character of history. Therefore, he should at least be the principal
character in the Christian congregation. If he can become this, it
will have political consequences. What happens in the congregation
happens in the midst of the world and for the sake of the world.
Worship is not a corner show, but comprises all universe and history. It is a prophetic sign of the truth behind the illusions of the
power games in the world, and the answer to the question who, in
the last resort, determines the destiny of the nations.[81]

From the beginning, the sign of this has been bread. There is one
bread and one church; that means: one humanity. The broken-down
walls are no abstractions, but economic realities. If, in Christ, there
is but one human race, then the food supplies of the earth, too, are
a common possession. The political consequences are not congruent
with any of the present existing political systems, and cannot even
be clearly defined for all situations and epochs, but they are no
utopia either: they are, instead, the "demands of the reality of realities."[82]

The consequences of the gospel for the life-style have, through
church history, been frequently applied "downwards." They have
entered many programs of adult education. The situation of one
who is right "down" must be seen as a common concern because it is
everyman's situation. As this situation has its focus *at the bottom*,
so responsibility has its focus *at the top*. Like the prophets and
Moses, the congregation must address the rulers, saying: "Let my
people go" (Ex. 5:1).

If the congregation is to be credible in this preaching, the gospel
itself must be turned "downwards" where it has its home. It is the
strategy of evangelism not to seek out "key persons," but the lost
ones; not slightingly and condescendingly, but in order to build
them up with the gift of a new identity. To those who in the eyes
of the world, and in their own eyes, are worth nothing, the gospel
gives a new dignity and a new pride. To have received forgiveness
means to be a child of God, and that is more than any of the dignities

of the world. The church may often have said so, but just as often has belied its statements by its actions. This has been true since the days of James (Jas. 2:2 ff).

In his context, many questions of style become burning issues. It is, for example, not appropriate to proclaim the dignity of Christians by distributing the gospel in luxury wrappings. It is a bad way of getting respect from the world to adorn church buildings like palaces. From his simple poor church in Montgomery, Martin Luther King, Jr., reached the whole world—something which cannot always be said for cathedrals. If the Christian congregation, in its responsibility for the poor and the sick, wants to set an example for the world, it should be difficult to get money for grand building schemes.

Without the faith, however, which accepts the presence of Christ in the individual and in the congregation, all these results of the gospel are nothing but new obligations, new indulgences, new lies. As I said in the beginning, there is in the Uppsala, 1968, documents not a trace of such possibilities.[83] Christianity is full of neurotic efficiency on the one hand, and of neurotic fearfulness, caution, and self-destruction on the other. (One of these neurotic characteristics is the accusation that the only attitudes to be found in the church are negative ones). Where is the well-known cheerful courage of the Lutherans, a courage which should be shaking the world with its piety and its deeds? So we come to the third effect of the presence of Christ and of his justification, namely: *resurrection and cheerful courage*.

I recall what I have said about the gospel and anonymous guilt.[84] We might think that this lost sense of cheerful courage might be regained by reducing or even abolishing the consciousness of sin and the confession of sins in the congregation. The opposite, however, is true. Because anonymous guilt remains anonymous, and therefore cannot be reached by the gospel, people try in vain to overcome their fear by deeds or by caution. Many rigidly set styles are nothing but a protective armor against such fear. But if the gospel is a power which works in the very depths of man, where anonymous guilt was prevalent before, then the direction of this work is given: it is a power working downwards, drawing the conclusion of the incarnation by identification. This identification, however, is an identification with people, not with style-patterns. Cheerful evangelical courage is an unreliable ally in the struggle between styles. "The wind blows where it wills" (John 3:8).

When Paul Tillich talks about the "courage to be" as the absolute faith, a faith in God beyond the judging and forgiving God, then he is talking about an abstract "I," and an abstract God. This "I" and this God have forgotten the world. It is without interest to them whether grass and birds live or die.[85] But even when faced with eternity, the apostolic faith cannot forget the flesh, the body, and the world. Therefore, it sets up prophetic signs of life in the world of death. The restoration of a sick or dead body is more than a sermon illustration on eternal life; it is the impact of the creative Word in its struggle with the powers of chaos, and an anticipation of the resurrection of the body.

Both the forgiving and the creating Word have their origin in the one Word, the Logos. Thus the revealed Gospel finds its way into the depths of the prophesy of creation where it had lived, hidden, from the beginning. Gustaf Wingren has described life in creation as cross and death, the life of the old man.[86] He has, thus, given an important correction to Einar Billing's doctrine of vocation. For Billing, God's mandate given in vocation was a sign of forgiveness.[87] This is not acceptable for all vocations and professions. If, on the contrary, our life in creation is a constant experience of death and of judgment, it does not mean that we just bear the yoke. It is rather a call to fight in the name of life, in league with the life-powers of creation. Those who have learned from the gospel to believe in forgiveness are given certain possibilities of recognizing these allies. Where Christ walks on earth, the sources of creation show themselves. That is why there is wine in Cana, and bread in the desert; that is why the sick ("those bound by Satan") are healed (Lk. 13:16). It is here that the cosmic power is named—the cosmic power which, at the same time both accuses and destroys. The victory of physical life is a victory over guilt and shame.

To shut oneself off from these allies can mean to shut oneself off from grace. Lars Ahlin tells of a marriage in which the man did not dare to receive the love of his wife until he had earned it, whereas the wife saw her justification by grace exactly in the giving of bodily love.[88] There is a flight from happiness which is a flight from God who, through the very gifts of this life, humiliates and kills our arrogant self. This "I" does not always mind particularly being an unhappy "I," as long as it can be a really big "I"; and that can often be achieved through martyrdom.

The style of the Christian congregation must have room for, and give voice to, the creative powers of body and earth. In this respect, too, it is a life-style. Those who want to hear it sung should meditate on the explanation to the first Article of the Creed in Luther's Small Cathechism. Other singers and poets, too, have something to give to theologians here. At a time when fields and oceans are being poisoned, the hymn about our Father's sparrow becomes a challenge against death (Mt. 10:29). At at time when the individual is being depersonalized, he must experience in the congregation that he is created to become co-creator with God; that is, for a type of work which fits into Billing's hymn of praise to vocation. The political and social consequences are clear: the Christian congregation should initiate the fight for the life for our fellow creatures, and the fight for man's right to create. Faced with the reality of congregational life, it is all the more necessary to make such statements.

This life-style also has a meditative side. There are ways which lead from life-style to mysticism—and back again. First, there is a common basis to evangelical faith and to mysticism, namely, the breaking away from neurotic activism. Second, the tranquillity of mysticism is not far from that of receiving faith. It is no accident that Luther published the *German Theology*, and wrote an introduction to it.[89] Third, the mystic is not as alone with God and as indifferent to the world as he has often been made out to be. Indeed, the experience of the unity of the cosmos has been called the principal mark of true mysticism.[90] Meditations on the evangelical texts are meditations on the lost and regained creation. Together with it, in it, with it as its body, the Christian congregation prays to God who is "on all sides, through and through, above and below, before and behind, so that nothing can be more truly present, and within all creatures . . ."[91]

The boundaries between times and worlds are broken down, between earth and heaven, between death and life. *Media morte in vita sumus.*[92]

The style of burials is revealing here. In a critical essay, Gustaf Aulén points out that the order of service of the Swedish church sees God as the one responsible for accidents and death.[93] The same phenomenon is apparent, for instance, in Hymn 175 of the *Evangelical Church Hymnal*: ". . . if you accept gladly what God does, then all sorrow will soon be stilled."

There is a Christian resignation to the works of death and the devil which is downright blasphemous and which also buries all natural worries under the label of "cheerful evangelical courage." Stoical composure, rather than taking seriously death (in Bonhoeffer's sense) and the hope of resurrection, has become the ideal.[94] First by individualizing, and then by repressing the consciousness of death entirely, the cheerful evangelical courage has lost its forms of expression. The biblical texts work with a consciousness of death which includes the whole of creation. They do not know a welfare society which could hide the presence of death. The biblical faith in resurrection is part of a cosmic eschatology. At times when one believes human "progress" to be worthy of eternity, it is easy to forget that death concerns the whole of creation, and, therefore, also poses the question of the resurrection of all things. Today, all the old questions return. A reinterpretation of eschatology as an individual and momentary "eschaton" is insufficient. The cheerful evangelical courage has to face the truth that the whole of humanity, and all the other creatures on this earth, will one day exist no longer. Only in this darkness will the old words about Christ as the life of the world regain their illuminating power. Here all styles fall away. Death is the great destroyer of style. But out of chaos there arises a new creation, and the congregation rises up in a song (Rev. 15:2 ff), something which is impossible without style or pattern. The contradiction between style and life shall be no more.

NOTES

1. *The Oxford English Dictionary*, see "style."
2. *Uppsala Speaks*, Geneva, 1968, N. Goodall, ed.; to be quoted by paragraphs and sections.
3. *Ibid.*, VI: 4.
4. *Ibid.*, VI: 7.
5. *Ibid.*, VI. 15.
6. *Ibid.*, VI: 18.
7. *Ibid.*, VI: 28.
8. *Ibid.*, I: 8.
9. 1 Pet. 2:18, according to B. Reicke, "De katolska breven," Stockholm, 1970, p. 39 f, 42 (our translation).
10. F. Mauriac, *Souffrances et bonheur du chrétien*, Paris, 1931 (our translation).
11. S. Lewis, *Babbitt*, 4th edition, London, 1932, p. 372 ff.
12. H. Koch, N. F. S. *Grundtvig människan diktaren folkledaren*, Stockholm, 1941, p. 78 f., 82 (our translation).

13. O. Hartman, *The Holy Masquerade*, Grand Rapids, 1964. Cf. The Pastoral Constitution of Vatican II, Chapter 43: The daily conduct of the priest is revealing the face of the church to the world.
14. L. Ahlin, *Natt i marknadstältet*, Stockholm, 1960, p. 154 ff (our translation).
15. *Uppsala Speaks*, VI, 13.
16. *The Book of Concord: The Confessions of the Evangelical Lutheran Church.* Th. G. Tappert, ed. and trans., Philadelphia, 1959, p. 314.
17. *Ibid.*, p. 33.
18. *Ibid.*, p. 314.
19. O. Hartman, "Kriminalpolitiken,'" *Predikan i nutidssamhället*, Uppsala, 1967.
20. *Ibid.*
21. K. Hagberg, *Den kristna tanken*, p. 102 (our translation).
22. H. Odeberg, *Fariseism och kristendom*, Lund, 1943, p. 102 (our translation).
23. *Book of Concord*, p. 536.
24. From "Suprematism as an Abstraction," 1922, in the program for an exhibition "concerning a universal art," Modern Museet, Stockholm, 1966.
25. A. Nygren, *Agape and Eros*, New York, 1969. See also A. Huxley, *Point Counter-Point*, London, 1928, p. 165.
26. So, e.g., Johann Arndt in his homily for the fourteenth Sunday after Trinity. These positions, however, seem to have been abandoned now, as, e.g., in *In Season and Out of Season*, sermons edited by H. R. Müller-Schwefe, Stuttgart, 1958.
27. *Svenska kyrkohandboken*, 1942.
28. Thus already St. Aelred, Abbot of Rievaulx, in Mignes *Patriologiae cursus completus, series latina*, Paris, 1944-66, and in *The Sunday Sermons of the Great Fathers*, M. F. Toal, ed. and trans. Chicago and London, 1955 and 1960, 1, p. 248 ff.
29. E.g., in *Jesus av Nasaret, attio originalplanscher av konstnären*, William Hole, Stockholm, 1930 (in original version, Eyre & Spottiswoode, London).
30. In spite of a critical attitude of the book, this also appears in G. Barczay, *Revolution der Moral* ("Revolution of Morals"), Zurich/Stuttgart, 1967. What is lacking here is a criticism of a social situation in which, for social reasons, pregnancies become distress situations. Different in Anne-Marie Thunberg, *Välfärd för Hoföda? Kris i abortfrågan*, Falköping, 1969.
31. C. Malmsten, *Mittens rike*, Stockholm, 1942, p. 229 (our translation).
32. *Ibid.*, p. 13 ff.
33. E.g., in James Joyce, *A Portrait of the Artist as a Young Man*, Stockholm/London, 1945, p. 159.
34. E.g., Arne Müntzing, *Biological Points of View on Some Humanistic Problems*, Lund, 1968, p. 14 ff.
35. G. K. Chesterton, *Orthodoxy*, New York, 1947, p. 267.
36. As seen psychologically by S. Freud, and above all by D. H. Lawrence.
37. *The Subversive Science*, New York, 1969, *passim*.
38. *The Ecumenical Review*, vol. XIV, no. 2, Jan., 1962, p. 183.
39. *Ibid.*, pp. 177 ff.
40. K. Anér, *Vår Lösen*, 1969, p. 289 (our translation).
41. H. Cox, *The Secular City*, SCM Cheap Edition, 1967, p. 126. My criticism no longer applies to Cox's essentially changed position in *The Feast of Fools*, Harvard University Press, 1969.
42. *Ibid.*, p. 21 ff., 268.

43. *Ibid.*, p. 148.
44. *Ibid.*, p. 32.
45. *Laurentius Petris Kyrkoordning av år 1571*, Stockholm, 1932, p. 14 (our translation).
46. *Ibid.*, p. 13.
47. T. S. Eliot, *The Sacred Wood*, 7th edition, London, 1950, p. 52 (our translation).
48. R. Bergh's "Experiment in Sigtuna: O. Hartman, *Jordbävningen i Lissabon*, Uddevalla, 1968, p. 41 ff.
49. *Book of Concord*, p. 46.
50. E. J. Sharpe, *Not to Destroy But to Fulfill: The Contribution of J. N. Farquahar to Protestant Missionary Thought*, Uppsala, 1965, p. 360.
51. H. von Glasenapp, *Der Hinduismus*, Munich, 1922, p. 62 ff.
52. E. Schlink, *Theology of the Lutheran Confessions*, Philadelphia, 1961, Chap. 7, esp. pp. 259 ff.
53. Gustaf Wingren, *Creation and Law*, Philadelphia, 1961, p. 117.
54. *Ibid.*, pp. 116-18.
55. Gustaf Wingren, *Gospel and Church*, Philadelphia, 1964, p. 119-20.
56. A.-M. Thunberg, *teologi revolution utveckling*, Stockholm, 1968, p. 65 (our translation).
57. *World Development: a Challenge to the Church*, 1968, I § 6.
58. *Appell an die Kirchen der Welt*. Dokumente der Weltkonferenz für Kirche und Gesellschaft, Stuttgart, 1967, p. 253.
59. *Book of Concord*, only in the German version: *Die Bekenntnisschriften der evang.-lutherischen Kirche*, p. 306 (our translation).
60. *The Uppsala Report*, p. 83.
61. F. Holmström-K. G. Llindelöw, *Kyrkans röst och statens*, Falköping, 1967, p. 20.
62. R. Tobias, *Communist Christian Encounter in East Europe*, Indianapolis, 1956, p. 144.
63. C. A. VII.
64. J. Bodamer, *Der Mensch ohne Ich*, Freiburg, 1958.
65. D. Riesman, *The Lonely Crowd*, New York, 1953, p. 28 ff.
66. O. Hartman, *Earthly Things*, Grand Rapids, 1968, p. 74 ff.
67. S. Hiltner, *Pastoral Counseling*, Nashville, 1949, p. 253 ff.
68. *Book of Concord*, only in the German version, *op. cit.*, p. 160.
69. See above, p. 215-16.
70. E. Billing, *Kyrka och stat*, Stockholm, 1942, p. 14 (our translation).
71. G. Vallquist, *Churches on the Move*, Philadelphia, 1970, p. 65 ff *et passim*.
72. E. Nyhlén, "Drömmar i Lutherrummet," *Vår Lösen*, 1970, p. 594 (our translation).
73. C. M. Lyckhage in *Vår Lösen*, 1964, p. 18.
74. *The Uppsala Report*, p. 83.
75. L. Ahlin, *Fromma mord*, Stockholm, 1952, p. 237.
76. "Purlie," Musical by Ossie Davis and Philip Rose, Winter Garden Theatre, New York, 1971.
77. The opposition between priest and layman which has not yet been overcome in the pastoral constitution of the second Vatican Council (Paragraph 43) is often eroded in attempts at liturgical renewal, even in the Roman Catholic church. It is all the more important to define the role of the ministry. When the Faith and Order Conference in Montreal in 1963 described the responsibility given to the "servant of the church" as an

attribute of the other members of the church, given to them for their service (Paragraph 98), this is in accordance with the wide scope and mixed kinds of activities which so often replace the real task of the priest—to bring forgiveness in the name of Jesus.

78. D. Hammarskjöld, *Markings*, New York, 1968, p. 149.
79. O. Hartman, *Earthly Things*, Grand Rapids, 1968, p. 84 ff, 159 ff.
80. *Ibid.*, p. 43 ff.
81. Cf. the Pastoral Constitution of the Second Vatican Council, paragraph 45.
82. This was said in dramatic form in my play presented to the 1968 General Assembly of the World Council of Churches of Uppsala, *On That Day*, Philadelphia, 1968.
83. Above pp. 211-12.
84. Above p. 231.
85. P. Tillich, *The Courage to be*, New Haven, 1957.
86. G. Wingren, *Creation and Law*, Philadelphia, 1961, pp. 131 ff.
87. *Ibid.*, p. 135. Cf. E. Billing, *Our Calling*, Philadelphia, 1965, p. 40.
88. "Yes, with a simple decision, she experienced . . . she could . . . hinder this traffic and from the source of life, stand alone . . . with her omnicompetence and her greed in the constant service of her own justification. . . ." L. Ahlin, *Natt i marknadstältet*, Stockholm, 1960, p. 249 (our translation).
89. Namely, to the second edition of 1518.
90. H. Sundén, *Älgskyttar, helgon och exegeter*, Halmstad, 1969, p. 60.
91. Luther in W.A. XXIII p. 134. *Luther's Works*, American Edition, vol. 37, p. 58. Cf. Y. Brilioth, *Nattvarden i evangeliskt gudstjänstliv*, 2nd edition, Stockholm, 1951, p. 158.
92. Luther's adaptation of the medieval hymn "Media vita in morte sumus," in his commentary on Gen. 22. E. Liedgren, *Svensk psalm och andlig visa*, Uppsala, 1926, p. 168.
93. *Svenska Dagbladet*, 19.11.1967.
94. D. Bonhoeffer, *Letters and Papers from Prison,* London and Glasgow, 1959, p. 50.

CONTRIBUTORS

Anna Marie Aagaard is lecturer in systematic theology at the University of Aarhus, Denmark.

Carl E. Braaten is professor of systematic theology at the Lutheran School of Theology in Chicago, Illinois.

Olov Hartman is the retired director of the Sigtuna Foundation, Sweden.

Theo Lehmann is a pastor in Karl Marx Stadt, German Democratic Republic.

George A. Lindbeck is a member of the faculty of the Divinity School of Yale University, New Haven, Connecticut.

Gérard Siegwalt is professor of systematic theology in the Faculty of Protestant Theology at the University of Strasbourg, France.

Kristen E. Skydsgaard is professor of systematic theology at the University of Copenhagen, Denmark.

Vilmos Vajta is research professor at the Institute for Ecumenical Research, Strasbourg, France.

Translations for this volume were provided by Mrs. Donata Coleman, Miss Margaret A. Pater, and Dr. Russell B. Norris.